TRANSPORT IN
THE INDUSTRIAL REVOLUTION

WILLIAM ALBERT
JOHN ARMSTRONG
PHILIP S. BAGWELL
JOHN A. CHARTRES
BARON F. DUCKHAM
MICHAEL J. FREEMAN
GORDON JACKSON
GERARD L. TURNBULL

TRANSPORT IN
THE INDUSTRIAL REVOLUTION

EDITED BY
DEREK H. ALDCROFT
MICHAEL J. FREEMAN

MANCHESTER UNIVERSITY PRESS

Copyright © Manchester University Press 1983
Whilst copyright in the volume as a whole
is vested in Manchester University Press,
copyright in the individual chapters and bibliographies
belongs to their respective author(s),
and no chapter may be reproduced whole or in part
without the express permission in writing
of both author and publisher

Published in Great Britain and
the United States of America by
Manchester University Press
at Oxford Road, Manchester M13 9PL, U.K.
and at 51 Washington Street, Dover, N.H. 03820, U.S.A.

British Library cataloguing in publication data

Transport in the Industrial Revolution
  1. Transportation — Great Britain — History —
18th century 2. Transportation — Great Britain
— History — 19th century
I. Albert, William II. Aldcroft, Derek H.
III. Freeman, M. J., 1950–
380.5'094   HE243

ISBN 0-7190-0839-5 (cased)
ISBN 0-7190-0979-0 (paperback)

Library of Congress cataloging in publication data

Main entry under title:

Transport in the industrial revolution.
  Bibliography: p. 210.
  Includes index.
  1. Transportation — Great Britain — History —
Eighteenth century — Addresses, essays, lectures.
2. Transportation — Great Britain — History —
Nineteenth century — Addresses, essays, lectures.
I. Albert, William. II. Aldcroft, Derek Howard.
III. Freeman, Michael J.
HE243.T74 1983   380.5'0941   82-62266

Printed in Great Britain
by Redwood Burn Ltd, Trowbridge, Wiltshire

CONTENTS

TABLES

ILLUSTRATIONS

PREFACE

Despite all that has been written in recent decades on British transport history during the industrial revolution, no single text examines, in turn, the progress of improvement in the four major transport sectors: road, inland water, coastal navigation and ports. Dyos and Aldcroft and Bagwell provide general surveys within their respective texts: *British Transport: an economic survey from the seventeenth century to the twentieth* (1969) and *The Transport Revolution from 1770* (1974), while at the other extreme there is a still growing plethora of material dealing with single transport sectors and with their many component parts. Between the two, however, a kind of 'no man's land' has arisen, resulting in a failure to recognise properly the inter-dependencies and interconnections which existed between waggon, barge and coaster, and an all too frequent tendency to view single sectors in an interpretative vacuum. The aim of the present volume is to bridge this gap. In commissioning a series of specialist contri-butions, in establishing some uniformity of treatment, and in under-pinning the whole with a broadly based introduction, it is hoped that students and researchers will gain a more realistic and balanced picture of transport evolution within the classic industrial phase. This is not to lay claim to having produced a semi-definitive volume; limitations of space alone prevented such a goal. Rather our aim has been to refine, update and expand the broad surveys of Dyos and Aldcroft and Bagwell against the ever-growing mosaic of detailed inventory and analysis.

No preface is complete without a list of apologies. The first must go to those whose interests lie in Wales and in Scotland, for with only a few exceptions, both countries have been omitted from the study — largely on grounds of space. Apologies must go also to those readers who expected to find in the introductory chapter a brief synopsis of contemporary economic and social change. It was felt, however, that few readers would come to a volume on transport development without some background knowledge of this kind. And since the literature is vast, anyway, there appeared to be no useful pur-pose in offering some replication of it. Our final regrets must be for the limited attention it has been possible to give to the transport/economy theme. If any single criticism can be levelled at the literature of British transport history, it is surely the deficient space accorded to this all-important relationship. Each chapter touches upon the theme and it has also been given some consideration in the introduction. In most cases, though, the emphasis has been towards isolating the more profitable areas of enquiry as distinct from offering definitive statements or conclusions. Thus it is to future students and researchers that we must look for providing answers to the many questions which remain.

The task of editing is always an exacting one. The editors wish to record their gratitude to the secretarial staffs at Leicester and Oxford for handling what after two and a half years of preparation has turned into a mountain of correspondence. The individual contributions were written over a period of about eighteen months, from early 1979 to mid-1980, and we are most grateful to the respective authors both for agreeing to contribute in the first place and for listening to our advice and criticisms as the scheme developed. Finally, we must register our appreciation for the many undergraduates and students who, often unwittingly, have contributed to the making of the book. Without the experiences and demands of teaching, it might never have appeared.

> *Department of Economic and Social History*
> *University of Leicester*
>
> *School of Geography*
> *University of Oxford*

1 INTRODUCTION
Michael J. Freeman

A transport revolution?

One of the commonest pitfalls for the student of transport development during the industrial revolution is the tendency to view the
internal trade and transport of the preceding eras as if looking back
to a pseudo-primeval society, as if there was some fundamental
discontinuity between 'pre-industrial' and 'industrial'. The temp-
tations of such a viewpoint are many, and perhaps not entirely without
foundation; it is a viewpoint, moreover, that has found favour well
beyond the confines of the transport sector, as any critical reader of
the textbook literature will know. But what it fails to appreciate is the
whole nature of the industrial transition, 'transition' being the
operative word, and more specifically the actual dynamics of transport
advance in the period. The point has been made forcibly by John
Chartres, who after detailed analysis of the London road carrying
business in the seventeenth century was led to question the 'binding-
mud analysis' of pre-industrial road transport.[1] He saw the London
business, in particular, as integral support for Wrigley's model of the
capital's role in transforming English economy and society between
1650 and 1750,[2] as well as underpinning in both the historical and the
operational sense the nation's carrier system at large. This view finds
echo in T. S. Willan's very much earlier work on river navigation. The
canal era, he wrote in 1936, should not be seen as a fundamental break
with the past, but rather as the natural and inevitable outcome of the
river improvements of the previous 150 years; canals fitted into and
augmented the framework of river navigation which had been created
and used during that preceding century and a half.[3]

The same concern for a 'long run' view of development features
very clearly in the chapters that follow on coastal shipping and ports.
The coasting trade long antedated the beginnings of modern industrialisation in the closing decades of the eighteenth century; even the
earlier river improvement schemes appear late by comparison. The
east-coast trades in coal and grain were already well established at the
end of the Elizabethan era, while the early significance of seawise
traffic, generally, is demonstrably seen in the Crown legislation of

1559 which defined the port towns through which all trade had to pass. Above all, it is perhaps in the 'commercial revolution', the acceleration in trade following the Restoration, that one finds the strongest argument for the deeper historical perspective.[4] The traditional Rostowian 'take-off' finds little or no support in the statistics of eighteenth-century port traffic.

Where, then, does this leave the conventional idea of a 'transport revolution' accompanying the 'revolutions' in industrial technique and organisation and in agriculture? It leaves it in some disarray. And the more so if one pauses to scrutinise more carefully the nature of contemporary transport advance. Few turnpikes, for instance, consisted of entirely new roads; by far the majority covered roads already in existence. The turnpike, moreover, did not replace the existing statute system of road maintenance; it merely supplemented it. Similar difficulties present themselves when one looks at the canal as an example of fundamental technological advance. While there can be little doubt of its significance in civil engineering terms and its importance in the realisation of scale economies in particular industries, the fact remains that the horse continued to be the means of traction and that one of the natural elements remained its fundamental basis, with all the attendant vagaries. Canals may have avoided the shoals and rapids of rivers, but they were far more liable to frost stoppage in sub-zero weather and water shortage in dry — the latter exacerbated by deficiencies of water supply engineering and the waste arising from lockage. In the shipping sector the absence of fundamental technological advance is even more striking. Ignoring for the moment the introduction of the steamship, which largely postdated the industrial transition proper, there was precious little development of the sailing vessel, given its widespread use. Meanwhile port facilities remained decidedly unsophisticated, even primitive, outside the major entrepots of Liverpool, Hull, Bristol and London with their growing numbers of enclosed docks. If we are to speak in terms of revolution, therefore, we need either to seek another historical period altogether or to recast our understanding of the word itself. The former is ostensibly the more just course, notably because the progressive application of steam power to land and sea transport from the 1820s constituted a much more fundamental and far-reaching technological advance, one which reduced and in certain cases eliminated dependence on the elements and animal power, so leading to a transformation in the pace, scale and conduct of trade. The steam engine affected all transport sectors.

That it failed to progress very far in road traction was due more to prohibitive turnpike tolls than to any technical weaknesses, as the widespread experimentation with steam lorries around 1900 testifies. It is thus in the middle decades of the nineteenth century, in Rostow's 'drive to maturity', that one sees radical change in the dynamics of the transport sector; not in the classic period of industrialisation.

Having assigned the idea of a 'revolution' to a later period than that covered by this book, what can be said about the nature of transport development at the time? One clue is to be found in the deep historical roots of the various transport sectors. The sequence of highway legislation, river navigation schemes, turnpike and canal promotions and dock and harbour improvements represented a continuous drive to upgrade existing systems of transport. What we see in the fifty years from 1770 was the culmination of a long, at times uneven but nevertheless perceptible movement towards greater efficiency, both in terms of basic infrastructure (the provision of networks and services) and in the institutional framework within which that infrastructure fell. The history of the road carrying industry is one long catalogue of minor improvements and adjustments — from John Taylor's famous *Carriers' Cosmographie* in 1637 to the veritable kaleidoscope of services which extended from London and the provincial centres by the eve of the railway age. Steadily during the eighteenth century packhorses were replaced by waggons, with all that meant in terms of greater capacity. Slightly later, it became the practice to change horses at set intervals along the route, a development which not only reduced journey times but encouraged greater frequency of services by enabling vehicles to be used more intensively. Besides these refinements in tractive effort there were improvements in the vehicles themselves: the adoption of the variable front axle, the introduction of rudimentary springing and the addition of brakes. Institutional advance was seen in the evolution of common working practices: in, for instance, the regularisation of transhipment arrangements and rules of payment. Progressively there emerged a distinct hierarchy of firms, serving the range of needs from long-distance inter-urban traffic to those met by the perfunctory village carrier. It was not a static hierarchy, of course, for the carrying business was as much prey to economic fluctuation as any other, if not more so by its very nature. Rather it was dynamic in structure, ever responsive to the shifts and pressures of the economy, and of specific transport requirements.

In the development of the waterway network a remarkably similar pattern can be traced. The drive towards greater efficiency began in making the rivers more navigable — through the construction of dead-water cuts, regulating sluices, pound locks and other devices. When the network endowed by nature had been fully utilised attention shifted to achieving wider coverage by means of artificial links between major drainage systems (e.g. the Trent & Mersey or Grand Trunk scheme) and enabling mineral resources to be tapped where there were no rivers (e.g. the Duke of Bridgewater's Worsley scheme). With one or two notable exceptions the first generation of canals were of the 'contour' variety, generally following a level course, however circuitous. Many of the earlier schemes were also of the 'narrow' type, with locks only 7 ft in width. As trade expanded, and rival modes of transport extended and improved, the contour principle gave way to an undulating one, requiring more locks and heavier engineering works,[5] while the standard lock width became 14 ft — the so-called broad canal. The underlying aim of these changes was a spatially more efficient waterway system, the search for which continued in the closing years of the canal era with the construction of shorter alternative cuts such as Cubitt's Birmingham & Liverpool Junction scheme, and experiments with inclined planes and lifts. For all this successive and sometimes much more than piecemeal improvement, the ultimate goal of visionary commentators such as John Phillips[6] was far from realisation by the 1830s. Some semblance of a canal network existed, but the inherent drawbacks of inland water as a means of transport, and the fact that alternatives were available, often with as many advantages, ensured that it would never become universal. The question of the 'mix' of transport technologies is fundamental to the period covered by this book and will be returned to below.

In summary, then, the picture of transport development is characterised not by phases of concentrated, radical change so much as a flowering of past efforts to upgrade and improve, the final working out of a continuous process of refinement and readjustment. And what makes this interpretation the more attractive is the way in which transport investment during the period emerges as an almost uninterrupted sequence of response to demand, clearly consistent with the complex, generally unpredictable, economic and political forces that shaped the nation's trade.

The 'geography' of contemporary transport demand

If there has been a past failure to grasp the true complexion of transport development in the period, it is equally the case that the background to it has been inadequate appreciation of the demand framework within which the development occurred. This does not refer to the notion of demand-led expansion, but rather to the evolving geographical pattern of demand, in a relative as well as absolute sense, and to its changing technical requirements. More broadly, the sequence and scale of contemporary advance has, in the first instance, to be seen against the 'operational milieu' within which it took place. At the general level this demands an awareness of overall economic, social and political capacities and trends, an already accepted *sine qua non*. At a more specific level, it means an appreciation of the practical forces and controls which moulded the character of transport development, often in readily identifiable ways.

The best known example of this kind of demand analysis is to be found in E. A. Wrigley's seminal paper on the supply of raw materials in the industrial revolution.[7] Canal development, he asserts, needs to be seen against the change from organic to inorganic raw materials, from vegetable or animal sources to minerals. The production of the former is areal; of the latter, punctiform. Transporting thousands of tons of coal from pitheads clustered within a few square miles of each other entails quite different problems from moving a similar weight of timber from an area of several hundred square miles. With coal there will be heavy tonnages moving along a select number of routeways; with timber, the reverse. Canals fitted into and were a necessary part of this shift in raw material supply and of the consequent change in the nature of transport demand. And in so far as the coastline may be considered an extension of inland navigation, the same analysis can be applied to the development of coastal shipping, notably the Newcastle coal trade. One might even extend Wrigley's argument to the emergence of the factory system. The concentration of labour and machinery under one roof as against the dispersal so characteristic of domestic industry clearly made very similar demands: the emphasis shifted from small-scale movement along a multiplicity of channels to capacity movement over a select few. This is not to say, however, that the adoption of the factory mode of production was a major driving force behind navigation and canal promotions. That lay indisputably in the needs of collieries and metal mines, as John Phillips made clear in 1803.[8]

Wrigley's analysis of raw material supply has found few counterparts in the marketing or distributive sides of the newly industrialising economy. Yet, as the present writer has tried to make clear elsewhere,[9] the shift in transport demand that Wrigley identified was to some extent paralleled in the contemporary transformation of the market. One may recognise a transition from an economy where markets were predominantly local and regional to one where they were far more national in their spread. The transport system it needed would be geared not to mass movement along a select few channels but to serving an enormous variety of locations over a multitude of routes. The canal represented the antithesis of this market transformation. It was, instead, one for which the evolving road carrying business was far more fitted. The point is made especially succinctly in the market patterns displayed in fig. 1, patterns which also provide clear testimony of the extent to which a national market for manufactures existed by this time. One should stress that any such reversal of Wrigley's thesis will not be without exceptions. Manufactures destined for major urban markets clearly form one, as do manufactured exports, given that they mainly passed through entrepots such as Liverpool, Hull and London. In each case, inland water was the more appropriate transport system for the reasons described above, though one should not forget that some of the major urban markets contained within them the seats of manufacture.

Mention of manufactured exports leads to the question of overseas trade and the way it developed over the period. For in the changing dimensions of the import and export trades from the early eighteenth century onwards one finds another set of influences on the framework of transport demand. It was not just a case of reinforcing the move towards a series of high-capacity routes. Imports and exports contributed to a wider and more 'connected' system of inland navigation, because so much manufacturing capacity was located well inland, making for substantial line-hauls to and from the major entrepots. The principal feature of foreign trade over the industrial phase was, of course, its expanding volume. There was no continuous upward cycle, as some would have us to believe, and different trades performed differently at different times. But as is noted in chapter 6, when fluctuations are averaged out, growth was *almost* continuous. What contributed to this expansion was the decline in manufactured imports, well under way by the early eighteenth century, and their replacement with raw material imports. Over the first three-quarters of the eighteenth century linen imports fell by about a third; all other manufactures by about three-quarters. Raw material imports, on the other hand, rose by some ninety per cent. This in itself had implications for the framework of transport provision, since the routes followed by linens, for example, upon landing at port would have been markedly different from those followed by imported flax: the one consigned to wholesalers and shopkeepers probably over a considerable range of country, the other to the linen and fustian centres of the northern industrial zones.

Complementary to the transformation in the import trade, there was a remarkable growth in exports, including re-exports, especially in the two decades following the War of American Independence. The runaway growth of the cotton trade in this context is especially well known. As chapter 6 records, by 1804–06 cotton goods accounted for over forty per cent of exports by value. The scale of cotton exporting, coupled with decline in merchanting outlets — witness the rise of the merchant emporium in Manchester — in many ways made the canal to cotton what it already was to coal. And the pattern was encouraged by the practice of delivering export cottons to the outports free of charge:[10] economy of scale in production and sale was matched in transport. The dramatic rise of cotton should not be allowed to obscure the growth of other export sectors, the most neglected surely being wool. Although woollen exports formed a decreasing percentage of total export, by value, over the course of the industrial revolution, they grew, nevertheless, and, what is more, represented a rising proportion of total production. In the West Riding the figure was well over two-thirds by the early nineteenth century, the American and later the South African markets featuring the most strongly. Hence trans-Pennine waterways such as the Leeds & Liverpool Canal found wool exports prominent among their traffic: for the same reasons that the Mersey & Irwell and Bridgewater navigations conveyed cotton exports in quantity from Manchester to Liverpool.

If one can see in the growth of the import and export trades a powerful reinforcement of the drive to develop inland navigation, one can find in the continuance of the domestic system of production a compendium of constraints and forces which worked in quite the opposite direction. It is sometimes thought that the domestic system disappeared rapidly in the path of the industrial revolution. As any student of the textile industries will know, however, the mode of

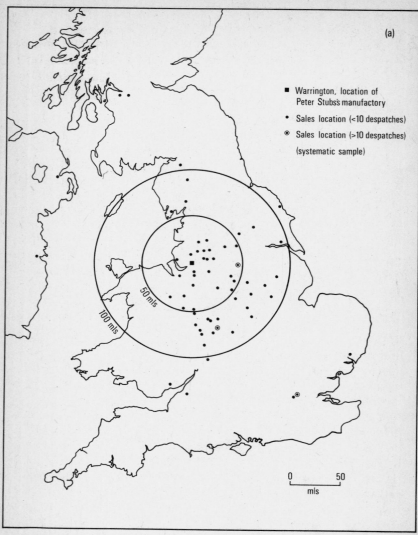

1 Market patterns for (*a*) a Warrington hand-tool maker; and (*b*) a Leeds linen manufacturer. From (*a*) Manchester Central Library Archives, Stubs Ms,

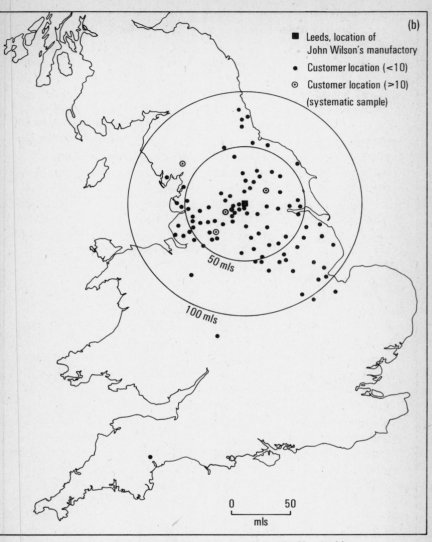

(b)

■ Leeds, location of
John Wilson's manufactory

● Customer location (<10)

⊙ Customer location (>10)
(systematic sample)

50 mls

100 mls

0   50
mls

L24/1 — Warehouse despatch book, 1811–15; (*b*) Leeds City Archives,
Wilson Ms, W/6 — Ledger, 1791–96

organisation which superseded it — the factory system — was very uneven, in cases even slow, in its spread. It came in carding and spinning well before weaving, and in cotton before wool. Indeed, the weaving of woollens remained within a cottage industry until well into the mid-nineteenth century. Thus, side by side with the cotton mills and woollen factories of the new industrial era, a vigorous domestic system was still to be found, with all that that meant in terms of the framework of transport demand. And to focus on textiles is not to miss the many other forms of industry — for instance, the small metal trades — where some sort of outworker system lingered similarly.[11]

Among the various forms of industrial organisation, the domestic system must be the most transport-intensive. To take woollen manufacture as an example: from the clipping of the wool from the sheep's back to its arrival in finished form in the draper's shop was one vast catalogue of movements. From the grazier to the wool factor, from the wool factor to the wool stapler, and from the wool stapler to the clothier represented but the simplest part of the procedure. It was in the processes of manufacture that the greatest mileage could often be registered. Heaton cites the case of a West Riding clothier at Askwith, near Otley, who obtained his wool at York or Wakefield.[12] When brought home, it was first sent out into the vicinity for combing; on its return, it went out again for spinning — in this case to Cheshire and north Derbyshire; when back from spinning it went out yet again for weaving. The cloth was despatched to market, only to begin yet a further stage of the cycle in terms of the various finishing processes. These were not necessarily carried on at the place of market. One can understand why Heaton referred to the 'many peregrinations' in the progress from raw wool to finished cloth.[13] The sequence called for a prodigious amount of travel and transport, but over as diverse a series of paths and scales as could be imagined. Some of the transport was by foot. But much was also by packhorse and waggon, progressively so as general conditions of transport improved. River navigations and canals featured in the movement of raw wool and in the distribution of cloth, especially for export, but inland waterways were ill suited to serve the larger part of the manufacturing process.

Demand preferences: the case against transport choice as simply a function of cheapness

In considering the 'geography' of contemporary transport demand, the feature to emerge most strongly is its heterogeneity, some would say an inevitable feature, given the economic metamorphosis. And this heterogeneity is perhaps no more clearly reflected than in the chapters which follow. The concomitant development and improvement of roads, inland waterways, coastal shipping and ports were directly related to so varying a framework of demand. Moreover, this variation was also to be found within each transport sector, as the respective chapters show.

The idea of the different transport sectors as being separate and to a considerable degree mutually exclusive parts of a whole is somewhat at odds with the recent efforts of econometric historians to evaluate the economic contribution of a single transport mode (most commonly the railroad) on the basis of the 'social savings' it achieved over alternative or earlier modes.[14] Readers who hope to find examples of such analysis in this book will be disappointed. Whatever the initial attractions of evaluating, for example, the economic contribution of the canals as against the road system, it is apparent upon closer scrutiny that such investigations are inappropriate in the context of the period. To indulge in such analyses of relative advantage is to misunderstand entirely the complexion and workings of the contemporary transport sector. The focus here should be not upon social savings but upon the different kinds of benefits, upon the net efficiencies each transport sector produced for the economy. Some substance of these has been demonstrated already in the previous sections.

The tendency, embodied in the social savings idea, to view the demand for transport as homogeneous, and to some extent likewise the supply, has characterised many conventional assessments of the functions performed by the different transport sectors in the industrial revolution. It has probably found commonest expression in the sphere of cost, one writer summing up his assessment of road haulage with the conclusion that because it was so expensive compared with canals the majority of goods were despatched by inland water.[15] What such reasoning fails to appreciate is that cheapness was by no means the overriding criterion. In the same way that the geographical pattern of transport demand contained sharply contrasting elements, met by a variety of transport sectors, so there was a similar variation in the type of transport service required. We may thus extend our earlier demand analysis to embrace the differing service needs of producers and consumers, of the kaleidoscope of industrial concerns and retail establishments which formed the pivot and *raison d'être* of the trading network.

It was none other than Adam Smith who pointed to the tremendous advantages of water carriage in raising the scale of industrial operation through its cheapness over land transport. One is bound to say that there is a wealth of evidence to be found in support. W. T. Jackman, still the foremost authority on transport development in modern England, reckoned that the cost of inland water conveyance was on average between one-fourth and one-half the cost of carriage by road.[16] Coastwise transport, meanwhile, could be cheaper than inland water by an equivalent proportion, as chapter 5 shows. Such cost differentials were most consistent in the movement of heavy, bulky, low-value commodities like grain, coal and other minerals; and this particular strength did much to explain the prominence of water carriage where these commodities were concerned — alongside, that is, those features arising from the spatial characteristics of production, discussed in the previous section. In the field of manufactured goods, or 'general merchandise', as contemporaries called them, the differentials were smaller but still often sufficient to register clear economic gains, particularly over substantial line-hauls. From these sorts of cost comparison it has frequently been a short step to dismissing the road network and the road transport system as insignificant to the industrial transition. What such conclusions overlook, however, is that other considerations were important: speed was one, regularity and reliability others. A comparison of road and inland water haulage will serve to illustrate the point.

Although both road waggon and canal barge were horse-drawn, typically at no more than walking pace, such parity did not extend to the respective journey times. Here the waggon was superior, mainly through the absence of such impediments as locks, and the greater incidence of working by night. Locks were obviously a greater nuisance on canals which traversed a major watershed. The Rochdale Canal had ninety-two locks in a length of only thirty-three miles, the Huddersfield, as chapter 4 notes, an incredible seventy-four in only twenty miles. The negotiation of the five-rise locks at Bingley on the Leeds—Liverpool usually took at least half an hour; moreover the time could be longer if there was already a barge in passage or others were waiting. The very existence of locks was thus as much a delaying influence as the need to negotiate them. Night working on canals was the exception rather than the rule throughout the industrial revolution. For various reasons, they were generally open from an hour before sunrise to an hour after sunset. Only from about the 1820s, with the introduction of 'fly boats' on some, did things begin to change. There were few restrictions of this nature on road transport services. From about 1780, following the improvements of the turnpike trusts, coach proprietors increasingly worked outside daylight hours, and waggon concerns imitated the example soon after. By 1800 scheduled waggons typically departed from major towns or cities at or after dusk, even though they may not have travelled throughout the night. It is exceedingly difficult to generalise about the specific effects of these disparities for journey time differentials. Suffice it to say that the waggon maintained a competitive edge, a line of reasoning which may justly be extended to road versus coastwise carriage, at least before advent of the steamship.

In both regularity and reliability, road transport maintained a similar advantage. Still confining ourselves for the moment to roads and inland waterways, one of the distinguishing marks of the system of organised waggon haulage was the frequency of service and the working to a specific timetable. Stagecoach operators undoubtedly set the tone here, but many of their practices came to be imitated, in varying degree, on the goods side as the demands of trade grew. A glance at any contemporary directory illustrates these features clearly. Waterway operations, while offering a much greater carrying capacity, offered neither a frequent nor a regularly scheduled service, at least not until the introduction of 'fly boats' towards the close of the canal age. Frequency of service was contradictory to the economies of scale achieved in a bargeload. A strict timetable was quite possible in principle, but in practice it was hindered by the comparative unreliability of canal working.

One hears much in the secondary literature — some truth, much untruth — about the execrable state of roads in the period: of mires which threatened to engulf horse and rider alike; of ruts so deep and tortuous as to defy all but the most intrepid of travellers. One hears less of the equivalent perils facing the canal or river-boat operator: the 'locking up' of the waterway by frost in a hard winter, the closures and periods of 'short-water working' which followed dry seasons, or the difficulties occasioned by burst banks, flash-flooding and a host of other hazards, not to mention stoppages occasioned by repairs. When a highway or turnpike was blocked, it was always possible to make a detour. The canal barge had no such means of escape. One reason why the hazard of frost in canal working has received so little attention is the assumption that the climate was much the same then as it is now. This was not the case. The frequency of 'cold' winters (those with a mean temperature below 3°C) was considerably greater, a hangover from a generally colder climatic phase in Tudor and Stuart times loosely termed the 'Little Ice Age'.[17] There is a wealth of information about frost stoppages among the records of canal companies and canal-using businesses. From the correspondence of Stubs Wood & Co., pin manufacturers, of Warrington, Lancashire, we learn that parts of the Trent & Mersey Canal, over which the firm obtained most of its material, were closed by frost for almost five weeks in the winter of 1814–15.[18] Across the Pennines, just twenty years earlier, John Wilson, a Leeds linen manufacturer, experienced similar difficulty in obtaining his supplies of Scottish linen from their landing place at Hull: 'the severe frost we have had for two or three weeks past, has stop'd the Navigation of our River [Aire] and it may be yet some time before we shall receive them'.[19] Here even the usually less vulnerable river navigations were being affected. The Huddersfield Canal was frozen up for thirty-seven days in the winter of 1822–23, for twenty-one days in that of 1825–26 and for seven weeks in the very severe winter of 1837–38.[20] Farther south, the Erewash, Derby, Cromford and Nottingham canals were impeded by frost for lengthy periods in each of the winters of 1813–14, 1819–20 and 1830–31.[21]

With the aid of the contemporary temperature record it is possible to derive some sort of quantitative assessment of the number of working days lost on canals through frost. The details are given elsewhere[22] and attention may be confined here to the results. Taking the Lancashire plain by way of example, it emerges that over the years 1771 to 1831 there are likely to have been stoppages of at least twenty days' duration in thirty winters and up to thirty days in ten of those. Away from the maritime air and on higher ground the figures would have been appreciably higher.

The problems of summer or autumn drought were no less serious. They were compounded on many waterways by deficiencies in water-supply engineering, deficiencies which grew more and more serious as traffic levels rose and newly founded urban water companies competed for supplies. Jackman lists a whole series of canals which were plagued by water shortages throughout their working life.[23] In such cases it often required only a slight shortfall in seasonal rainfall for difficulties to arise. And with an incidence of hot summers greater than we experience today,[24] it is no surprise to discover frequent and sometimes prolonged drought stoppages on many waterways, not to mention the times when barges could only be partly laden. In the summers of 1818 and 1826 the Huddersfield canal was forced to close its summit section for thirty-nine and sixty-two days respectively.[25] The Leeds—Liverpool recorded almost exactly similar conditions in 1824 and 1826.[26] In reporting the state of works on the new Birmingham & Liverpool Junction Canal in the summer of 1824, Thomas Cubitt held out little hope of an early opening, owing to the 'long continued drought of the present season, which has caused an entire suspension of business on some canals and great want of water on others'.[27] When we add to frost and drought the interruptions due to floods, burst banks and the necessity for repairs, it is clear that inland waterway working was anything but reliable. Users had to accept the consequent irregularities of delivery and supply, or anticipate them by stockpiling, or turn to land carriage. Of course, it would be foolish to imagine that road transport did not suffer from bad weather, particularly in heavy snow or times of flood. But the hazards of frost and drought brought none of the consequences faced by the waterways. By hardening road surfaces, they could actually make carriage easier.

These distinctive contrasts in regularity and reliability reappear in any consideration of road alongside coastal carriage. With the exception of a few heavily trafficked routes, coasting vessels operated to no clearly defined timetable, and in the case of many of the lesser ports they could be decidedly uncertain. In dealings with a Colchester wool factor in the early years of the nineteenth century Robert Jowitt & Son, Leeds woollen merchants and manufacturers, observed that wool shipments sent coastwise from Colchester to Hull or Selby might be better sent first by land to London, *then* by coaster to Hull: 'the freight is much lower there [London] and ships sailing weekly and oftener. They are more dilatory at your port than any we have to do with.'[28] John Wilson, the Leeds linen manufacturer, had rather similar grounds for dissatisfaction on the Dundee—Hull route in the early 1790s, one of his main channels of raw linen supply. It was not a problem of dilatoriness, simply that there was but one vessel working the route. 'I wish you had two ships in this trade,' he wrote to his Hull shipping agent in May 1790.[29] Regularity of working was not, of course, easily attainable under sail, the more so given the unpredictability of the English weather. The Dover Strait was renowned for its difficult winds, which sometimes held traffic up for months at a time. And the apparently more sheltered east-coast route could often become prey to violent storms. In January 1803 Robert Jowitt & Son heard that a vessel bound from Dover to Hull with sixteen packs of their fleeces had been driven right up to South Shields.[30] Two years later the *Rochdale*, with seven packs aboard, was reported 'on shore near Lowestoft'.[31] The 'risks of the sea' could be covered by insurance, but this served to reduce the cost advantages, the more so when wharfage dues were added, and the additional ton-mileage incurred on a less direct route than land carriage could usually offer. Where sea freights were exceptionally low, as between London and Hull, the advantages might remain strong after such deductions. In other cases the picture might be very much less favourable.

The question of the full economic cost of water carriage, whether coastwise or by inland waterway, is seldom acknowledged or investigated (see chapter 4). In the movement of raw cotton between Liverpool and Manchester around 1815, consignments by waggon cost only half as much again as by waterway when carting costs for the latter were taken into account.[32] One thus needs to be wary of bland generalisations about the vastly lower cost of water alongside road carriage. Indeed, there were sometimes instances where a near parity of charges prevailed, as indicated in a letter from a Leeds dyer to a dyestuff merchant in London in 1799: 'be so good as forward us 50 lbs Cochineal soon as possible pr *Rockingham* [coaster] and if you think it [i.e. the cost per *Rockingham*] will be no lower send us a bag by Jackson's waggon'.[33]

To conclude, it is necessary to pose the question: under what circumstances might cheapness of transport be forsaken for greater speed, regularity or reliability? The circumstances were many, intricately bound up with the nature of the industrialising economy. The frequent fluctuations in the state of trade, the almost constant advent of new firms and processes, made a flexible production capacity, and more specifically an ability to capitalise quickly on an advancing market, almost a *sine qua non* of survival and success. The faster and more reliable road transport system was a key to that flexibility. Where conditions of bulk and weight permitted, it enabled increased supplies of raw materials to be obtained with the minimum loss of manufacturing time. Thus, upon the cessation of hostilities in 1815, M'Connel & Kennedy, the giant Manchester spinners, ordered cotton from Liverpool brokers to be conveyed by road rather than water, the carrier being placed on forfeiture of carriage charge if consignments were not delivered within a stated time.[34] A similar pattern could prevail in product sales, a sudden upturn in the market or a run on a particular category of goods being met by a temporary shift to land carriage when cheaper water conveyance was the 'norm'. It was for this reason that William Lupton & Co., the well known Leeds woollen merchants, sometimes chose to send their American exports by Hartley's or Welsh's waggons to Manchester and then by water to Liverpool, rather than sending them by the Union Company which offered a through service over the Leeds—Liverpool canal.[35]

Disregarding periods of economy buoyancy, the time factor could be important in its own right. Undue time in transit, or undue delays, could mean lost manufacturing capacity and lost sales. This in turn could result in a growing debt, with rising interest payments to accompany it. Thus in their difficulties over the shipment of wool coastwise from Colchester, Robert Jowitt & Son remarked that 'the interest of money' was as much as the land carriage to London.[36] Some smaller manufacturers led such a hand-to-mouth existence that they had no choice but to employ the quicker and more reliable means of transport. For them the risk of incurring debt or debt interest was unthinkable. They waited on receipt of bills for goods sold before any further material could be purchased. Thus economic survival was often circumscribed by the facility with which trading operations could be carried out.[37]

The time factor could also take on special significance in any manufacturing operation for which the market was highly competitive. Sales success depended not just on competitiveness in quality and price but also on the efficiency of distribution. This was an attribute which the road transport system was by far the more capable of providing. Such considerations became all the more valid where products were of a high value in relation to their bulk or weight; in their case transport cost had little or no importance. John and Joseph Holroyd of Sheepscar, Leeds, who had the reputation of being among the best dyers of woollen cloth in the West Riding, relied on land carriage almost exclusively in the assembly and despatch of their material, even to markets as distant as London.[38] What underlines the point is that it was not Holroyd's themselves who paid carriage. It is possible, therefore, to find circumstances where speed, regularity and reliability could figure not only as a temporary preference in transport decision-making but as a permanent, integral element of production. These balancing arguments in favour of land carriage may be added to those in the geographical analysis of demand in section two.

Transport and economic development

It would be inappropriate to introduce a book of this kind without some reference to that 'cinderella' of themes, the relationship between transport and economic development. Until the 1960s the prevailing view of transport's role in economic growth was a very positive one. Transport was seen as a leading economic sector of itself, *engendering* growth. And not only in terms of 'forward linkages' — economic benefits stemming from the ability to convey commodities in greater volume, more quickly and at reduced cost — but also in terms of 'backward linkages', the derived demands of transport development in terms of new construction, new operating equipment and new employment. Lord Lugard, in 1922, asserted that the development of Africa could be summed up in one word: 'transport'.[39] Almost forty years later, W. W. Rostow felt justified in claiming the railroad to have been the most powerful single initiator of take-offs into self-sustained growth.[40]

From various writings on the subject after about 1960 it emerged that this traditional interpretation was founded in very few cases on any close, quantitative analysis of the evidence or on any proper investigation of the mechanics of economic growth. Upon examination it transpired that the grounds for a 'positive' view of transport's role were shaky, at the least; there was a case not only for seeing transport as playing a 'permissive' role but also for regarding it as a 'lagging' sector. The permissive view is usually first associated with A. O. Hirschman, in his *Strategy for Economic Development*.[41] Not in any way incompatible with this, though, are the several reinterpretations of the railroad in American economic growth, generally taken to represent the 'lagging' view. Foremost of these is undoubtedly R. W. Fogel's thesis in which he concluded that the railroad was not a vital ingredient of American economic growth and that the transport demands of the evolving economy might just as easily have been met by an improved and extended inland waterway system.[42]

The debate which followed reinterpretations of this kind was extended and controversial;[43] indeed, it continues even now.[44] What seems to be emerging is that there can be no universal rules concerning the relationship between transport and economic growth. It is necessary to recognise that there is scope for positive, permissive and even 'negative' (i.e. transport investment being misdirected investment) viewpoints. Above all, it must be accepted that the nature of the relationship may vary over space and through time — from one region and from one country to another, and over the historical continuum. Variability through time is to some extent inevitable, given the 'lumpy' nature of so much transport investment, capacity often being added in fits and starts rather than evenly over the years. The 'geography' of economic growth, meanwhile, is a theme which has recently been attracting considerable attention among economic historians and development economists, even if, to quote John Langton, it has yet to match Walter Isard's contention that 'a well balanced economic history must explicitly consider spatial processes and the evolving web of interregional relationships'.[45]

Against these considerations, it is useful at this stage to recall Hirschman's ideas about the relationship between 'social overhead capital' (investment in transport and power) and 'direct productive activities'.[46] Investment in the two sectors, he suggested, may well follow an unbalanced sequence. In one case, investment might be channelled first into the expansion of DPA, simply making more intensive use of existing transport resources. Here, transport investment comes only when congestion arises and the benefits of a new infrastructure are demonstrably evident. In another case the position may be almost reversed, transport taking the initial investment and investment in DPA expected to follow from the consequent gains to producers. In transport terms, the first alternative is referred to as 'development by shortage', the second as 'development by excess'. Fig. 2 illustrates the two possibilities diagrammatically, the evenly spaced curves representing successively greater levels of DPA, the straight line $Y-Z$ an exactly balanced sequence of transport investment.

What light do the findings of this book cast on the relationship between transport and economy as examined above? The balance of opinion seems to fall very much in favour of Hirschman's 'development by shortage' view. Before offering evidence in support, however, it is useful to stress one essential difference between many of the transport improvements being examined here and that major focus of debate, the railroad. As stressed earlier, the steam railway represented a fundamentally different technology compared with existing systems. It made fundamentally different demands upon the economy, in particular in its need for vast supplies of heavy industrial materials in construction and operation. From Mitchell's figures, the railways' demand for iron for permanent way alone was almost thirty per cent of total estimated pig-iron production in the years

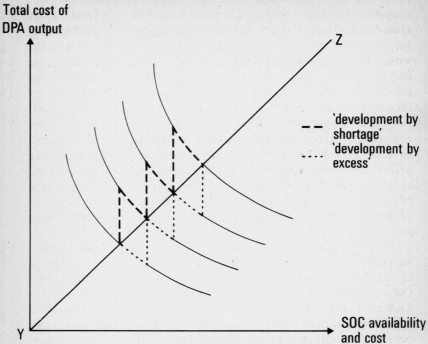

2 The relationship between SOC and DPA. After A. O. Hirschman. *Strategy of Economic Development*, Yale University Press, 1958

1844–51.[47] One finds few parallels within the transport sectors under consideration here. Turnpiking certainly required little in the way of manufactured inputs. Canal and dock construction were notable more for their demands on man and animal power to build extensive earthworks. In terms of derived demands, therefore, one sees a much lesser impact — at least until steamship operations began to establish a new pattern after 1820. Of course, this should not lead us to gloss over the enormous labour demands of transport during the period. The railway 'navvies', as is well known, got their name from the earlier army of canal builders, while road transport gave permanent employment to vast numbers of people, including the many involved in supplying animal feedstuffs: the complexities of the coach and carrier network as conveyed in chapter 3 were repeated in the underpinning structure of offices, warehouses, inns and stables. If one looks at the full range of derived demands, however, the railroad's precursors had a more restricted impact.

The 'development by shortage' view perhaps finds its clearest support in chapters 2 and 4. Almost all the earlier turnpike schemes, up to about 1750, were clearly responses to growing traffic levels and the severe difficulties they presented for road maintenance. As chapter 2 notes, the trusts here need to be distinguished carefully from other forms of transport improvement which were 'more unambiguously positive innovations'. In this context, moreover, it is curious how contemporary travellers' descriptions of the appalling state of the roads have so often been taken to indicate limited traffic levels. What they may equally reflect is a *rising* volume of traffic, a trend the turnpike trusts were clearly directed to accommodate. During the 1750s and 1760s one can discern a slight shift in this relationship — according to Albert, largely the influence of the 'demonstration effect'. As the pace of trust development increases there is evidence of a kind of 'creative disequilibrium'. Turnpike promotion became necessary to 'mitigate any comparative disadvantage brought about by road improvement in other areas'. The term 'mania' is often used to characterise the developments of these years, but it implies an irrationality that is probably more imagined than real. Certainly there were lunatic schemes, as well as schemes which were to make sense only later.[48] This was not, however, the broad tenor of development. Besides, there is evidence of a marked upturn in road traffic during the two decades concerned. After 1770 the development slowed, and in some regions one can observe a process of infilling and the setting up of alternative routes. In the north of the country, though, turnpiking was of a more substantive nature, explained by the fact that the newly rising industrial areas had figured comparatively little in the earlier phases. As chapter 2 notes, over the period 1791–1836 Lancashire and Yorkshire accounted for 32 per cent of new turnpike Acts.

The sequence of waterway development offers a broadly similar picture. Leaving aside Willan's point about the canal era being a perfectly logical progression from the earlier drive to improve rivers, analysis of the timing of canal promotions supports the view that they followed periods of trade expansion — as congestion and undercapacity made their appearance. It was once commonly thought that the timing of canal investment was mainly a function of capital supply and the cost of credit.[49] When interest rates were low and borrowing was cheaper, money flowed more readily into transport schemes when they promised greater returns. J. R. Ward has since discredited this idea.[50] Over the short and medium term, canal development was more closely correlated with the growth of traffic than with movements in the rate of interest. When trade flourished in the 1750s, 1760s, early 1770s and early 1790s canal schemes flourished too. By contrast, when trade slackened, as from the mid-1770s to 1790, the number of waterway projects also fell. Indeed, Ward even went so far as to observe that any measure of correlation with interest rates probably reflects no causal connection at all.

It would be wrong to be carried away completely by the traffic-led view of development here. The demonstration effect described by Albert, for instance, had some counterpart in the years of canal mania, while there were more than a few 'economically suicidal' or 'downright lunatic' schemes at the time. What helped to cloud the position further was the widening geography of canal finance after 1790. Whereas canal promotions up to then had been financed almost entirely locally, the pattern from 1790 proved rather different, as chapter 4 demonstrates. Money was forthcoming from areas far removed from the scene of schemes themselves. In short, canals became a form of speculative investment — in a way that turnpike trusts were never to become. Although one might see in this change support for a more positive interpretation of transport improvement, it seems that little of the new investment was founded on any careful analysis of profitability, and in consequence the number of mania schemes which eventually proved a dismal failure was considerable. A few created their own stimulus, but the speculative boom tended to remove development from any rational economic perspective.

Outside turnpike and canal promotion, the 'development by shortage' view is echoed in the sphere of harbour and dock improvement. At the major ports of Liverpool, Hull and London the sequence was a long catalogue of response to demand, while at lesser ports a large proportion of the increasing trade was accommodated simply by using existing capacity more intensively. As chapter 6 notes, attempts by landowners and traders to 'steal a march on their fellows' by founding or finding new ports were frequently disappointed. So complexly interconnected was the relationship between ports and their traffic becoming that attempts to manipulate it were bound to run into trouble. In fact this has been a characteristic of port development even in more recent times.

Finally, in the provision of road transport services one can find further threads to strengthen the above interpretation, in road haulage particularly — as shown in chapter 3. However, it is important not to overlook the low unit capitalisation of much road service capacity, especially compared with turnpike, canal and harbour ventures. It permitted a responsiveness to fluctuations in trade that was more inherent than specific and hence does not present a really satisfactory comparison. This factor undoubtedly lay behind the evidence of supply-induced expansion in the formative years of the coaching business, as identified in chapter 3. Much at variance with the other transport sectors, even including road haulage, the sophisticated and mature structure in coaching by 1820 may have owed much to the creative energies of the early operators. But here, of course, one is dealing with a relatively new dimension in transport. By comparison with freight, the market for passenger travel in 1750 was comparatively untested. Travel was not then a consumer good, in the way it was to become seventy or eighty years later. Experiment and creativity, supply-led expansion, were thus to some extent inevitable features.

Towards a contextual as distinct from a compositional perspective?

One of the special problems of studying transport as an economic sector is that in some ways it has little real existence. It exists simply as a mechanism of trade, performing a service as distinct from producing goods — excepting, that is, some passenger transport. An inevitable result has been that much writing on the subject is cast in a heavily institutional mould. Without conscious and concerted effort to see the sector in its wider context, it has been too easy simply to focus on improvements of the infrastructure, operating arrangements and such elements as competition, the latter an especially prominent feature of the British transport scene. Earlier the case was stated for seeing transport development in England during the industrial revolution in the light of the framework of demand, in terms of both the evolving geographical pattern and the nature of the service required. Whilst this goes some way towards broadening the perspective, it still fails to embrace the full 'milieu' of which transport forms a part. The scale and nature of trade, for instance, remain largely unexplored. From Wrigley and others we may have a fairly clear conception of its broader dimensions. We know comparatively little about its more detailed structure, about the complex relationships and flows which made up the industrial metamorphosis.

It would be misleading to suggest that the study of trade is a universally grey area. The work of Ralph Davis and others on English overseas trade confirms the point eloquently,[51] while chapters 5 and 6 are as much concerned with trade as with more institutional elements. Few will deny, however, the chronic inattention to internal trade, an omission which in fact extends over a considerably longer period than that examined here.[52] The main explanation is the dearth of sources. Records of inland transport concerns are notoriously uninformative about the life-blood of their business, the commodity movements that provided their *raison d'être*. One may infer a little from the scale and pattern of transport provision, but to try to read from it any hard-and-fast conclusions would be exceedingly dangerous. If the transport institutions are unforthcoming of information on trade, it is logical to look instead to the consumers, to the merchants and manufacturing groups for whom transport services were essential. The sources here are much more plentiful and present an altogether different perspective. Space does not permit a detailed illustration of the possibilities that emerge. Figure 3, however, gives an idea of the sort of trading relationships that characterised an emerging industrial region such as the West Riding. When pictures of this kind are juxtaposed with the evolving spectrum of transport services the real significance of transport improvement will be easier to grasp, as also will be an understanding of the nature of regional economies and the dimensions of regional economic change. What is especially striking about fig. 3 is the extent to which the West Riding's trade relations had penetrated and, more broadly, how far economic exchange and specialisation had advanced by around 1800.

These changes in the scale and pattern of trade were part of that wider transformation of economy and society sometimes called the rise of industrial capitalism or, more simply, the process of modernisation. There was an alteration in the relations between groups within society; there were alterations in the prevailing value systems, in the way in which people responded to change, and in a whole host of other things, not least being tides of taste and fashion. The sequence of transport improvement needs to be interpreted as much within this socio-economic context as in the stricter field of trade evolution. Albert takes an important step on this path in his assessment of popular opposition to the turnpike trusts. The trusts need to be seen as part of that 'sweeping away ... of the traditional social order and replacing [it] with institutions and relationships more appropriate for an emergent industrial capitalism'. In the imposition of tolls the trusts 'redefined a fundamental property relationship', replacing a communal institution with one based on monetary payment. In a different vein but no less relevant is H. J. Dyos's interpretation of canal development as part of the broader process of substituting capital for labour.[53] And canal investment might be similarly regarded in connection with the evolution of the money market. At times the transport sector appears little more than an extension of the new socio-economic system, the upper echelons of the coaching business offering perhaps the best case in point. The 'mails' and their immediate counterparts existed primarily to meet the needs of merchants, manufacturers and the business community as a whole. They developed from the last quarter of the eighteenth century in response to the quickening pace of the economy, to the evolving order of merchants and industrialists to whom an efficient and deepening contact network was a fundamental necessity. The ability to track market prices closely, to buy or sell when profit margins were greatest, to achieve a quicker and more reliable circulation of capital, to read the opportunities for expansion — all these things hinged upon the coaching system. It was not simply a matter of facilitating contact and speeding up the conveyance of letters, the latter bearing information on prices, transmitting orders and bills of payment, and establishing terms of trade. Alongside this, there was the intensive traffic in parcels and small packages, that in trade samples above all. Stagecoaches were used for conveying samples ranging from raw cotton and wool to yarn, thread and cloth,

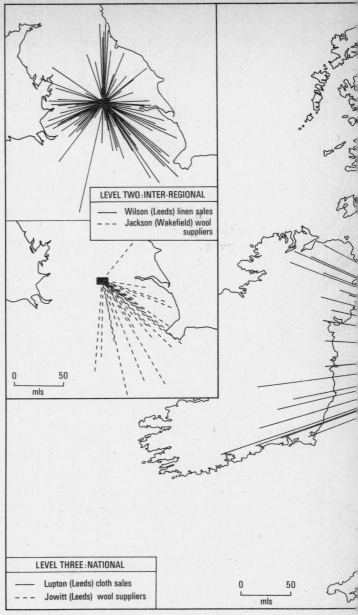

LEVEL TWO: INTER-REGIONAL

—— Wilson (Leeds) linen sales

- - - Jackson (Wakefield) wool
      suppliers

0   50
   mls

LEVEL THREE: NATIONAL

—— Lupton (Leeds) cloth sales

- - - Jowitt (Leeds) wool suppliers

0   50
   mls

3 Trading relationships (domestic) of the West Riding of Yorkshire, c. 1790–
   1815. From Ms records of five sample businesses, viz. Robert Jowitt & Sons,
   Leeds wool merchants (University of Leeds, Brotherton Library); Robert
   Clough, Keighley worsted spinners and manufacturers (Brotherton Library);

LEVEL ONE: INTRA-REGIONAL

—— Jowitt (Leeds) wool sales
---- Clough (Keighley) sales of
       worsted yarn and cloth

KEIGHLEY

LEEDS

Br

Hfx

0   5
  mls

John Wilson & Sons, Leeds linen manufacturers (Leeds City Archives);
Joseph Jackson, Wakefield woolstaplers (Wakefield District Archives);
William Lupton & Co., Leeds woollen and worsted manufacturers and
traders (Brotherton Library)

from bar iron to precision tools, and from hops to drinking ale.[54] Thus in a way that was never as true in any of the other transport sectors, a part of the coaching business not only echoed the socio-economic transformation but was manifestly part of it.

Wider considerations such as these understandably find little room in the chapters that follow. It is to be hoped, however, that their mention will direct future researchers to more broadly based investigations: towards seeing transport as the measure of the relations between places; to an appreciation of the social and political milieu within which transport provision is generated. In this way the so far illusory goal of 'roles and relations' may be more nearly approached.

Notes

The author acknowledges the financial support of the Social Science Research Council in making possible some of the research from which this introduction stems.

1   J. A. Chartres, 'Road carrying in England in the seventeenth century: myth and reality', *Economic History Review*, 2nd ser., XXX, 1977, pp. 73–94.

2   E. A. Wrigley, 'A simple model of London's importance in changing English society and economy, 1650–1750', *Past and Present*, XXXVII, 1967, pp. 44–70.

3   T. S. Willan, *River Navigation in England, 1600–1750*, Oxford University Press, London, 1936, pp. 138–40.

4   See R. Davis, 'English foreign trade, 1660–1700', *Economic History Review*, 2nd ser., VII, 1954, pp. 150–66; and *id.*, 'English foreign trade, 1700–1774', *Economic History Review*, 2nd ser., XV, 1962, pp. 285–303.

5   An interesting attempt to quantify this change is to be found in J. H. Farrington, *Morphological Studies of English Canals*, University of Hull Occasional Papers in Geography No. 20, Hull, 1972.

6   J. Phillips, *The General History of Inland Navigation ... etc.*, London, 1792.

7   E. A. Wrigley, 'The supply of raw materials in the industrial revolution', *Economic History Review*, 2nd ser., XV, 1962, pp. 1–16.

8   J. Phillips, *The General History of Inland Navigation*, London, 4th ed., 1803.

9   M. J. Freeman, 'Road transport in the English industrial revolution: an interim reassessment', *Journal of Historical Geography*, VI, 1980, pp. 17–28.

10   See M. J. Freeman, 'Transporting methods in the British cotton industry during the industrial revolution', *Journal of Transport History*, 3rd ser., I, 1980, p. 67.

11   See, for instance, T. S. Ashton, *An Eighteenth Century Industrialist: Peter Stubs of Warrington, 1756–1806*, Manchester University Press, 1939.

12   H. Heaton, *The Yorkshire Woollen and Worsted Industries*, Clarendon Press, Oxford, 1920, pp. 335–6.

13   *Ibid.*, p. 395.

14   A brief survey of the field is contained in P. O'Brien, *The New Economic History of the Railways*, Croom Helm, London, 1977.

15 P. S. Bagwell, *The Transport Revolution from 1770*, Batsford, London, 1974, p. 60.

16 W. T. Jackman, *The Development of Transportation in Modern England*, Cambridge University Press, 1916, II, p. 729.

17 For details see H. H. Lamb, *Climate: Present, Past and Future*, Methuen, London, 1977, II, pp. 461–73, 569–70.

18 Manchester Central Library Archives, Stubs Wood & Co. Ms, L24/2 — Correspondence and Orders.

19 Leeds City Archives, Wilson Ms, W/3/17 — Letter book, 1792–95.

20 Wakefield District Archives (Goodchild Loan Ms), Aldam Collection — Reports of the Committee of the Huddersfield Canal Company, 1823, 1826, 1838.

21 See G. G. Hopkinson, 'The inland navigations of the Derbyshire and Nottinghamshire coalfield, 1777–1856', *Journal of the Derbyshire Archaeological and Natural History Society*, LXXIX, 1959, p. 37.

22 Freeman, 'Road transport', pp. 23–5.

23 Jackman, *Development of Transportation*, I, pp. 429–31.

24 See Lamb, *Climate*, p. 571.

25 W.D.A. (Goodchild Loan Ms), Aldam Collection — Reports of the Committee of the Huddersfield Canal Company, 1819, 1827.

26 C. Hadfield and G. Biddle, *The Canals of North West England*, David & Charles, Newton Abbot, 1970, I, p. 179.

27 W.D.A. (Goodchild Loan Ms), Aldam Collection — Report of the Committee of the Birmingham and Liverpool Junction Canal Navigation, 1834.

28 University of Leeds, Brotherton Library, Jowitt Ms, 31 — Letter book, 1802–05.

29 L.C.A., Wilson Ms, W/3/16 — Letter book, 1790–92.

30 U.L.B.L., Jowitt Ms, 31 — Letter book, 1802–05.

31 *Ibid.*

32 Freeman, 'Transporting methods', pp. 70–1.

33 L.C.A., Holroyd Ms, H3 — Letter book, 1784–1827.

34 Freeman, 'Transporting methods', p. 70.

35 U.L.B.L., Lupton Ms, 82 — General Ledger, 1812–19; 91 — Personal Ledger, 1819–26. In the years 1820–26 the account for Welsh & Co. was £172, that for the Union Company, £921.

36 U.L.B.L., Jowitt Ms, 31 — Letter book, 1802–05.

37 See, for example, Freeman, 'Transporting methods', p. 71.

38 L.C.A., Holroyd Ms, H3 — Letter book, 1784–1827.

39 F. D. Lugard, *The Dual Mandate in British Tropical Africa*, Blackwood, Edinburgh, 1922, p. 5.

40 W. W. Rostow, *The Stages of Economic Growth*, Cambridge University Press, 1960, p. 55.

41 A. O. Hirschman, *Strategy of Economic Development*, Yale University Press, 1958.

42 R. W. Fogel, *Railroads and American Economic Growth: Essays in Econometric History*, Johns Hopkins University Press, Baltimore, Md, 1964. A comparable study is A. Fishlow, *American Railroads and the Transformation of the Antebellum Economy*, Harvard Economic Studies, Cambridge, Mass., 1965.

43 For a selection of its dimensions see P. Temin (ed.), *New Economic History*, Penguin Books, Harmondsworth, 1973; also O'Brien, *The New Economic History*.

44   See, for instance, R. W. Fogel, 'Notes on the social saving controversy', *Journal of Economic History*, XXXIX, 1979, pp. 1–54.

45   J. Langton, *Geographical Change and Industrial Revolution: Coalmining in South West Lancashire, 1590–1799*, Cambridge University Press, 1979, pp. 1 and 260.

46   Hirschman, *Strategy of Economic Development*, pp. 83–97.

47   B. R. Mitchell, 'The coming of the railway and United Kingdom economic growth', in M. C. Reed (ed.), *Railways in the Victorian Economy*, David & Charles, Newton Abbot, 1969, p. 22.

48   See, for example, M. J. Freeman, 'Turnpikes and their traffic: the example of southern Hampshire', *Transactions of the Institute of British Geographers*, new ser., IV (1979), pp. 415–16.

49   See T. S. Ashton, *The Industrial Revolution, 1760–1830*, Oxford University Press, London, 1968 ed., pp. 7–9.

50   J. R. Ward, *The Finance of Canal Building in Eighteenth-century England*, Oxford University Press, London, 1974, pp. 161–9.

51   See n. 4.

52   See J. A. Chartres, *Internal Trade in England, 1500–1700*, Studies in Economic and Social History, Macmillan, London, 1977, pp. 9–12.

53   H. J. Dyos and D. H. Aldcroft, *British Transport: an Economic Survey from the Seventeenth Century to the Twentieth*, Leicester University Press, 1969, p. 102–3.

54   The surviving correspondence of contemporary firms such as Peter Stubs, Warrington hand-tool manufacturer (M.C.L.A., Stubs Ms, L24/1 — Orders and General Correspondence), M'Connel & Kennedy, Manchester cotton spinners (John Rylands Library, M'Connel & Kennedy Ms — Letter books, Letters, 1796–1831) and Joseph Jackson, Wakefield woolstapler (W.D.A.: Goodchild Loan Ms, Jackson Ms — Incoming correspondence, 1809–25) abound with references to this traffic in samples.

2 THE TURNPIKE TRUSTS
William Albert

Now Turnpikes are grown much in Fashion
The Hardest Tax in all our Nation —
For where Wine & Women & Stock-jobbing past,
The Turnpike must help us at last.
3 July 1727   — *Kingswood colliers' letter to the turnpike*

Several of these turn-pikes and tolls have been set up of late years, and
great progress had been made in mending the most difficult ways, and
that with such success as well deserves a place in this account ... —
Daniel Defoe, *A Tour through the Whole Island of Great Britain*, 1723

I wish with all my heart that half the turnpike roads of the kingdom were
plough'd up, which have imported London manners, and depopulated
the country — I meet milkmaids on the road, with the dress and looks
of strand misses; and must think that every line of Goldsmith's Deserted
Village contains melancholy truths. — John Byng, *The Torrington
Diaries*, 1781[1]

The turnpike trusts which spread throughout Britain in the eighteenth
and early nineteenth centuries are an important, well known but often
misunderstood feature of the industrial revolution. That contemporary opinion was divided on their purpose and merit is suggested
by the quotations above. In this chapter the development of the turnpike system in England will be considered under four main heads: the
trusts' emergence from the communal system of parish repair; the way
the turnpikes developed geographically; management, road repair and
finance; and finally the role of the new bodies in the unprecedented
economic and social changes of the period.

The origins of the turnpike trusts

Genesis
A number of aspects of the origins of the turnpike trusts deserve
attention. In the first place it must be understood how the new
authorities evolved from the existing parochially based road repair
system. This is important not only to establish their legal provenance,
but also because it helps explain both the structure and the location
of the early turnpike authorities. Secondly, there is the question of
who promoted and who opposed the collection of tolls, and why.

It is best considered in this section, for the trusts were not simply an administrative innovation. They were an administrative innovation brought into being by a small section of the community in what it saw as its own best interests. In this sense they were an important socio-political as well as economic phenomenon, and must be seen as a vital element in the process that saw the remnants of traditional society cleared away and replaced by the logic of the market — a logic which was the very basis for the triumph of industrial capitalism.

During the Middle Ages, and most probably before, the upkeep of the king's highway was a local responsibility. In 1555 this common-law obligation was clearly delineated and codified.[2] In a modified form it remained the basis of road maintenance for almost three hundred years. By the 1955 Act, and subsequent amending legislation, parishes were made liable, on pain of a fine at the local Quarter Sessions, for the repair of the roads within their jurisdiction. They were to appoint surveyors, who could not refuse the post, and ensure that under the latter's supervision each parishioner either laboured six days a year on the roads or, if he satisfied the property qualification, sent a team and two men. As might be imagined, a system based on coerced labour directed by coerced labour never proved very satisfactory. Beatrice and Sidney Webb wrote,[3] 'In England, at least, this Statute Labour seems in the sixteenth and seventeenth centuries to have been performed with the utmost remiss. Whether there was ever a time in which this work was commonly done with any degree of conscientiousness or exactitude we may well doubt.'

So long as wheeled traffic was local and infrequent the failings of the parish system probably did not give rise to serious problems. But as traffic steadily began to increase in the seventeenth and eighteenth centuries the inability of certain parishes to maintain their roads, especially those along the main through routes, became more apparent. To help remedy the situation a number of general measures were adopted in the late seventeenth century. Restrictions were imposed on the weight of waggons and the number of animals permitted in draught, while in 1662 and 1670 justices of the peace were given the power to levy a rate to supplement statute duty. This provision was finally made permanent in 1691.[4] For some roads the new powers were still not sufficient, however, and it was on one of them that the first experiment with tolls took place.

The first Act granting authority to collect tolls from those who used the roads to finance repairs was passed in 1663 for a long section of the Great North Road between Stilton in Huntingdonshire and Wadesmill in Hertfordshire.[5] This was an important and heavily travelled route, which some parishes had been finding it difficult to maintain since at least the early seventeenth century. Various solutions had been tried. Fines were imposed, statute duty increased and re-apportioned, rates levied, etc., but to no avail. On three occasions local justices and the parishes had sought permission to raise money by a toll on road users, and Parliament finally agreed to a temporary measure in what must have been seen as exceptional circumstances.[6] The Act of 1663 was to remain in force for only eleven years, and it was to be thirty-two years before the next turnpike authority was formed. Under the Act the justices became responsible for collecting tolls and supervising repairs, in line with their role in the parish repair structure. It is clear that the powers granted in this first Act were meant as a short-term supplement to statute labour and not a replacement for it. No major new system or restructuring of the old one was envisaged.

Because of unsettled political conditions it was not until 1695 that the next authority was created.[7] This too was justice-controlled, as were the five subsequent trusts set up before 1706. In that year an important change took place when the road between Fornhill and Stony Stratford was turnpiked and placed under the control of thirty-two appointed commissioners.[8] This novel arrangement soon gained popularity: not only did it help assuage local opposition by devolving control to those who lived near the roads, but the justices' many other duties had undoubtedly made it difficult for them to administer the turnpike roads efficiently. With a single exception all the turnpike authorities established from 1714 were of this type. The trustees, as they came to be known, were enabled to erect gates, collect tolls and borrow money, and given a range of other powers to maintain the roads in good order.

The new *ad hoc* bodies were to function for only twenty-one years, at which time the roads would revert to parochial control. But invariably the trusts were able to get their powers extended for a further term, and frequently augmented as well. Initially envisaged as providing a temporary supplement for statute labour, the turnpike trusts thus came to replace the parishes as the principal agency for maintaining the country's main roads. They did, however, remain wedded to the system from which they had emerged, for the parishes still had to provide statute labour or pay an agreed sum in lieu. If the trusts did not repair their roads properly it was the parishes who were ultimately liable and could be fined.

Support and opposition

The obtaining of a turnpike Act was the result of local initiative, most frequently from those responsible for the upkeep of the road under the existing system. The numerous petitions in support of turnpike schemes came from a variety of groups, but mainly parishes, town councils, merchants, farmers and landowners. It is generally assumed that all this improving activity was intended to secure better transport facilities; while this was often the case, in the late seventeenth and early eighteen centuries particularly the desire to impose tolls can be seen as a negative response to increasing use of the roads. The trusts were essentially a means of enabling local people to shift the burden of repair on to those who used the highways and avoid having to pay rates or fines. This may have been entirely reasonable, but it clearly distinguishes the trusts from most other forms of transport improvement, which had more positive aims. The point should not perhaps be pushed too far, but it does provide an interesting insight into the nature of the turnpike trusts. It also can be seen as very much of a piece with the general policy of maintaining the roads by restricting their use, a central plank in highway legislation from the seventeenth to the early nineteenth centuries.

Another important insight into the kind of change the trusts represented can be had by looking at the opposition to them. Pawson has argued that too much has been made of both parliamentary and popular opposition, and that essentially the trusts were an 'uncontroversial' administrative innovation.[9] His excessively deterministic analysis and a judicious juggling with dates lead him to a conclusion which ignores the inherently revolutionary nature of the trusts. It is this broader question which must be considered.

The slow spread of tolls before the second decade of the eighteenth century can be explained partly in terms of opposition, either locally — which meant no petitions would be drawn up — or at Westminster, where many early requests for turnpikes were refused. For example, the first trust's gate at Stilton caused so much local opposition that it was never erected; the right to take tolls on the Huntingdon and Cambridge section of the road lapsed after eleven years, and even in Hertfordshire toll collection was suspended for a number of years. At the same time, Parliament turned down at least eighteen schemes

between the early 1660s and 1714, although many of the roads concerned were subsequently turnpiked.[10] However, once the idea
became more widely known, the formal precedent more clearly
established and the trusts recognised as institutions, parliamentary
opposition did decline. The same appears also to have been true
locally, especially when it became apparent that local interests could
be protected by appointing 'worthies' of the district as trustees and
obtaining concessions for local traffic.

There were, however, some quite violent popular risings against
the turnpikes. In Bristol, for example, rebellious coal miners and,
later, farmers destroyed gates in and around the city in 1727, 1731 and
again in 1748. In Ledbury there were serious disturbances in 1734 and
1735, while in 1753 some fifteen people were reported to have been
killed during riots against turnpike trusts in the Leeds—Bradford area.
These and other popular outbreaks were complex affairs and have
been discussed in more detail elsewhere,[11] but it is true that so full-
blooded a reaction was infrequent. The chief reason was that the
legislation was drafted so as to protect local interests and ensure that
the main burden fell on those passing through. The latter generally
had no base from which to arouse widespread or purposeful
resistance. Their antipathy was shown by assaulting collectors or
simply by avoiding the toll gates, both quite common occurrences.
Furthermore the limited mileage of most trusts, together with what
E. P. Thompson refers to as 'the total situation of power and
deference in the countryside',[12] worked against there being more
widespread popular resistance.

Despite the fact that it erupted rarely, the general hostility should
remind us that however necessary or effective the trusts may have been
they were the creation of the economically and politically powerful,
and were perceived as such. 'The turnpikes,' records John James,
'were, by the lower classes, universally regarded as an obnoxious
regulation — more adapted for the convenience of the wealthy portion
of the community ...'.[13] Like parliamentary enclosures, they redefined a fundamental property relationship. Both devices were important in transforming the character of the countryside as commons
gave way to fenced fields and the roads were blocked by toll gates.
In most cases the men behind the fences and the gates were the same
— the improving gentry. The turnpike trust must, therefore, be seen
as an integral part of the revolutionary changes of the period, changes
which were sweeping away the last vestiges of the old social order

and replacing them with institutions and relationships more appropriate to an emergent industrial capitalism. The trusts were not only part of this process but can be seen as appropriately symbolic of it. They replaced a communal institution with one based on cash payment, and the fact that social and economic relations were no longer mediated by custom and tradition but increasingly by the market was a dominant feature of those years.

These remarks should not be construed as criticism of the turnpikes or those who promoted them, only as a necessary corrective to historical accounts which see the emergence of the trusts — or, for that matter, most of the other far-reaching changes of the period — as socially and politically disembowelled 'economic issues'. Pawson, for instance, can write, 'Such an alteration [the turnpikes] could only take place with the agreement of the community through its representatives in Parliament.'[14] Even the lowly turnpike trusts deserve a greater degree of historical sagacity than this. Their economic significance was considerable, but without a full appreciation of how they fit into the broader framework of capitalist transformation they appear in the end as little more than one-dimensional 'improvements' — part of Mathias's mythical 'industrial revolution by consent'.[15]

The growth of the trusts

The timing of development

In their classic study the Webbs claimed that the turnpikes did not form 'radiating arteries of communication' but were scattered, unconnected and only by the end of the century formed something approaching a national network of improved roads.[16] This view has remained unchallenged until recently, when more detailed analysis of turnpike legislation has revealed a very different picture. Although there was no national plan as such, local initiative seems to have reflected fairly well the pattern of most heavily used roads. This gave rise in the first period of growth to a concentration on the main roads leading from London, as well as a considerable degree of interconnected development in some provincial areas. Before considering the geographical spread of the trusts it is necessary to say something about the overall timing of development.

Using new turnpike Acts as a measure, it appears that the growth of the system can be roughly divided into four periods, the last of which spanned three distinct sub-periods (see fig. 4). The first, until

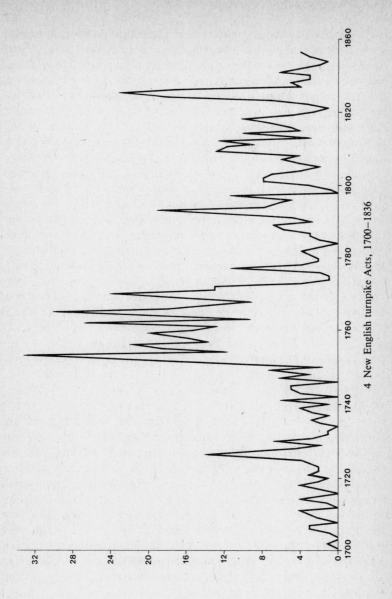

4 New English turnpike Acts, 1700–1836

1750, was one of slow, uneven growth. It was followed by the years of the 'Turnpike Mania', which lasted from about 1750 to 1772. There were then almost two decades of relative quiescence, and finally a long period in which renewed activity was concentrated in the widespread speculative investment booms of the early 1790s, 1809–12 and the mid-1820s. It has to be remembered that we are talking about the formation of new authorities, not the total mileage turnpiked or aggregate levels of investment in road improvement. Although the number of turnpike Acts is often taken as an indicator of investment it is at best an indifferent measure, for roads varied in length, terrain and traffic density, and the amount spent on substantive improvements — as opposed to normal maintenance — could vary from year to year.[17] As to mileage, this is important in gauging the extent of the system and must be considered. Pawson has calculated that in the first period there was a proportional relationship between the percentage of the eventual (1836) number of Acts and mileage, while during the mania period 40 per cent of the Acts accounted for 52 per cent of the eventual total mileage.[18] This is important in showing that the significance ascribed to these years is well deserved, and it points to the fact that on the whole the post-1790 trusts tended to be smaller. Accounting for the aggregate pattern of trust formation is not an easy task, as local considerations were probably more important than national economic trends, at least during most of the eighteenth century. Nonetheless some general points can usefully be made as to the fluctuations in the overall level of trust formation.

One general influence which has been adduced as an important determinant is the rate of interest. Ashton argued that for projects '... concerned with building and means of communication ... it [the rate of interest] is of the greatest consequence'.[19] Pressnell observed that in judging their effects it is necessary to consider the entire structure of rates, both long and short-term. 'The rise and fall of public utility investment appears to fit broadly into a framework of widening and narrowing respectively of the "normal" spread between interest rates.'[20] However, while years of large-scale trust formation were generally also times when interest rates were low, there was no significant correlation at or near the principal turning points. For example, interest rates were low for two decades before the 'Turnpike Mania' and were still low when the boom ended in 1772. Not until the 1790s do they seem to assume an active, rather than a permissive, role.[21] In those years and in the early decades of the new century trust formation clearly took on a more speculative character.

Looking at the periods individually, some tentative conclusions can be offered to explain the fluctuations. As argued above, before the second decade of the eighteenth century a general unfamiliarity with the new authorities and opposition both locally and at Westminster were important in retarding the spread of trusts. The adverse conditions agriculture faced during the second quarter of the century also affected road improvement, since most roads were in rural areas and landed interests were probably the most important source of capital for the turnpikes. Indeed, Little has argued that for the economy as a whole these were years of economic 'deceleration'[22] and as such were not conducive to greater investment in road building. From the 1750s conditions began to improve, and it was growing prosperity — and probably an increase of traffic — that stimulated turnpike activity in the 1750s and 1760s. There was also the influence of the 'demonstration effect', for during this period there were many examples of groups of interconnected trusts being established within the space of a few years. The setting up of trusts had more than a local effect, as there is evidence that this type of improvement gave rise to what might be termed a creative disequilibrium. By securing a turnpike promoters may have sought to mitigate any comparative disadvantage brought about by road improvement in other areas while at the same time realising similar savings for their own district. Finally, the trusts formed from the early 1790s onwards, while appearing to owe much to speculative interest, seem by their location to have been a response to the demands of expanding urban areas and the northern industrial regions, the latter having hitherto seen relatively little turnpike activity. Over the whole period 1791–1836, for instance, the counties of Yorkshire and Lancashire accounted for 32 per cent of the new turnpike Acts passed.

Geographical spread

For an improvement such as a turnpike trust, where local conditions, needs and initiative were so vital, an analysis of changes in the aggregate level of enabling legislation can give but a very general idea of why certain roads were turnpiked. To get a more precise picture the geographical spread of the trusts over time must be considered. Using the same periods as above, we find that in the years before 1750 a high percentage of activity was concentrated on the busy main roads to London (see fig. 5). On the thirteen routes which have been identified there was variation in the timing of legislation, but a general

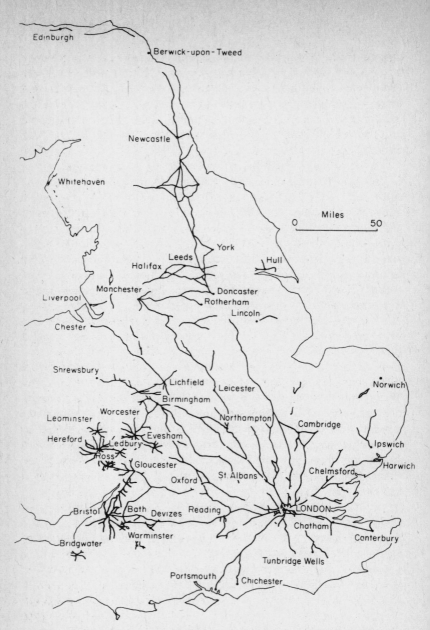

5 The turnpike road network in 1750. From E. Pawson, *Transport and Economy*, Academic Press, London, 1977, p. 140

pattern does emerge.[23] Before the second decade of the century most new trusts were near London, with eighteen of the twenty-five main route Acts within forty miles of the capital. During the 1720s there was activity all along the main roads, and by 1730 almost 900 miles of the total route mileage of 1,563 had been turnpiked. In the next decades most of the remaining roads came under trust control, and by 1750 only 182 miles remained free of toll gates.

Besides the activity on the main London roads, in the years before 1750 there was quite important development in the Severn and Wye valleys and in the West Riding. In the west a number of town-centred trusts were established, which instead of controlling a stretch of highway were given power over a network of roads leading into the town. Authorities of this type clearly demonstrate a spirit of improvement on the part of the promoters, generally the town councils, who probably felt that better roads would assist local commerce. Such trusts were set up in Bristol, Warminster, Leominster, Ledbury and Hereford, among other places. These developments took place mainly in the mid-1720s. In the 1730s some important trans-Pennine routes were turnpiked, and in the following decade a network of turnpike roads was established near Leeds, Halifax and Wakefield.

It is important to consider the growth of the turnpike system before 1750 separately, for, as fig. 5 shows, in this period, far from being 'scattered' or 'unconnected' as the Webbs claimed, a fairly comprehensive system of turnpiked main roads as well as important provincial networks had been established. One of the principal reasons for this pattern of growth was the pervasive effect of the London market, not only on the roads around the city but farther afield. Defoe observed that '... this whole Kingdom, as well the people, as the land, and even the sea, in every part of it, are employed to furnish something, and I may add, the best of everything to supply the city of London with provisions'.[24] Indeed, many petitions for a turnpike cited the heavy traffic en route to London as a main reason for seeking relief. Being so heavily travelled, and therefore so expensive to maintain, it is understandable, given the nature of the existing system of repair, that these routes should have been the first to receive attention. Similar pressures were felt on roads leading into some provincial centres and help account for development here. It is also significant that many towns in the Severn and Wye valleys were on navigable rivers, and the problems caused by vehicles carrying goods to and from these river ports are mentioned in many turnpike petitions.

It is impossible to assess the 'Mania' period with the same care as the preceding years, since from 1750 activity spread rapidly to most parts of the country, over 500 trusts being formed to cover more than 15,000 miles. This was also the time of extensive turnpiking in Wales, and trusts were set up in the border country and central valley of Scotland.[25] By 1772 the skeletal structure of improved roads in England up to 1750 had been considerably elaborated (fig. 6). The pattern of growth suggests that the existing trusts had had an important influence on expansion: once turnpiking had begun it tended to generate further local interest. For example, except for the far western counties, which saw their first phase of activity in the 1750s, most new trusts were linked to or very near existing toll roads. Moreover a considerable number of trusts were formed as parts of simultaneously established interconnected groups of roads. Thus, six interlinked authorities were set up in the Carlisle–Penrith area in 1753, and around Norwich ten trusts were established in 1769 and 1770. In the east and north Midlands twenty-four of the twenty-five trusts created in the 1750s were linked to one another and an extensive network of turnpike roads had been established there by the early 1770s.

In the 1770s and 1780s the overall rate of growth declined, and what few trusts were formed were distributed more or less evenly throughout the country. Of those created during the long years of the French wars — possibly owing to the demands arising from the conflict — fourteen were in the Durham and Northumberland coalfields, fifteen in Kent, near the ports of Dover, Hythe, Folkestone, Margate, Ramsgate and Deal; and in London five important trusts were established, three of them near the docks. There was also a good deal of activity in the expanding cotton textile region, where an elaborate fourteen-trust network connected Bury, Blackburn, Rochdale, Bolton, Manchester and other towns. In the post-war period, besides the many small urban trusts, there was a significant concentration in Yorkshire and Lancashire, where twenty-four of the fifty-nine trusts formed during the speculative boom of the mid-1820s were located.

A number of important points arise from this brief survey. Firstly, the formative years of development before mid-century were extremely significant in that, with the exception of the roads from Exeter and Norwich to London, all the main arterial routes had been almost completely turnpiked. This pattern of development derived to a large degree from the fact that the new authorities were originally seen as supplementary to the system of parish repair, and it was on the most

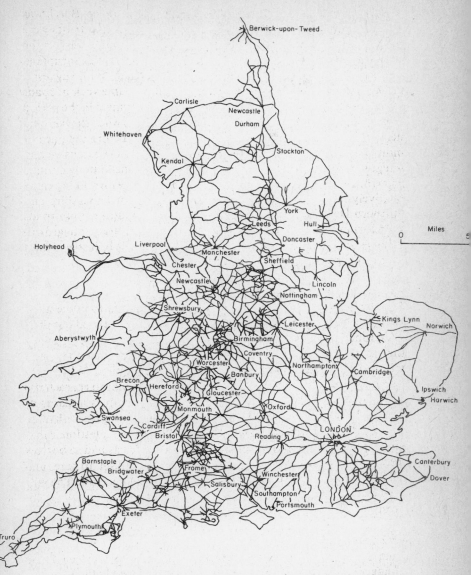

Berwick-upon-Tweed
Carlisle
Newcastle
Durham
Whitehaven
Stockton
Kendal
York
Leeds
Hull
Doncaster
Holyhead
Liverpool
Manchester
Sheffield
Chester
Newcastle
Lincoln
Shrewsbury
Nottingham
Leicester
Kings Lynn
Norwich
Aberystwyth
Birmingham
Coventry
Worcester
Northampton
Cambridge
Banbury
Brecon
Hereford
Ipswich
Gloucester
Harwich
Swansea
Monmouth
Oxford
Cardiff
LONDON
Bristol
Reading
Barnstaple
Canterbury
Bridgwater
Frome
Winchester
Dover
Salisbury
Southampton
Portsmouth
Exeter
Plymouth
Truro

0   Miles   5

6 The turnpike road network in 1770. From E. Pawson, *Transport and Economy*, Academic Press, London, 1977, p. 151

heavily travelled routes that the parishes needed assistance. But, it was not only from a desire to shift the burden of repair that trusts were formed. The creation of the town-centred trusts in the west in the 1720s, and the fact that promoters quite often got roads turnpiked that were well outside their immediate jurisdiction, both suggest a positive desire for transport improvement. The framework of roads improved before 1750 served as a basis for development in the period of extensive turnpiking during the 1750s and 1760s when the national network was being filled in. By the early 1770s, before the pace of industrialisation began to quicken, there was a quite extensive and integrated system of turnpike roads ready to facilitate economic growth. It does seem, however, that more intensive turnpiking came relatively late to the northern industrial areas. In Lancashire and northern Derbyshire, for example, many of the intra-county roads were turnpiked in the period 1789–1810, this relatively late growth being probably due to the fact that the cotton textile industry did not begin to expand rapidly until 1780.

The operation of the trusts

To judge how effective the trusts were it is necessary to understand how they were managed and the way in which they carried out their main function — road repair. The early historical accounts, especially that of the Webbs, tended to perpetuate the idea that they were mismanaged and that their repairs left much to be desired. While there is some truth in these accusations, it would be a mistake to characterise the turnpike system as a whole in this way, for by the standards of the time the trusts can be said to have carried out their duties with more than a reasonable degree of success. Another related question is that of finance. At most stages of their existence the trusts had to borrow money, to cover the costs of obtaining their Act, to set up gates and toll houses, or to improve roads in advance of toll receipts. The way in which the money was raised provides a clearer picture of the interests which supported the new authorities.

Administration

Once the change-over from justice control had been effected, the management of the new road authorities was placed in the hands of appointed trustees. They were generally local men of substance, mainly landowners but also members of Parliament, merchants and local mayors or aldermen acting ex-officio. If most Bills contained a long list of trustees it was primarily to expedite their passage through Parliament and mollify local opinion; only a handful of men would be active in running the trust. The trusts were self-perpetuating bodies and could appoint new members to replace those who died or declined to serve. The only restraint was a property qualification. The trustees' powers were fairly extensive, and from the 1740s virtually unchecked, as an earlier provision giving the justices of the peace a regulatory role ceased to be included in new Acts. They could erect gates, collect tolls, buy land, mortgage the toll yield, divert the course of the road, and most other things thought necessary for maintenance and improvement. Not until 1822 was a degree of outside control imposed, when the government required annual accounts be sent to the county clerk of the peace,[26] although it gave him no power to deal with trusts that were being mismanaged. Formally the trusts' existence was only temporary, but when their twenty-one-year term neared expiry they were invariably granted renewal Acts, often with greater powers and/or additional roads.

Each Act prescribed the date and place of the first meeting and the number of trustees needed for a quorum. By the General Turnpike Act of 1773 trusts were required to hold four general meetings a year, although many failed to comply. On the whole it seems that, with the exception of the first occasion, when decisions were taken about the appointment of officers, setting up the gates, and raising money, few meetings were held and attendance was low. The larger provincial trusts and those in London did show fairly reasonable levels of participation, but in many areas trusts seem to have been effectively controlled by a small group of men. It is interesting to note that in some districts there was a considerable degree of interlocking control, with the same trustees running more than one trust. Such was the case from the mid-eighteenth century in parts of the West Riding, and in 1833 it was claimed that the seven turnpikes out of Winchester were controlled by the same trustees, as were five or six near Stamford in Lincolnshire.[27]

Given that in most cases the trustees were not assiduous in their duties, success rested to a large degree on the choice of the principal officers — the treasurer, clerk and surveyor. The first of these posts was generally the most important, as it involved collecting, holding and distributing funds and keeping the accounts. The job was generally, though not always, given to a trustee, and from the late eighteenth century a note of greater professionalism was introduced by the growing tendency to appoint local bankers to the position. The advantages the trust derived from the banker's reputation and his financial connections help explain why the practice became popular. By 1834 bankers were acting as treasurers for at least 419 of the 1,037 trusts.[28]

After that of treasurer, the post of surveyor was the most important and influential. As most trustees probably had little practical experience, whether the roads were well maintained or not depended on the skills and diligence of the surveyor. Before the nineteenth century there seem to have been few qualified men the trusts could turn to, nor were road-mending techniques very sophisticated. There was therefore little the trustees could do but hope to find someone who was at least honest and had practical skills. While there is no doubt that there were many fraudulent and incompetent surveyors, the improved state of the turnpike roads in the eighteenth century suggests that some at least were reasonably competent.

The writings of John Loudon McAdam, the most influential and articulate critic of the trusts' standards of management and repair, contain many charges of 'unknowledgable' surveyors being employed and give the impression that the nineteenth-century practitioners were no more skilled than their eighteenth-century counterparts. 'Surveyors are elected because they can measure; they might as well be elected because they can sing; but they are more commonly elected because they want a situation.'[29] Quotable as it is, this caustic comment should not be taken at face value, for McAdam decried any system but his own. Furthermore, it appears that as the number of turnpike trusts increased there did emerge a group of professional road surveyors who, while perhaps less skilled than McAdam and his sons, at least offered a more considered approach to their work than the part-time amateur. Together with the banker treasurers, the increasing employment of professional surveyors suggests that by the nineteenth century the administration of the trusts had begun to assume a more professional character, a trend also apparent in other local authorities at the time.

Besides keeping their roads in good repair, the trustees' chief preoccupation was the collection of tolls. This seemingly simple matter was vastly complex and troublesome. In the first place the schedule of tolls was inordinately complicated. In addition to different charges for each category of vehicle and number of horses drawing, there were partial concessions for some types of waggons or those carrying particular goods, full exemptions for others, and extra charges for waggons laden over a certain weight or using wheels of certain dimensions. There was also the problem of toll evasion, something extremely difficult to guard against. It fell to the gatekeepers to interpret and apply the complex scale of charges, and it is not surprising to find that travellers frequently complained about them, or that there were many cases of fraud. It was because of this latter problem and to avoid the inconvenience of having to administer toll collection that many trusts resorted to leasing, or 'farming', gates for a fixed yearly sum. This practice has been the subject of criticism, for the Webbs and Jackman claim that the lessees colluded at the toll auctions to lower the price they had to pay.[30] While it may have happened on occasion, the trusts had adequate safeguards and there is little evidence that the practice was widespread. On the whole it would seem that toll farming was advantageous to the trustees, freeing them of the worry of toll collection and guaranteeing a steady income.

During the eighteenth century those who farmed the tolls seem to have operated on a relatively small scale and were often gatekeepers themselves. By the nineteenth century, however, professional toll farmers began to appear. For example, of those bidding for the Wibsey Low Moor trust's gates in 1839, fourteen gave their profession as toll farmer.[31] Two men stand out as the most important. One was Joshua Bower (1773–1855), a Hunslet glass manufacturer and colliery owner who leased many gates in the West Riding and the rest of the country. The other was Lewis Levy, who in concert with various associates was reputed to be in control of three-quarters of the gates in London in 1825.

Before turning to the question of how well the trusts maintained their roads it is necessary to try and assess the effectiveness of their administration, since they have been strongly attacked for inefficiency and waste. Many of the parliamentary committees that were convened in the first decades of the nineteenth century to look into their affairs came to the conclusion that they were badly run, in that little money went to repairs and heavy debts were being incurred. Both Jackman and the Webbs have perpetuated this view, which it should be added seems to have derived from the testimony of John McAdam, whose evidence clearly shaped many of the committees' findings and who generally denounced all systems save his own as misconceived. There are grounds for reconsidering the accepted opinion.[32]

The Webbs saw the level of indebtedness as the most serious short-coming, since it meant that most of the trusts' income had to be devoted to interest and debt repayment as against expenditure on repairs.[33] But, as Pressnell has observed, it would be wrong to consider the existence of a debt as *a priori* grounds for assuming unsound financial management.[34] Unlike the canals or the railways the trusts could not raise funds by issuing shares, and if large-scale improvements were to be carried out the only way it could be done was by raising money against future toll receipts. This mortgage debt should, therefore, be seen more as a form of capital than as a debt *per se*. If interest payments were being met and did not absorb a disproportionate share of income it can be said that the trustees were discharging this aspect of their responsibilities reasonably well.

Conscientious handling of the debt did not necessarily mean that a trust was being well run. The proportion of income devoted directly to repairs is equally, if not more important. It provides a fair indication of the attention the trustees were giving to their primary task, although it says nothing about the effectiveness of the repair techniques themselves.

It is not until 1834 that we have detailed information on a nationwide basis to assess the two aspects of trust performance. The returns made to Parliament in this and four succeeding years show that, overall, the trusts devoted 67 per cent of their income to repair expenditure, 20 per cent to interest payments and only 8.5 per cent to administrative expenses.[35] Given their particular legal and administrative structure, these were quite respectable results. Using information from the first national report in 1821 (much less detailed than the 1830s reports) and returns from 1837, it is possible to be somewhat more precise.[36] Assuming that to be well run a trust had to spend at least 55 per cent of its income directly on repairs, not more than 20 per cent on interest payments, and to have no more than three years' arrears of interest, the results in table 1 are obtained. The 1821 data (which give average figures for three years) only provide information on income, interest payments and arrears, and hence may overstate, in this case, the number of trusts in a favourable position. The calculations lend some support to the traditional view of the trusts' performance as lacklustre but also show that a substantial number of them, and much road mileage, were being competently administered. Furthermore, if we consider the viewpoint of the road user, whose main concern was the amount actually spent on the roads, the picture

Table 1 Well run and badly run trusts

Year	No. of trusts	(%)	Mileage	(%)
Well run trusts				
1821	376	(39.6)	7,613	(42.5)
1837	426	(40.7)	9,275	(47.6)
Badly run trusts				
1821	573	(60.4)	10,289	(57.5)
1837	621	(59.3)	10,212	(52.4)

Source. P.P., 1821 (747) IV, 343; 1839 (447) XIV, 299.[36]

is somewhat brighter, as in 1837 597 trusts controlling 12,218 miles of road were devoting more than 55 per cent of their income to repairs.

It is difficult to provide strictly comparable figures for the eighteenth century, but Pawson, using the same criteria, has assessed the accounts of a number of trusts in the period. His findings are more or less consistent with those for the nineteenth century, and he concludes, '... there was no marked change in the overall financial position between the eighteenth and nineteenth centuries, at any rate in respect of road repair expenditure'.[37]

The preceding analysis suggests that, while mismanagement was a problem, to characterise the entire system as badly administered would be a misrepresentation. Judged by present-day standards the trusts may seem to have been inefficient, but in the early nineteenth century modern administrative techniques were in their infancy, and the trusts did not lag behind other public authorities in adopting and developing new ideas. When it is remembered that, unlike most other transport improvements, they were run as a non-profit-making public service by volunteers for no direct personal gain, the fact that they performed as well as they did is remarkable.

Repairs and maintenance

The trusts were set up to provide better roads, but most trustees probably had no more idea about the practical business of highway engineering than the parish surveyors they superseded. This is not particularly surprising, as the technology saw no substantial advance until the nineteenth century, and there were few experienced or knowledgable surveyors whom the trusts could hire.

In general it seems that throughout most of the seventeenth and eighteenth centuries ideas about how to keep the roads in a fit state centred less on methods of repair than on restricting their use. This can be seen in the number of petitions claiming excessively heavy loads and/or narrow wheels as the cause of the trusts' difficulties. The attitude was reinforced by Parliament, which from the early seventeenth century passed a series of Acts limiting weights, wheel widths and the number of horses permitted in draught. The General Turnpike Act of 1773[38] contained twenty-eight clauses relating to wheels, weights, carriage construction, etc., and the numerous parliamentary committees which met from the 1790s to consider the problems of the roads spent almost all their time deliberating over how they could best be protected. Not until McAdam came on the scene about 1810 and began to promote his ideas did the emphasis on restriction begin to be superseded by greater attention to the methods of road making.

This is not to suggest that he had no predecessors, for there were a number of treatises available.[39] But, none was of much practical use or showed any great advance on seventeenth-century practice, with its stress on achieving a convex surface and covering it with materials such as flints, gravel, or furnace dross. McAdam's breakthrough was to determine the right degree of convexity, to be precise about the type and quantity of materials, and to set out clear administrative guidelines. His methods were successful because he seems to have studied the problems and devised relatively cheap and simple solutions. It is also important to realise that his system achieved popularity because it allowed, and indeed was largely based on, the exploitation of pauper labour — men, women and children employed at piece rates on breaking stones to a uniform size. This recommended itself to the trusts, especially in the post-war years when such labour was readily available.

As in the case of administration, it was McAdam's criticism of the trusts' repair procedures and the weight his views carried with parliamentary committees that had helped to create the impression that the turnpikes were poorly maintained. This does not, however, seem to have been true. The minute and account books of the trusts show considerable attention not only to surfacing (the main repair activity) but also to improved drainage, widening, easing gradients, erecting markers and other improvements. The trustees may have had to rely on traditional practices until McAdam and Telford began to propagate more 'scientific' ideas, but at least they were able to employ them more intensively than the parish surveyors, and they were able to bring longer stretches of road under unified control. Moreover they replaced unwilling and inefficient statute labour with wage labour, and this probably increased the effectiveness of the old methods. It is clear that there were many cases of badly managed trusts, of fraud by surveyors or contractors, and much general waste and inefficiency. But the improved condition of the roads under the trusts' care attests to their efficacy.

Judging that condition is a difficult task, for we must depend very largely on travellers' accounts. Whilst their observations may have been accurate, they were influenced by the season, the weather, and the mode of conveyance, among other things. It is also clear that during the eighteenth century standards changed, adding to the difficulty of making a comparative evaluation. On the whole, though, contemporary writings show unequivocally that the turnpikes marked a considerable advance.

Commenting at a time (the 1720s) when the turnpike trusts were first beginning to appear in any number, Daniel Defoe was fulsome in his praise:

... it must be acknowledg'd they are very great things, and very great things are done by them; and 'tis worth recording, for the honour of the present age, that this work has been begun, and is in an extraordinary manner carry'd on, and perhaps may, in a great measure be completed within our memory.[40]

Arthur Young is often assumed to have been a stern critic, but Edwin Gay has shown that of the 940 miles of turnpike road he covered during his northern tour in 1771 he found 490 good, 210 'middling' and only 240 miles bad.[41] W. T. Jackman's comprehensive compilation of travel and agricultural reports brings further confirmation that the trusts brought about great improvement.[42] Pawson has shown that at the end of the eighteenth century, of the thirty-three counties surveyed by the Board of Agriculture, twenty-one had turnpike networks classified as good or excellent, eight as middling or variable, and only four as bad.[43] Increasing traffic, stable or falling carriage costs, and heavier permitted loads all indicate improved conditions.[44]

Despite the seemingly overwhelming evidence of eighteenth-century improvement, Richard Edgeworth wrote in 1813 that there were only twenty miles of well repaired road in the entire country, and the 1819 parliamentary committee concluded that the state of the turnpikes was generally defective.[45] These views can be questioned, but they do reflect much higher standards, the result of continuous improvement throughout the previous century, and, of course, the new techniques given currency by McAdam and Telford. As the Webbs observed,[46] 'What were then the best-kept turnpikes, once thought something like perfection, came now to be deemed only passable, whilst the condition of the worse sort of road is again felt to be an intolerable public nuisance.' Yet, while there were undoubtedly problems on certain roads, the 1840 report, which contains returns from 706 trusts, shows only 13 per cent to have been in a bad state.[47] While the problems of assessment must be kept in mind, it can be said that from quite early in their existence the trusts were carrying out their functions with a fair degree of success.

Finance

Their revenue came from tolls, but the need to undertake work in advance of income meant that most trusts had to raise money. Borrowing was permitted by their enabling Acts and took the form of interest-bearing mortgages secured on the proceeds of the gates. Proprietory interest and profits were inappropriate for concerns which operated on the 'king's highway', and no shares could be issued. Unlike the canals and railways, the turnpikes did not usually need large sums for fixed capital expenditure. However, it is important to consider this aspect of their operations, as an appreciation of where the money came from will tell us who supported the new ventures. They attracted many small investors, who may not have been directly concerned about better roads, and were therefore an important channel for mobilising local savings. Both these points are directly related to the question of how the turnpike trusts are to be seen in terms of the wider issue of capital formation during the industrial revolution. In this sense they are an essential element in considering the influence of the turnpikes on economic development.

In terms of the way it was carried out the financing of the turnpike trusts can be divided into two periods — the years before and those after 1750.[48] In the first there was little pre-enactment borrowing, and loans were solicited on an *ad hoc* basis when necessary. They tended to be few and relatively large; most lenders were trustees. After 1750 the pattern began to change as those seeking to promote a trust obtained promises of financial support before an Act was obtained. By the 1760s this practice was widespread, and a clause began to appear in the Acts dealing with the enforcement of subscriptions. In many cases the loans were divided into small sums — £25, £50 or £100 denominations — which gave greater opportunities for the investor with modest resources and broadened the base of financial support.

While it is often difficult to identify the occupations of those who lent the trusts money, it appears from surviving documents that the most important group of investors both before and after 1750 consisted of gentlemen, landowners, yeoman and tenant farmers and members of the aristocracy. In the later period, as the trusts became more numerous and investment in them more open, there was an increase in funds from merchants, manufacturers, artisans and shopkeepers. Merchants and manufacturers had much to gain directly from better roads, as did landed interests; widows, spinsters, clergymen, local charities, etc., probably saw the trusts as a reasonably secure and remunerative investment.

It is not difficult to understand the attraction to landed interests. Good roads improved a district's competitive position and were a vital complement to enclosure, which turnpikes seem to have preceded in some areas. Easier access to markets, lower transport costs and the chance to shift the burden of repair on to road users recommended the trusts to the small owner-occupier and tenant farmer as well as to the larger landowner. The direct returns, in the form of interest payments, may have been important to some of the smaller men, but it would seem that on the whole it was the indirect benefits that attracted the support of the landed classes. This was probably true also of merchants and manufacturers, many of whom could have earned a higher return on their capital in their own businesses. Herein perhaps lies the reason why some well known industrialists who were active in promoting turnpikes extended only a modest financial commitment. In 1764, for example, Josiah Wedgwood, along with other pottery manufacturers, promoted the Burslem–Newcastle under Lyme trust but only subscribed £150. In 1756 Edward Knight became a major investor in the Ludlow Second Trust, which ran near his ironworks at Bringwood, but his contribution was overshadowed by that of local landowners. At the end of the eighteenth century Samuel Oldknow was involved in a number of transport schemes near his mills at Marple and Mellor, including four turnpikes and the Peak Forest Canal. Records suggest that he made only token investment in the road projects. Of two trusts set up in the cotton textile region — Chapel en le Frith to Entreclough Bridge (1802) and Glossop to Marple

Bridge (1806) — the first received only minority support from manufacturers, and in the latter case their investment was matched by that of local landowners and farmers.[49]

It is important to note that, although the landed interest continued to be the most important source of funds, by the end of the eighteenth century those who had no direct interest in improved roads and lent money simply for the return (generally 5 per cent) became increasingly prominent. This is clear from many trust documents and suggests, among other things, rising middle-class savings. The importance of this source of funds, which Ward has shown to have been so vital for canals,[50] has been underestimated, but it is clear that it was of growing significance. The more speculative character of trust formation from the 1790s may have owed much to the amount of capital available locally and the desire of the modest saver to realise a return on it. The turnpikes were able to mobilise these funds, which may not have been available to more risky direct investment in industry or commerce, and apply them in creating a form of social overhead essential for economic expansion. Postan wrote that during the industrial revolution '... the reservoirs of saving were full enough, but the conduits to connect them with the wheels of industry were few and meagre'.[51] The trusts can be seen as significant 'conduits' channelling local savings into improved roads which benefited agriculture and industry alike.

The turnpike trusts drew funds from a wide spectrum of investors — from the rich and powerful noble landowners to lowly labourers, from Parliament (the Exchequer Loan Commission was established in 1817) to village tradesmen. It is clear, however, that it was the landed interest which provided the bulk of the requisite capital. This is not particularly surprising, for, although industry was expanding, urban and industrial areas were still small islands in a sea of agriculture. Moreover, as Flinn has observed, 'Since wealth in surplus to normal consumption requirements was highly concentrated in the landed classes, if more capital was to be made available for economic expansion it was from this class above all that it would come.'[52] In considering the relationship between agricultural improvement and industrialisation it is important to bear in mind that it was the capital and initiative of the agricultural sector that did most to provide an infrastructure of improved roads so necessary for industrial growth. This is another example of the way in which such growth was dependent on the prior capitalist transformation of agriculture.

The turnpikes and the economy

As has been argued, in terms of their administrative competence and as road repairers the turnpike trusts achieved a higher degree of success than has generally been acknowledged. Moreover, far from covering scattered and unconnected bits of road, from the mid-eighteenth century a quite respectable network of main roads had already been turnpiked, and this was substantially extended in the next two decades. But what were the benefits and how were they distributed? And what was the relationship between the development of the turnpike trusts and the rise of industrial capitalism?

The general propositions about the link between transport improvement and economics are fairly well known. Discussion here will be confined to isolating as far as possible the particular effects of road improvement. Given the highly interrelated nature of the transport network, this is not an easy task. It is perhaps best to consider first the benefits, direct and indirect, that came from better roads and then turn to the broader issue of road improvement and capitalist development.

The direct benefits can be defined as the savings realised by road users — greater speed, reliability, ease of travel, carrying capacity, etc. They are extremely difficult to quantify, because there is little information on private road users, and for professional road hauliers and coach proprietors better roads were only one factor influencing their charges. While improved roads might allow economies to be realised, it was the manner in which the road services responded — in terms of competition, differentiation of services, carriage construction, etc. — that ultimately determined the charges for goods and passengers.

To the extent that better roads made it possible for carriers to haul heavier loads with the same number of horses, or fewer, to reduce wear and tear on animals and equipment, to make journeys more quickly and thus save on variable costs, and to use their equipment more intensively, it can be said that the trusts contributed to lowering the cost of road transport. There is evidence that all these factors were operative and can be linked with improved roads. Daniel Defoe wrote in the 1720s:

The benefit of these turnpikes appears now to be so great, and the people in all places begin to be so sensible of it, that it is incredible what effect it has already had upon trade in the countries where it is more completely finish'd; even the carriage of goods is abated in some places, 6*d*. per hundred weight, and in some places 12*d*. per hundred, which is abundantly more advantageous to commerce than the charge paid amounts to, and yet at the same time the expense is paid by the carriers too, who make the abatement; so that the benefit in abating the rate of carriage is wholly and simply the tradesmen's, not the carriers.[53]

Some thirty years later another observer claimed, '... carriage in general is now thirty per cent cheaper than before the Roads were amended by Turnpikes'.[54] While the extent of the reduction may be questioned, evidence from the justices' assessed rates for carriage tends to confirm both claims and shows a significant fall in road transport charges during the first half of the eighteenth century (table 2).

Table 2   **Average per ton mile assessments made by justices**

Decade	Assessment	Decade	Assessment
1690s	14s 8d	1760s	13s 2d
1700s	16s 4d	1770s	12s 0d
1710s	–	1780s	11s 7d
1720s	14s 5d	1790s	12s 4d
1730s	13s 5d	1800s	14s 0d
1740s	14s 3d	1810s	15s 3d
1750s	13s 3d	1820s	14s 9d

Source. Pawson, *Transport and Economy*, 1977, p. 296, and a reworking of material in Albert, *The Turnpike Road System*, 1972, pp. 260–2.

The writer who adduced a 30 per cent saving attributed it to faster, easier travel and reduced costs because carriers could haul heavier loads with the same number of horses. The assertion is supported by changes in the maximum weights permitted by various highway Acts from the early seventeenth century.[55] In 1621 the limit had been set at 20 cwt, in 1667 it was increased to 30 cwt in summer, and by 1741 it stood at 60 cwt. By 1765 it had doubled again, while the number of horses allowed had fallen from seven in 1662 to only five in 1751. Heavier loads drawn by fewer animals indicate a direct benefit for road users (although improved vehicle construction was also an important factor), and underlines the significance of trust development before 1750. The trend of falling road haulage charges continued throughout the century. Together with the considerable increase in the speed of passenger transport — Jackman estimates a saving of a third to a fifth between 1750 and 1830[56] — and the gradual elimination of seasonally differential charges, it points to substantial direct benefits continuing to be realised from the improved roads.

The indirect benefits are impossible to measure, but they were as great, if not greater than, the direct benefits. They include such things as the growing size of the market and the increase in specialisation and scale of production it allowed; the savings engendered by faster, more reliable transport which lessened the need to hold large raw material or finished goods inventories and so freed capital for more productive use; the effect on agricultural improvement; the breaking down of regional isolation, which contributed to the process of socio-economic transformation — all important factors which by their nature are impossible to quantify in any meaningful way. However, to indicate the importance of improved roads some of their principal effects on industry and agriculture can be briefly mentioned.

All agriculture relied on road transport in some degree, to carry produce to the nearest local market or to navigable water for transhipment. Improved roads which offered easier, cheaper and more reliable access to markets, and to inputs such as marl or lime, were therefore important in the process of agricultural transformation. That the benefits the new authorities could give rise to were well appreciated at the time is shown by a letter from the agent of a Lincolnshire estate in support of a local turnpike scheme:

That Boston is a Sea Port of no small Consideration to which Place the Road is proposed from Wainfleet, which is within One Mile of your Estate a very valuable Intercourse will be established. That Sheep may always be sent to Smithfield Market w'ch sometimes are greatly impeded by bad Roads in the Spring ... That Wolle may at all Times be sent either to Southern or Northern Markets for that Article which can now only be effected in the Summer.

On these Considerations was the Estate my own I should prefer the Completion of a Turnpike to the Present very uncertain State of the Road on which the Permanence of Business so much depends on Seasons.[57]

By improving market access the turnpikes helped to break down local and regional marketing patterns and self-sufficiency, and so gave an added spur to the commercialisation of agriculture. This did not, however, suit everyone, as a remark of Adam Smith's demonstrates.

It is not more than fifty years ago, that some of the counties in the neighbourhood of London petitioned against the extension of the turnpikes into the more remoter counties. These remoter counties, they pretended, from the cheapness of labour, would be able to sell their grass and corn cheaper in the London market than themselves, and would thereby reduce their rents, and ruin their cultivation.[58]

A comment suggesting a somewhat similar chain of events was made a few years earlier by Arthur Young.[59] 'I find all sensible people attribute the dearness of their county to the turnpike roads; and reason speaks the truth of their opinions ... but make a turnpike road through their county and all cheapness vanishes at once.' As Pawson observes,[60] although the new turnpikes may have benefited farmers they were '... certainly not beneficial for the rural non-farm population, for the inhabitants of the market towns and villages who did not grow much food'. The point is an important one; unfortunately he does not develop it, but it is one key to a more profound understanding of the relationship between road improvement and capitalist transformation.

By putting districts in easier contact with markets turnpikes helped to increase rent values. For example, Grigg claims that the Sleaford–Tattershall trust contributed in the late eighteenth century towards the rise in rents near Billinghay in Lincolnshire,[61] and there were undoubtedly many similar cases in other parts of the country.[62] There was also an important connection between turnpikes and enclosures, although the exact nature of the relationship is not completely clear, as so many factors influenced both. Unimproved transport facilities could have been put under greater strain by increased quantities of goods coming from enclosed lands, but there is evidence to suggest that it was improved roads that provided the basis for enclosure. In Leicestershire, for example, turnpiking generally preceded parliamentary enclosure, and the great majority of the enclosures in the 1760s and 1770s were within one to three miles of a turnpike road. The phenomenon may have been more general, as the sharp rise in turnpike legislation in the 1750s preceded the more intense period of enclosure of the following two decades.[63]

For industry better road transport was important both locally and in terms of an improved national system. The significance of a larger market for specialisation and economies of scale has already been mentioned. Quicker, easier communication by improved roads, allowing more expeditious exchange of information, orders for goods, etc., was also vital for the development of a more sophisticated industrial structure.[64] Much long-distance industrial traffic went by water, but such was not always the case. Describing the western cloth centre of Frome, Defoe remarked,[65] 'I call it an inland town, because it is particularly distinguish'd as such, being not only no sea-port, but not near any sea-port, having no manner of communication by water, no navigable river at it or near it. Its trade is wholly clothing, and the cloths they make, are, generally speaking, all conveyed to London.' This applied to most other cloth towns in the area and helps account for the early turnpike activity near Devizes, Chippenham and Calne, and the virtually complete turnpiking of the western road to Bristol by 1728.

Since even short hauls of bulky low-value commodities such as iron ore or coal could increase their price inordinately, it was in the interest of industrialists to improve roads near to them. There is ample evidence that they did. In north Staffordshire the road between Lawton and Tittensor (turnpiked in 1713) was used by carts carrying iron ore to the Lawton, Dodington and Vale Royal furnaces, and the road from Lawton to Cranage (turnpiked in 1731) for taking iron to the forges at Cranage. The influence of local ironmasters is evident here, for on both roads iron ore was given concessionary rates, while, on the latter, pig iron, coal and charcoal were granted lower tolls. Judging from the many petitions, the carriage of iron, coal and iron-wares was an important factor in the turnpiking of roads to the north and west of Birmingham. It is not difficult to multiply the examples of direct involvement of manufacturers in road improvement. The case of the merchants and manufacturers of Leeds has already been mentioned, as has that of Josiah Wedgwood, Edward Knight and Samuel Oldknow.

Empirical observation of the links between better roads and industrial or commercial change, or discussions of direct and indirect benefits, are only one dimension of the relationship between the development of the turnpike trusts and the socio-economic transformation which took place in this period. To take the analysis this far and no further is to accept that the interaction of economic factors is not only the principal explanation for transport improvements but the only aspect of the wider effects of those improvements worth considering. This is a form of crude economic reductionism which tends to obscure more than it explains. It is, of course, not to be denied that the improved roads brought benefits, as did many other changes during the industrial revolution. But in both cases, at least in the short and medium terms, the benefits accrued mainly to those who used their superior political and economic weight to push through the requisite changes in their own interest.

With regard to the turnpike trusts it has been argued above that they were far from being an uncontroversial administrative reform.

They represented an important redefinition of a communal property right, and until a way of placating local opposition was devised — toll concessions and the appointment of local men as trustees — they did not meet with widespread acceptance. The trusts not only brought the 'freedom' of the king's highway into the market but also provided the means by which the market could succeed in sweeping away the remnants of what E. P. Thompson has identified as the paternalist model of marketing and manufacture,[66] a model inconsistent with the needs of capitalist development. We need only recall Young's comment about turnpikes and 'the dearness of their county' to appreciate the role of improved roads in drawing agricultural commodities out of local markets and thus contributing in times of dearth to local shortages, serious hardship for the poor and widespread rioting. As Thompson has shown,[67] these uprisings against high food prices, which occurred in 1709, 1740, 1756–57, 1766–67, 1773, 1782, 1795 and 1801, were reactions against what was popularly seen as the undermining of the traditional moral economy by the demonstrably unequal functioning of the 'free' market. This is not a marginal issue. It was at the heart of the industrial revolution.

In 1663 the first tentative steps were taken to provide temporary assistance for parishes in repairing a portion of the heavily travelled Great North Road. By the early decades of the eighteenth century this temporary device had begun to spread to other areas and assume a considerable degree of permanence. In 1750 the country already had 143 turnpike trusts, responsible for over 3,000 miles of main road, and by the 1830s the number had grown to well over 1,000, controlling more than 20,000 miles of road and collecting £1½ million in tolls. Only with the coming of the railways did the importance of the trusts begin to fade. The situation was summed up in an 1851 report to Parliament, in which it was observed:

In 1833 Turnpike Roads were the chief means of communication throughout the kingdom for the transit of goods and passengers; much expense and skill had been bestowed in adapting the roads to the increased traffic of goods, and the more speedy passage of the mails and stage coaches. From this period railways had gradually superseded the use of Turnpike Roads for the conveyance of goods and passengers, except for short distances and local convenience, and the Turnpike Roads in a large majority of the counties are assuming more the character of ordinary highways.[68]

Although the turnpike trusts became outmoded in the Victorian era, it must not be forgotten that this most ubiquitous institution, an important feature of the landscape for over 150 years, had been one of the central pillars on which the industrial revolution was based.

Notes

1   Colliers' letter, D15/2, Gloucestershire Record Office; Daniel Defoe, *A Tour through the Whole Island of Great Britain*, II, London, 1962, p. 119; *The Torrington Diaries*, ed. C. Bryan Andrews, London, 1935, I, p. 6.

2   2 and 3 Philip and Mary, c. 8. See S. and B. Webb, *English Local Government: the Story of the King's Highway*, London, 1913, pp. 14–61, and W. T. Jackman, *The Development of Transportation in Modern England*, 2nd edn., London, 1962, pp. 32–68.

3   Webb and Webb, *King's Highway*, p. 28.

4   W. Albert, *The Turnpike Road System in England, 1663–1840*, Cambridge, 1972, pp. 15–16.

5   15 Car. II, c. 1.

6   Albert, *Turnpike System*, pp. 17–20.

7   Shenfield to Harwich in Essex (7 and 8 Wm. III, c. 9) and Wymondham to Attleborough in Norfolk (7 and 8 Wm. III, c. 26). A full list of all new turnpike Acts passed between 1663 and 1836 can be found in Albert, *Turnpike System*, pp. 202–23, and in E. Pawson, *Transport and Economy: the Turnpike Roads of Eighteenth Century Britain*, London, 1977, pp. 341–60. The former list includes only English Acts, while the latter includes Welsh and Scottish ones, though only to 1800.

8   6 Anne, c. 4.

9   Pawson, *Transport*, pp. 76, 118.

10   Albert, *Turnpike System*, p. 21.

11   W. Albert, 'Popular opposition to turnpike trusts in early eighteenty-century England', *Journal of Transport History*, new ser., V, 1979.

12   E. P. Thompson, *The Making of the English Working Class*, London, 1968, p. 240.

13   J. James, *The History and Topography of Bradford*, London, 1841, p. 155.

14   Pawson, *Transport*, p. 84.

15   Peter Mathias, *The First Industrial Nation*, London, 1969, p. 4.

16   Webb and Webb, *King's Highway*, p. 125.

17   For an interesting attempt to measure the level of investment in trusts see John Ginarlis, 'Road and Waterway Investment in Britain, 1750–1850', unpublished Ph.D. thesis, University of Sheffield, 1970, chapters 3, 4 and 6.

18   Pawson, *Transport*, pp. 114–15.

19   T. S. Ashton, *Economic Fluctuations in England, 1700–1800*, Oxford, 1959, p. 84.

20   L. S. Pressnell, 'The rate of interest in the eighteenth century', in *Studies in the Industrial Revolution*, ed. L. S. Pressnell, London, 1960, p. 208.

21   Albert, *Turnpike System*, pp. 120–31.

22   A. J. Little, *Deceleration in the Eighteenth Century British Economy*, London, 1976, *passim*.

23   For further detail on the geographical extension of the trusts see Albert, *Turnpike System*, chapter 3, and Pawson, *Transport*, chapter 6. The information for this section is drawn from these two sources.

24   Defoe, *Tour*, I, p. 12.
25   Pawson, *Transport*, pp. 153–4.
26   3 Geo. IV, c. 126, arts. 78–80.
27   Albert, *Turnpike System*, pp. 62–4.
28   L. S. Pressnell, *Country Banking in the Industrial Revolution*, Oxford, 1956, pp. 269–70.
29   *Parliamentary Papers (P.P.)*, 1810–11 (240) III, 855, p. 31.
30   Webb and Webb, *King's Highway*, p. 139; Jackman, *Development of Transportation*, pp. 682–3.
31   List of Bidders, HAS–59, Halifax Central Library.
32   Albert, *Turnpike System*, pp. 85–7.
33   Webb and Webb, *King's Highway*, p. 135.
34   Pressnell, *Country Banking*, pp. 367–8.
35   *P.P.*, 1840 (256) XXVII, I.
36   *P.P.*, 1821 (747) IV, 343, and 1839 (447) XXIV, XLIV, 299. For full details of this analysis see Albert, *Turnpike System*, pp. 230–6.
37   Pawson, *Transport*, p. 229.
38   13 Geo. III, c. 84.
39   For example, William Mather, *Of Repairing and Mending the Highways*, London, 1696, or John Scott, *Digests of the General Highway and Turnpike Laws ...*, London, 1778.
40   Defoe, *Tour*, II, pp. 120–1.
41   Edwin Gay, 'Arthur Young on English roads', *Quarterly Journal of Economics*, XLI, 1927, pp. 545–51.
42   Jackman, *Development of Transportation*, pp. 81–101, 285–302.
43   Pawson, *Transport*, p. 269.
44   See below.
45   Richard Edgeworth, *An Essay on the Construction of Roads and Carriages*, London, 1813, p. vii, and *P.P.*, 1819 (509) V, 369, p. 4.
46   Webb and Webb, *King's Highway*, p. 165.
47   *P.P.*, 1840 (280) xxvii, 15, appendix.
48   This entire question is considered in Albert, *Turnpike System*, chapter 5, upon which this section is based.
49   All the above from Albert, *Turnpike System*, pp. 105–7.
50   J. R. Ward, *The Finance of Canal Building in Eighteenth Century England*, Oxford, 1974.
51   M. M. Postan, 'Recent trends in the accumulation of capital', *Economic History Review*, VI, 1935, p. 2.
52   M. W. Flinn, *The Origins of the Industrial Revolution*, London, 1966, p. 47.
53   Defoe, *Tour*, II, p. 129.
54   *The Farmers and Trades Apprehensions of a Rise upon Carriage*, London, 1752, p. 5.
55   Albert, *Turnpike System*, p. 181.
56   Jackman, *Development of Transportation*, pp. 683–701.
57   Letter from J. Bourne to William Drake, 1 October 1766, TYR 4/1/49, Lincolnshire Archives Office.
58   Adam Smith, *An Inquiry into the Nature and Causes of the Wealth of Nations*, ed. Cannon, New York, 1937, p. 25.

59   Arthur Young, *A Six Weeks Tour through the Southern Counties of England and Wales*, London, 1768, p. 260.
60   Pawson, *Transport*, p. 317.
61   David Grigg, *The Agricultural Revolution in South Lincolnshire*, Cambridge, 1966, p. 44.
62   Pawson, *Transport*, pp. 317–18.
63   Albert, *Turnpike System*, pp. 115–16.
64   Pawson, *Transport*, p. 309.
65   Defoe, *Tour*, I, p. 280.
66   E. P. Thompson, 'The moral economy of the English crowd in the eighteenth century', *Past and Present*, L, 1971.
67   *Ibid.*, p. 79.
68   *P.P.*, 1851 (18) XIVIII, p. 3.

3 ROAD TRANSPORT
John A. Chartres & Gerard L. Turnbull

Assessments of road passenger and goods transport during the industrial revolution have long suffered from being presented from the perspective of the railways. In their traffic carrying capacity and in their resultant impact on the economy and the landscape the railways cast a shadow over the road transport system from which few have been able to escape. In part this is a response that can be readily understood. Whereas derelict canals provided a vivid testimony to *one* of the railways' precursors, the road transport system vanished almost without trace; when memories faded there was little to press its claims on the attention of historians. In another sense, however, the perspective offered by the railways is quite misleading.

Undoubtedly railways transformed the transport system and had powerful effects on the entire economy. Yet they were of small economic importance before 1840, by which time the country had travelled far along the path of industrialisation. The contribution of transport to that progress was vital, that of road transport as much as any other. Road transport services, for passengers and goods, formed an extensive and well developed segment of the wider transport industry and contributed positively to industrial growth. Indeed, some of the trends observable in their development, especially the growth of passenger traffic and the quality of freight services for conveying produce and merchandise, are highly informative clues to the origin of railways themselves. Had more attention been paid to road transport as a precursor of rail the resultant perspective would have demonstrated that some of the developments long regarded as creations of the railway had been anticipated on the roads. Indeed, one of the railway promoters' objectives was to steal the strengths and traffics of road transport. This chapter attempts to provide some of that missing perspective. It deals first with road passenger transport and then with road haulage.

Passenger transport

The early years of railways in England saw a pattern of traffic which in many ways surprised contemporaries. Despite the claims of their promoters that by invading the monopoly of the canals they were intended primarily to cut the costs of goods carriage, much of their revenues before 1850 derived from passengers. In consequence, a large part of the 'social saving' attributed to them before 1865 by Hawke was derived from passenger travel. If his analysis of the market for railway conveyance is correct, then it suggests that the demand for travel was highly income- and price-elastic. In short, reductions in the cost of travel would generate rapid growth in the volume of traffic, especially in competition with the expensive and economically less efficient stagecoach system.[1]

Was this rapid advance of relatively short-haul passenger travel so surprising in the context of the road passenger-carrying business of the preceding century? It seems hard to accept that passengers' response to changes in real income or the cost of travel should not have been similar before the advent of the railway. In the later nineteenth century, travel of all kinds became an important consumer good, and it is clear that the position was much the same during the industrial revolution. As incomes in general rose between 1750 and 1850, and as those of middle-income groups in particular rose substantially in real terms, so too expenditure on the luxury of travel increased at least proportionately.[2] Parallel with the creation of 'satanic mills' or deep mines was the development of the popular spas, from Bath to Harrogate, the seaside resorts such as Brighton and Scarborough, and the further advance of the major inland towns as centres of resort and entertainment.[3] All these were served primarily by advances in the provision and organisation of road passenger transport.

To these important symbols of the 'superfluity' characterising at least part of the economic growth of later eighteenth-century England more mundane demands on the coaching industry can be added. As well as being a consumer good of considerable importance, travel was for the individual also a producer good: it represented an intermediary between producer and merchant, middleman and retailer, town and country. This was clearly central to the evolution of the carriage of goods, discussed below, but vital also in the growth of passenger travel. Commercial travel — even travellers — merchants, factors and others came to enjoy better links with the capital and with the major provincial towns by the expansion of road traffic, as much in personal communications as in the transit of goods.[4] Above all, it is the link with the focus of new tastes and fashions, the capital, that stands out as the driving force in this process of integrating the home market. London was the great hub of road passenger carriage before 1800, transmitting its tastes, fashions and demands to the nation through the coaching system and the unofficial postal service it represented.[5]

In these several ways, therefore, the development of facilities for the relatively rapid transit of passengers about the country was an integral part of the process of industrialisation. Its growth in one sense reflected the income changes which formed the base of growth in the home market in the years before 1780.[6] This further indicates that, along with tobacco, sugar and other familiar symbols of rising domestic consumption, personal travel may have had a relatively high price and income elasticity of demand. This in turn helps to resolve the paradox of the early railway, promoted for goods carriage but profiting more from the passenger. The links formed between the provinces and the capital through the road passenger services which developed thus reflected and further generated the great internal division of labour represented by the industrial revolution.

The London trade

The options facing the individual wishing to travel in England in 1750 were limited by his purse, by the type of journey he wanted to undertake, and by his personal geography. For those wishing merely to get to the nearest market town, unofficial local carriers, horseback or foot represented the most likely choices.[7] At the other end of the spectrum, the Londoner wishing to visit Salisbury, Birmingham or Oxford could travel by a variety of coaches or diligences, fast or slow, by postchaise or similar private hire vehicle, or, more cheaply, in the great waggon of the road haulier. Similar options faced the inhabitant of Exeter or Manchester wishing to make the return journey to the capital, but in 1750 there was not yet so great a range of means for travel between the provincial capitals. In 1750 the stagecoach system linking London with the major provincial centres was already over a century old, when the provincial network scarcely existed. It is therefore logically with this leading sector of passenger travel that we must begin.

London's links with the provincial capitals by coach, the public and scheduled passenger carrier, can be traced back to the middle years of the seventeenth century. Rapid growth in stagecoach services took place in the later years of the century so that by 1715 over 800 services a week were leaving London for provincial centres.[8] The measurement of subsequent growth raises several logical problems for both passenger and goods carriage, and before considering the nature of growth it is important to consider some of these issues.

The output of the public road transport industry can be reconstructed in a global sense only from published guides to services. These are themselves fragmented, and no one series can cover the whole of the period between 1715 and 1840, not even for the more limited years of the industrial revolution. The estimation of output thus involves the awkward jointing of data series. Further, there are difficulties, common with directory-type sources, of double or multiple entries, misleading or perhaps even fictitious entries and so on. All these factors must be borne in mind when considering the implications of the estimates discussed below.[9] Taking this into account, two measures have been employed in the assessment of the passenger carrying business: the *service quotient*, a quantum of the weekly frequency of coach departures to specific centres; and estimated weekly *passenger mileages*, being the quotient further modified by variables representing the capacity of the coach and the distance of the destination from London. The simplicity of the former is perhaps outweighed by the better fit of the latter measure to real resources and travel: it deflates the growth attributable to the short-distance and suburban stages, which would otherwise distort the 'output' of the industry.

For present purposes it proved impossible to generate statistics representative of the total output of the London stagecoach or goods carrying industries, and sampling has been adopted. For present purposes the services from London to thirty-eight major provincial centres were analysed for the years 1715, 1765, 1773, 1796, 1816 and 1840. This partial estimate of services may have led to certain biases in the figures presented later in the chapter, but should represent the broad pattern of change in both sectors of road transport. The sample towns are plotted on fig. 7, together with the boundaries of the 'region' employed in the assessment of changes. So far as possible, destinations chosen for the analysis are exclusive: the figures for services to them represent the minimum of double counting. For example, in the Lancashire and Cheshire zone there was always a great deal of overlap in services running to Liverpool and Manchester, and hence the former is taken as a sample town for the analysis of coach, and the latter for goods, services. In addition, as is obvious from the map, some allowance is made for the distance decay of services from

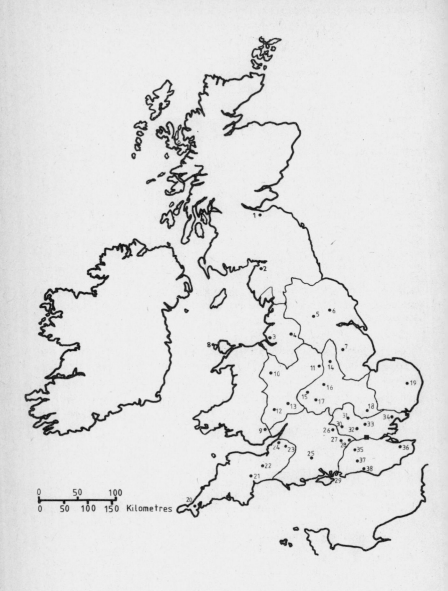

the capital by the rather greater density of sample towns taken for the southern and eastern parts of the country.

It is on this basis that the summary figures of growth in passenger-carrying services have been calculated (table 3). They invite some

Table 3   Growth in passenger services to selected provincial centres, 1715−1840

Year	Service quotient	Index (1796 = 100)	Passenger miles ('000)	Index (1796 = 100)
1715	158	10	67	7
1765	279	18	123	12
1773	376	24	183	18
1796	1,596	100	1,040	100
1816	2,060	129	2,043	197
1840	1,765	111	2,369	228

Source. The Merchants and Traders Necessary Companion, 1715; J. Osborn, *A complete Guide to all Persons who have any Trade or Concern with the City of London and Parts Adjacent*, 10th edn., 1765; H. Kent, *The Shopkeeper's and Tradesman's Assistant*, 1773; R. and H. Causton [successors to H. Kent], *The Shopkeeper's and Tradesman's Assistant*, 1796; Henry Kent Pauston, *Kent's Original Tradesman's Assistant*, 1816; *Robson's London Directory, Street Key, and Conveyance List for 1839*, 19th edn., 1839.

rather surprising conclusions and offer contrasts with the expansion of road haulage. In the first half of the eighteenth century the industry was still growing fairly rapidly, measured by both service quotient and passenger miles. Growth averaging over 1½ per cent per annum in the first half of the century was low by comparison with that visible

7 Sample towns employed in the estimation of trends in the output of coaching and road haulage, with regional boundaries. *North and Scotland:* 1 Edinburgh, 2 Carlisle. *Cheshire and Lancashire:* 3 Liverpool, 4 Manchester. *Yorkshire and Lincolnshire:* 5 Leeds, 6 York, 7 Lincoln. *Wales:* 8 Holyhead, 9 Monmouth. *West Midlands:* 10 Shrewsbury, 11 Derby, 12 Hereford, 13 Worcester. *East Midlands:* 14 Nottingham, 15 Birmingham, 16 Leicester, 17 Warwick, 18 Cambridge. *East Anglia:* 19 Norwich. *South-west:* 20 Falmouth, 21 Exeter, 22 Taunton, 23 Bath, 24 Bristol. *South and West:* 25 Salisbury, 26 Oxford, 27 Reading, 28 Windsor, 29 Portsmouth. *Northern Home Counties:* 30 Aylesbury, 31 Bedford, 32 St Albans, 33 Hertford, 34 Colchester. *South-east:* 35 Guildford, 36 Canterbury, 37 Horsham, 38 Brighton.

in the last quarter but rather higher than that which characterised much of domestic industry and transport in the period. More significantly, the figures of table 3 reveal that it was a period in which services were expanding rather faster in geographical spread than in absolute number. The rate of growth in passenger mileage between 1715 and 1765 indicates that the expansion of routes was as marked a feature of the early growth of the industry.

In the context of the economic history of Britain between 1750 and 1850, the growth in output of the passenger carrying industry as revealed here still seems remarkable. Output rose faster and in a more sustained manner than in most other trades and industries. Even so, the most rapid growth coincided with the period of the classical industrial revolution — the second half of the eighteenth century — and in terms of the service quotient ceased after 1816. This is probably rather misleading, and expansion almost certainly continued into the 1830s, the final observations being slightly distorted by the early impact of the railway.[10] Even so, it is clear that by the end of the Napoleonic wars the basic network of links with the capital was established. Subsequent expansion was marked by growth in the carrying capacity of coaches, as is indicated by the continued if retarded growth of the passenger-mile figures in table 3. In addition, as will be seen below, the early nineteenth century witnessed the proliferation in the capital of the short-stage, the forerunner of the omnibus.

The provinces

These conclusions are generally confirmed when we disaggregate the figures and consider the pattern of change on a 'regional' basis (table 4). As we have already made clear, the regions employed in the table are not wholly satisfactory in that they are based on groupings of counties, but they do offer a broad correspondence with the major zones and routes served. What further aspects of growth are illustrated on this regional basis?

It is clear from table 4 that by 1765 certain parts of the country were already relatively well provided with services compared with our index base year of 1796. These may perhaps best be considered as areas of the leading sector of the early modern economy, including as they did many of the major towns and areas of economic growth in the earlier eighteenth century — Norwich, Bristol, Coventry and Birmingham, Leeds and Sheffield. By contrast, in 1765 the North and Wales were relatively underdeveloped, and consequently achieved

Table 4 Growth in road passenger services to selected provincial centres, by region, 1715–1840

Region	1715 PMW ('000)	1715 I	1765 PMW ('000)	1765 I	1773 PMW ('000)	1773 I	1796 PMW ('000)	1796 I	1816 PMW ('000)	1816 I	1840 PMW ('000)	1840 I
Northern Home Counties	6.2	20	8.1	26	13.5	43	31.3	100	65.9	211	46.2	148
South-east	5.5	4	9.6	7	11.5	8	146	100	216.3	148	184.8	127
East Anglia	4.1	21	6.1	31	6.1	31	19.9	100	22.6	114	51.5	259
East Midlands	8.9	8	14	13	21	20	107.3	100	215.2	201	267.4	249
South and West	13.4	7	28.5	15	28	15	192.3	100	236.4	123	199.2	104
West Midlands	5.6	13	12.3	27	16.9	38	45	100	149.9	333	179.4	399
South-west	15.2	7	17.2	8	55.4	26	214.7	100	555.7	259	453.3	211
Lancashire and Cheshire	–	–	7.4	14	8.7	16	54.4	100	90.6	167	121.1	223
Yorkshire and Lincolnshire	8.2	18	19.4	43	21.1	47	45.4	100	200.6	442	211.6	466
North and Scotland	–	–	–	–	–	–	139.1	100	216.4	156	508.9	366
Wales	–	–	0.8	2	0.8	2	44.5	100	73.7	166	145.9	328
Total	67	7	123	12	183	18	1,040	100	2,043	197	2,369	228

Notes. Regions are as drawn in fig. 7, and are composed as follows. Northern Home Counties: Bedfordshire, Buckinghamshire, Essex, Hertfordshire, Middlesex; South-east: Kent, Surrey, Sussex; East Anglia: Norfolk and Suffolk; East Midlands: Cambridgeshire, Huntingdonshire, Leicestershire, Northamptonshire, Nottinghamshire, Rutland, Warwickshire; South and West: Berkshire, Dorset, Gloucestershire, Hampshire, Oxfordshire, Wiltshire; West Midlands: Derbyshire, Herefordshire, Shropshire, Staffordshire, Worcestershire; South-west: Cornwall, Devon, Somerset; North and Scotland: Cumberland, Durham, Northumberland, Westmorland, Scotland; Wales includes Monmouthshire.

Source. As for table 3.

rather faster growth later in the century. Explanations in terms of regional economic growth and of metropolitan influence and pull, not felt very much at the periphery, leave an apparent anomaly in the South-east. In absolute numbers of coach departures (the service quotient) the region ranked equal third to the South-west, behind the South and West and the northern Home Counties. It had grown early to satisfy the Canterbury and Dover trades, and the south-western route into Surrey, towards Guildford. Few other demands were placed on the passenger carriers of the area until the resort trade of Brighton and Margate started to exert an influence towards the end of the century.[11] Broadly speaking, of the three regions nearest to the capital, it was the two northern and western ones, containing major centres like Windsor, Reading, Oxford, Aylesbury, Colchester and St Albans, that grew faster before the 1770s.

Subsequent growth was more consistent across regions. The industry grew rapidly in capacity in the last quarter of the eighteenth century and also continued to spread its coverage to the peripheral zones. Between 1773 and 1816, in our observations, the system reached maturity and completion, with the most rapid advances coming in the industrialising areas of the Midlands and the North. By contrast, old areas of importance in the South-east, South and West and East Anglia relatively stagnated. By 1816 many regions had reached a level of services exceeding that of our final observation, 1839–40. By the latter date the railway was already pegging back services in the metropolitan zone, and continued growth was confined to the peripheral regions. Perhaps by a displacement effect, it was fastest at the greatest distances from the capital as the north of England, Scotland, Wales and, through Holyhead, Ireland were brought into the network.

All of which tends to confirm the view suggested by so many historians of the early modern period that it was the capital which played the major part in the growth of the eighteenth-century economy. Such metropolitan prejudices would have been markedly reinforced by a consideration of the coach services between the provincial capitals in the 1750s and 1760s, for at that date they were virtually non-existent. As in so many relatively underdeveloped economies, travel to and through the capital long remained a substitute for direct inter-regional links. Indeed, there are numerous examples of failed inter-provincial services, even from the beginning of this period of expansion. In an apparently favourable context, Messrs Ettrick & Harle attempted to establish a stagecoach service between Durham and Sunderland and Newcastle in 1748. Within a fortnight, having covered only 23 per cent of costs, the partners abandoned the scheme and provided a post-chaise instead. This, too, failed within a month.[12]

Until very late in the century, then, the level of regular demand for coach travel between provincial centres remained quite inadequate to sustain services in any way comparable with those to and from the capital. Broadly speaking, it was only in the last quarter of the century that these links were added to the coach network, illustrated in fig. 8. The basic inter-provincial links of the 1790s were of very recent vintage, and clearly reinforce impressions derived from the London stages of the importance of growth later in the century.

Suburban traffic

This lag in development of the provincial network was mirrored also in the zone closest to the capital. The only town capable of developing an extensive system of suburban stages, proto-omnibuses, before 1800, or even before 1830, was London, since for our period the true suburb arose only in the capital. Although the suburban development of the capital dated from before 1700, when Highgate, Hampstead and other villages on the western fringes were beginning to develop suburban characteristics, there is little evidence of coach services to the outskirts before the middle of the century.[13] Once started, the suburban services grew rapidly, as is illustrated by table 5.

The development of suburban stages and early omnibus routes mirrors the pattern of London's own growth very effectively. Before 1773, with crossings of the Thames only into Southwark across London Bridge, and at the western end of the metropolis across Fulham, Westminster, and the Blackfriars footbridge, the zones most heavily served were much as would be expected. The prime 'commuter' territory of south-west Middlesex stood out in absolute terms, with eastern Surrey and the Kentish zone of the capital following a distance behind. At the opposite end of the period the easy penetration of Surrey offered by the three new bridges built between 1816 and 1819 is demonstrated in the rapid growth of suburban coaches to Brixton, Kennington and Camberwell. The general demand for suburban residences which grew during the later eighteenth century led to the overall pattern of growth in these services: the specific direction of development was determined, much as H. J. Dyos indicated, 'by improvements in communications, particularly, the

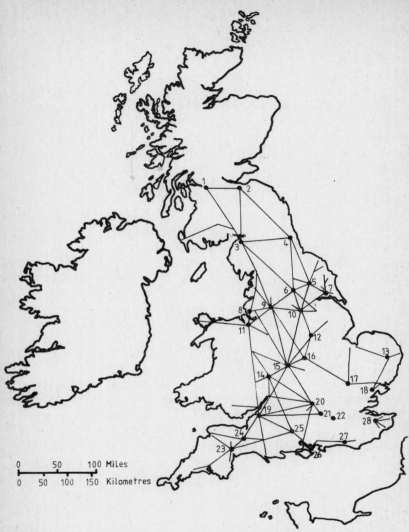

8 Inter-provincial coach services, c. 1790. 1 Glasgow, 2 Edinburgh, 3 Carlisle, 4 Newcastle upon Tyne, 5 York, 6 Leeds, 7 Hull, 8 Liverpool, 9 Manchester, 10 Sheffield, 11 Chester, 12 Nottingham, 13 Norwich, 14 Worcester, 15 Birmingham, 16 Leicester, 17 Cambridge, 18 Colchester, 19 Bristol, 20 Oxford, 21 Reading, 22 Guildford, 23 Exeter, 24 Taunton, 25 Salisbury, 26 Portsmouth, 27 Brighton, 28 Canterbury.

Table 5 Estimates of the growth of London's suburban stagecoach services, 1765–1840

	1765		1773		1796		1816		1840	
	PMW	I	PMW	I	PMW	I	PMW	I	PMW	I
Middlesex										
South-west	3.3	7.5	10.2	23.3	43.7	100	43.0	98.3	109.5	250.3
West	0.2	20.8	–	–	1.0	100	3.3	326.4	27	2,683.3
North-west	0.5	6.3	2.9	38.9	7.3	100	16.9	230.9	54.4	742
North	0.4	2.5	4.6	27.9	16.6	100	15.7	94.8	41.4	249.7
North-east	–	–	7.7	83.6	9.2	100	5.4	58.3	45	487.3
East	–	–	0.5	20.5	2.5	100	5.9	238.6	19.5	790.9
Sub-total	4.4	5.4	25.9	32.2	80.4	100	92.7	115.3	296.9	369.4
Surrey										
South-west	0.5	3	2.7	15	18.2	100	13.5	74.6	49.3	271.3
South	0.2	2.4	0.7	9.7	6.9	100	4.9	70.9	83	1,200.7
South-east	0.6	11.7	1	19.2	5	100	8.9	177.4	18.5	367.6
Sub-total	1.3	4.3	4.4	14.5	30.1	100	27.4	90.9	150.8	500.7
Kent	1	3.3	2.8	9.2	30.2	100	23.2	77	56.8	188
Essex	0.7	6.6	5.8	53.4	10.9	100	13.6	124.8	35.9	328.5
Total	7.4	4.9	38.9	25.7	151.6	100	157	103.5	540.3	356.5

Source. As for table 3.

the creation of certain bridges and the cutting of new roads'.[14] The pattern is easily identified in fig. 9 and table 3.

The causes of growth

These indicators of the extent and phasing of growth in coach services between London and the provinces, the major provincial centres, and between the capital and its developing suburbs require explanation. What was the cause of this growth? One answer lies in a form of Say's law in that the supply may have created its own demand. The evidence of the price of travel certainly suggests that the demand was relatively price-inelastic but that it became less and less so over the period under consideration. The evidence of fares must therefore first be considered (table 6).

It must at once be admitted that the data available on stagecoach fares are unsatisfactory. It is hard to ensure comparisons of like with like, but so far as possible this has been done both in the town-based series and in Dr Pawson's price series, which appear as the 'composite' element in table 6. These can be compared with the two major price series available for the period, the Phelps-Brown and Hopkins 'basket of consumables' and the Schumpeter—Gilboy consumer goods series. Both suggest that during the years of growth up to and during the Napoleonic wars the cost of travel rose less than that of either proxy for the general price level. Thereafter, admittedly on a poor data base, our figures indicate a reversal of the process as in the 1820s and 1830s the general price level fell and coach fares to Manchester rose.

As indicated earlier, part at least of the problem of analysing price: demand functions is specifying like units for comparison. Between 1750 and 1840 the output of the passenger-carrying business became gradually differentiated as 'flying machines', 'caravans' and, from the 1780s, 'post coaches' were added to the range of vehicles available to the traveller. The variety of vehicles and their distinctiveness can be illustrated with a number of simple examples. By the 1750s and 1760s there were 'coaches' or 'machines' on the road, together with a 'flying' variant. They were distinguished in price, speed and capacity, and may have sustained different elements of the passenger market. Flying coaches or machines charged slightly higher prices in the 1760s and 1770s, made earlier departures to enjoy a longer effective travelling day, and restricted the number of passengers, commonly limiting also the weight of luggage by setting 7 lb or 10 lb as a threshold beyond which 1*d* per mile excess was charged. By contrast, at the other

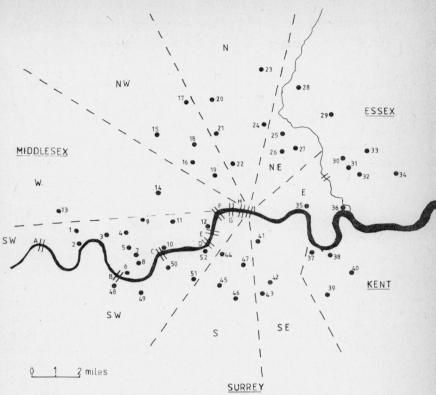

9 London suburban coach services. *Middlesex*, south-west: 1 Turnham Green,
2 Chiswick, 3 Hammersmith, 4 Earls Court, 5 Brompton, 6 Fulham, 7 Walham
Green, 8 Parsons Green, 9 Kensington, 10 Chelsea, 11 Knightsbridge, 12 Westminster; west: 13 Acton, 14 Paddington; north-west: 15 Hampstead, 16 Camden
Town, 17 Highgate, 18 Kentish Town, 19 Somers Town; north: 20 Hornsey,
21 Holloway, 22 Islington, 23 Tottenham, 24 Newington; north-east: 25 Clapton,
26 Hackney, 27 Homerton; east: 35 Limehouse, 36 Blackwall. *Essex:* 28 Walt-
hamstow, 29 Leyton, 30 Stratford, 31 West Ham, 32 Plaistow, 33 Forest Gate,
34 East Ham. *Kent:* 37 Deptford, 38 Greenwich, 39 Lewisham, 40 Blackheath.
Surrey, south-east: 41 Walworth, 42 Peckham, 43 Dulwich; south: 44 Kennington, 45 Brixton, 46 Herne Hill, 47 Camberwell; south-west: 48 Putney,
49 Wandsworth, 50 Battersea, 51 Clapham, 52 Vauxhall. *London's bridges*
(west to east): *A* Kew (opened 1759), *B* (Fulham (1729), *C* Battersea (1772),
D Vauxhall (1816), *E* Westminster (1750), *F* Waterloo (1817), *G* Blackfriars
(1769), *H* Southwark (1819), *I* London.

Table 6 Indices of coach fares compared with measures of the general price level, 1752–1832

Decade	Manchester	Birmingham	Bristol	Newcastle	Leeds	Composite	Prices		
							P–B & H	S–G	
1750–59	100	97.8				87.5	89.3	94.1
1760–69	100	100	100	100	100	100	100	100
1770–79	102.8	119.6	101.6	99.3	93.1	96.4	114.5	110.3
1780–89		102.2	93.4			113.9	117.2	105.5
1790–99		133.2	100			127.9	141.8	136.6
1800–09	141.4					160.7	209.5	187.2
1810–19				138.3	155.8		227.5	200.6
1820–29							173.6	
1830–39	186.9						162.8	

Source. W. T. Jackman, The Development of Transportation in Modern England, 3rd edn., 1966, appendix 6, pp. 702–15; J. Osborn, A Complete Guide, 1765; composite fare series from E. Pawson, Transport and Economy, 1977, p. 296; E. H. Phelps-Brown and S. V. Hopkins, 'Seven centuries of the prices of consumables, compared with builders' wage-rates', Economica, new ser., XXIII, 1956, pp. 296–314; the Schumpeter–Gilboy index of consumers' goods, from B. R. Mitchell and P. Deane, Abstract of British Historical Statistics, Cambridge, 1962, pp. 468–9.

end of the market, 'slow coaches' and caravans emerged for those not prepared to pay a premium for what in eighteenth-century conditions was rapid transit. Effectively the distinctive types evolved in the coaching business early in the period were still there at its demise in the 1840s: at the top were the premium-priced mail or flying coaches; beneath them a broad middle band of coaches and diligences offering perhaps a second-class service; next the 'old' or 'slow' coaches explicitly making a virtue of lower price or relative obsolescence; and at the bottom the caravans or their equivalent, offering half-rate travel to passengers prepared to accompany goods or parcels traffic. As expansion occurred, then, a range of different options were offered, and the choice open to the road passenger widened significantly.

It is worth considering the implications of these conclusions for the structure of the industry as it evolved. Expansion in this period was rapid, often sustained in a 'pioneering' phase by supply-induced demand, but was not guaranteed success. Output expanded at a rate well beyond that by which fares rose against the general price level, and although demand seems not to have been very price-elastic it became more so during the second half of the period. Passengers were able to choose from a widening range of coach types and conditions: at the upper level the post-chaise or private hire, and at the bottom a humbler range linked with goods transport. Part of the explanation of the changing output : price relationship observed earlier lies in the gradual development during the second half of the eighteenth century of real competition. All these developments tended to foster the gradual concentration of the industry into larger units as the requirements of speed, investment and competition demanded greater resources. Hart's assessment of the great concerns which had evolved by the 1820s — those of Sherman, Chaplin and Horne — may, however, have concealed the general trend to larger firms, visible from the 1750s onward when innkeepers first consolidated their control over the coaching business and then, as individuals or partners, gradually gained control over entire routes.[15] The early features of our period — an industry of risk, uncertainty, ease of entry, and the rapid expansion of the pioneering era, especially marked by the provincial and suburban services — disappeared during the late eighteenth century as many influences produced a more mature industrial structure. The pressures of speed, competition, qualitative change, taxation and shifting price conditions made for greater barriers to entry to the business and, at least on some roads, led to the development of large firms. While these great concerns may have controlled a substantial proportion of the premium traffic to and from the capital by 1830, the extent of oligopoly must not be exaggerated: the industrial structure was marked in 1840 by many larger firms than that of 1750, but it was never sufficiently concentrated as a whole to lose its competitive character.[16] In this may lie the explanation of the rather unusual price : output relationship.

Coaching and the economy

In conclusion we must consider briefly what differences these developments in passenger carriage made to the economy as a whole. At one level, probably at the upper end of coaching, they provided increasingly rapid transit for the merchant factor and the business community at large, thus providing a parallel service for industry and commerce to that offered by goods services. Gains in speed of communication for such groups at perhaps reduced relative costs must have added significantly to business efficiency. At all levels, from 'quality' travel by post-chaise to that in the humbler caravan, the developments provided a new and increasingly attractive consumer good. Clearly one must not underrate the contribution of the leisure industry to the economic growth of the period. Sherman's *Red Rover*, the development of Bath, Brighton or Scarborough, and the creation of an extensive interlocking network of post-chaises may represent as powerful a symbol of economic growth as domestic consumption of cotton goods, at least before 1800. In Gilboy's terms, demand factors in industrialisation, personal travel and the associated leisure industries had a powerful multiplier effect. Paradoxically, the more satisfactory explanation of their development may lie in the creative impact of the suppliers of coach and passenger travel facilities. The 'frippery and vice' represented by the huge expansion of personal travel may therefore add significantly to the more direct communication benefits to business and jointly represent an important factor in England's industrial growth.

The haulage of goods

Improved road passenger transport, then, contributed powerfully to business and commercial organisation during the industrial revolution. But what of the great flow of manufactured goods and articles which were an integral component of the industrial growth of the period? Did their production and marketing owe anything to the haulage side of the road transport industry? Contrary to the trend of much historical writing, road haulage made a positive contribution. In order to see how and why, the context must be outlined briefly.[17]

Transport serves manufacturing industries in two main ways: first, it enables raw materials to be assembled at least cost at the most economic site for processing them; secondly, it minimises the interval between their conversion into finished goods and their sale in the final market. The demand for transport services follows a complex pattern, set ultimately by the needs and characteristics of the traffic to be conveyed — its bulk, value, urgency, ease of handling, risk. The services have, therefore, to be equally complex, some catering for the bulk, low-priority traffic at a cheap rate, others meeting more specialised needs at appropriately higher prices. Into this latter category fell products such as textiles and light metalwares which figured prominently in the rise of manufactures during the industrial revolution. It was in meeting the needs of this type of traffic that road goods transport was especially important.

Road goods transport has long been neglected, apparently for two reasons. The first is an unstated but nonetheless implicit belief that the packhorse and road waggon, so much less dramatic than steam power, lacked the capacity to cope with the impressive statistics of industrial growth; the second, an explicit contrast between the cheapness and efficiency of water transport against the expense and limitations of road haulage. Both judgements rest on a negative view of the condition and cohesion of the road network, a view which recent research, reviewed in chapter 2,[18] has done much to dispel.

The assumption that road transport could not cope with the traffic must be abandoned. By later standards the output of the economy in the mid-eighteenth century was quite small in physical terms and although, compared with previous experience, it was growing relatively quickly, many of the measures of output used — e.g. millions of pounds' weight, instead of tons, of raw cotton consumed — convey an exaggerated impression of scale. Everitt was surely right to warn, especially for the early phase of the industrial revolution, against overconcern with northern industrial towns and to stress that 'a great deal of industrial development [took place] in the smaller market towns of England', the product of the workshop rather than the factory.[19] The road waggon, even the 'flying' variety, may lack the dramatic quality of the canal barge, but there is little doubt that up to the end of the eighteenth century it carried a significant share of the nation's traffic.

Moreover the growth of output, as well as being relatively modest in scale, was geographically dispersed. Much of the product traded beyond purely local markets consisted of light manufactures, produced in many different parts of the country. They were easily transported by the waggons and packhorses of the common carriers, the specialist suppliers of public road haulage services, and were of a high enough value to absorb the carrier's charges. Certainly road transport was not cheap: crude ton-mile rates usually point to a wide margin in favour of water transport. Ton-mile figures, however, do not tell the whole story. To reckon the full cost by water several other charges have to be added — wharfage dues and porterage, for example. And since water routes were often considerably longer than the alternative land routes, and coastal shipping in particular was liable to disruption by war and bad weather, there were many circumstances in which road transport was not a lot more expensive when all these considerations were taken into account, and it was a good deal more reliable. Road haulage was not confined only to the most valuable traffic, or used as a last resort when 'normal' means, usually water, had failed. On the contrary, the common carriers met a regular and well defined segment of the demand for transport services. In no other terms is it possible to account for the extensive network of carrying services observable by the mid-eighteenth century and the way they demonstrably grew during the industrial revolution.

Indeed, by the mid-eighteenth century the carrying trade was already well enough established to have developed a recognisable and clearly defined structure.[20] The services provided by the common carriers combined to form a network which covered the whole country. It was composed of separate strands, each the specialised business of a distinct group of operators who, with few exceptions on present evidence, confined their activities to their own particular category of business. Like Gaul, the trade was divided into three parts — the London trade, in which the biggest enterprises were to be found; that between the major provincial centres, a lesser though still substantial line of business; and, at the base, the local, short-distance trade in which a host of small-scale operators provided the essential linking services which extended the haulage network to every town and most villages. The majority of traffic originating was local, perhaps conveyed no more than a dozen miles or so, and was dealt with by the local carriers, supplemented by a variety of other agents who engaged in road haulage on an *ad hoc* basis. Traffic for a more distant market was handed on to the appropriate London or provincial carrier, or, in the reverse direction, entrusted to a local carrier for final delivery. Thus, without any operator transgressing the bounds of his own line of business, the different strands of services interlocked to form a coherent, integrated system of transport. Each of the three strands will be considered in turn.

The London trade

At the head stood the London trade, the longest established, its antecedents reaching back at least to the late fourteenth century, and, certainly in terms of traffic conveyed, by far the most important. The London carriers were the 'blue riband' operators. Their businesses were the largest; they employed the biggest horses and waggons, and hence the most capital; their organisations were the most complex. Like other carriers, they initially conducted their business from inns and inn yards, but the need to provide specialist facilities and develop, especially in London, local collection and delivery services, in addition to point-to-point conveyance, soon led the biggest of them, carriers from major provincial centres like Russell of Exeter and Pickford of Manchester, to acquire premises of their own. In London some inns were converted to the carrying business: Russell took over the Bell, Friday Street, and Pickford's acquired the Castle, Wood Street.[21] At the same time specially built carriers' warehouses and offices were being erected in most provincial centres. By the 1820s and 1830s some of these comprised extensive complexes of buildings, occupying prime central sites. In 1837, for example, the assets of Marsh & Swann, London, Cambridge and Norfolk carriers, came under the auctioneer's hammer: besides the 100 waggon horses, twenty-one assorted waggons and vans, and 'sundry other waggons, capital sprung carts, drugs, trucks, and other carriages' advertised for sale, there was a large central site, some two-fifths of an acre in extent, on which stood a house, stables, offices, covered yards, warehouses, granaries, collarmakers', blacksmiths' and wheelwrights' shops.[22] The London carriers ranked among the most important of the urban trades.

The foregoing provides a brief glimpse of the main characteristics of the London carrier's business. To assess the structure and development of the London trade as a whole, it is necessary to turn to estimates of its output, as measured by the volume of services supplied per week and, more particularly, the measure on which most of the subsequent analysis rests, the volume of ton-miles per week.

The various estimates, for the trade as a whole and broken down by regions, are presented in tables 7 and 8.

Here, as with the passenger figures, the evidence is bound to pose some difficulties. Four different sources,[23] albeit surveys of the same industry, are unlikely to harmonise smoothly. Although too perfect a fit would be grounds for suspicion, it is reasonable to expect that errors and omissions should cancel each other out such that some confidence could be placed in the overall pattern. Indeed, at the aggregate level the data appear to present few problems: the estimates indicate a regular upward trend, much as might be expected. The regional ton-mile estimates, however, make it plain that discrepancies between series do exist — for example, the sharp swings in the East Anglia series between 1765 and 1773, and the whole of the Yorkshire and Lincolnshire series. While the very real danger of presuming a regular upward trend and viewing deviations from it only as 'problems' must be resisted, no satisfactory explanations of the fluctuations suggest themselves. It is possible that some of the shifts represent real adjustments to differing traffic levels or the changing force of competition from water transport. Possibly, too, there were changes in modes of operation which, say in East Anglia, by raising productivity reduced the number of units required. Just as likely, however, there are errors in the data. In both cases, especially East Anglia, the absolute level of recorded services, on which all the other calculations rest, is relatively low, so that a small error would have a disproportionate effect on the ton-mile estimates and the index numbers derived from them.

Two final cautions are in order concerning possible distortions in the estimates. Although the sample data are adequate to the purpose, it appears that, while they pick up the longer-distance carrier services well enough, they discriminate against the regions closest to London, especially the northern Home Counties and the South-east. The full data would almost certainly modify the rates of change indicated by these figures, but the overall pattern, which is the primary concern here, is unlikely to be significantly affected. Secondly, no attempt has been made to allow for the influence of the trade cycle. There is bound to have been some effect, if only in the volume of traffic conveyed: how far service levels were sensitive, and adjusted, to shifts in the cycle is not known.

The summary estimates for the London carrying trade, table 7, demonstrate several interesting contrasts with the passenger trade.

Table 7 Output of the road haulage industry in London: services and ton miles per week, to selected provincial centres, selected years 1715–1840

Year	Service quotient	Index	Ton miles	Index
1715	108	37	13,279	10
1765	175	60	80,356	59
1773	183	62	84,752	62
1796	294	100	135,996	100
1816	574	195	275,356	203
1840	1,081	368	458,516	337

Note. The ton-mile estimates rest on the following assumptions: for 1715 a payload of 1.2 tons per service (a weighted average derived from the proportion of packhorse and waggon services); from 1765 onwards, four tons per service (all by waggon), the legal maximum set by Parliament in that year. Permissible weights increased later in the century, but by how much cannot be determined. These assumptions perhaps overstate the 1715 and 1765 estimates, understate those for 1773 and 1796 and are possibly neutral in 1816 and 1840.

Source. As table 3.

By 1715 road haulage had reached a higher stage of development, a reflection of its much longer history. Moreover carrying services already covered the whole country, whereas the remoter parts were still devoid of coaches. During the eighteenth century carrying progressed more slowly than the passenger side, but its capacity for further growth was greater. By the turn of the century the output of the coaching trade, measured by services, was approaching its peak; road haulage, in contrast, was to experience four decades of vigorous expansion. The other marked difference concerns seasonality. Seasonal differences in both service and price remained part of the coaching trade until the end of the eighteenth century, but were not significant in road haulage. There is no support here for the prevalent textbook view of impassable winter roads bringing road traffic to a halt.

Other features of the haulage estimates invite comment. The contrast between the service quotient and ton-mile indexes in 1715 and their differential growth to 1765 points to a predominance of shorter-distance services at the earlier date and a relatively greater growth of more distant provincial services during the intervening fifty years. The regional series, table 8, provide support for this; the two regions to

progress at a rate above the average, in terms of ton-miles, were
Lancashire and Cheshire, at twice the average, and Yorkshire and
Lincolnshire, at about a third higher rate. Both, however, would have
contributed more mileage than tonnage to the index.

There was no significant change between 1765 and 1773, but the
latter date marks the stage at which competition from canal transport
began. Certainly by 1796 an effect would be expected: much of the
Midland and Northern canal system was complete, although London
was still dependent on its unsatisfactory link with the system at Oxford
by way of the Thames. The expansion that took place is therefore all
the more striking. Rapid industrial growth evidently provided
adequate traffic for both road and canal, though data for the 1780s
might well indicate that the former lagged behind during that decade.
By the mid-1790s the onset of war, always a stimulus to road transport, would have offset some of the effects of canal competition.

Industrial growth, war up to 1815, and the legacy of war, helped
also to explain the vigorous expansion of road haulage after the turn
of the century. The war focused attention on the state of the roads,
and improvements begun during those years were continued afterwards, notably by the McAdam and Telford. Better road conditions
meant less wear and tear on vehicles and horses, and this, together
with an end to the wartime inflation of fodder and horse prices, caused
the real costs of road haulage to fall. For this reason, and by force
of sharp competition within the industry, carriage rates were lower
in the 1820s and 1830s than they had been for some years.[24] As a consequence road haulage was able, within limits, to draw traffic away
from the canals. In addition the better roads enabled more efficient,
lightweight vehicles — sprung carts and vans — to be introduced for
both short and long distances. In all, then, there was a marked increase
in the efficiency and competitive power of road haulage in the early
nineteenth century, sufficient to explain the sustained increase in the
estimated output of the industry up to the advent of railways. Road
haulage retained considerable volumes of lucrative traffic, on which
railway promoters cast envious eyes.[25]

Road haulage was also a growing industry within the confines of
London itself. As with passenger transport, the physical extension of
the capital and the strengthening of ties with the hinterland stimulated
the introduction of short-haul cart and caravan services, a close
parallel to the short-distance coach and 'bus' services already described. Only a handful of cart services were listed in 1773, but by 1796

the nucleus of an extensive network, serving an inner ring of some twenty miles, had already grown up and was supplemented by a few faster, caravan services to more distant parts of Essex, Suffolk and Hampshire. By 1816, a couple of decades before the same features appeared in provincial centres, the adjacent Home Counties of Middlesex, Surrey, Essex and Kent, in that order of importance, absorbed over 95 per cent of an estimated weekly output of 1,800 cart and caravan services. The subsequent trend was for these services to increase substantially in number and to become more intensively local.

The provinces

It is clear from the regional series (table 8) that the summary figures hide a great deal of regional variation. Different parts of the country participated in the national economy, as represented by contributions to the London market, in differing degrees, and shifts between road and water transport are most likely to be reflected at the regional level. Some of the recorded fluctuations in individual series probably reflect deficiencies in the data but others were more likely real; the fall in the West Midlands series between 1773 and 1796 may well be attributable to canal competition, in which case both the smallness of the fall and the extent to which it was subsequently reversed would be striking. The strength of the expansion from 1796 to 1840 comes out in all the series. Comparisons of the relative shares of output between the regions, however, point to certain limitations in the ton-mile measure, although it is the measure of output usually employed for road haulage. It does not discriminate between tonnage and mileage and hence indicate where the burden of traffic to be conveyed actually fell. The East Midlands, the South-west and the three northern regions together contributed the greater portion of ton-mileage, 75 per cent in 1765 and about 60 per cent in 1840; their share of total services was less, 55 per cent and 40 per cent, and their share of total tonnage probably even less still. However, although these figures tend to underplay the contribution of other regions[26] — the northern Home Counties, the South-east and the South and West, for example — they do help to explain why the long-distance provincial services were costly to mount and why those who operated them needed large resources.

The provincial and local sectors of the carrying trade escape this problem: since ton-mile estimates cannot be attempted, our analysis can employ only the service quotient. Examination of the structure of the carrying trade from provincial sources demonstrates that the

Table 8 Regional distribution of road haulage output in London: estimated ton miles per week, selected years, 1715–1840

	1715		1765		1773		1796		1816		1840	
	TMW	Index	TMW	Index	TMW	Index	TMW	Index	TMW	Index	TMW	Index
Northern Home Counties	784	24	3,180	98	2,268	70	3,240	100	5,220	161	13,080	404
South-east	308	6	1,688	31	1,424	26	5,500	100	12,248	223	27,920	508
East Anglia	814	36	2,712	120	904	40	2,260	100	5,424	240	14,012	620
East Midlands	2,342	13	14,544	79	16,008	87	18,452	100	35,604	193	51,392	279
South and West	834	5	5,348	32	8,448	51	16,492	100	27,828	169	39,076	237
West Midlands	1,199	15	6,496	79	9,204	111	8,272	100	39,932	483	63,556	768
South-west	2,984	11	18,800	70	15,972	59	26,920	100	57,176	212	108,652	404
Lancashire and Cheshire	670	5	9,672	68	6,696	47	14,136	100	20,832	147	27,528	195
Yorkshire and Lincolnshire	1,254	22	9,896	173	12,548	219	5,724	100	16,680	291	29,808	521
North and Scotland	1,780	7	7,504	30	10,796	44	24,796	100	45,320	183	50,184	202
Wales	310	3	516	5	516	5	10,204	100	9,092	89	33,308	326
Total	13,279	10	80,356	59	84,752	62	135,996	100	275,356	203	458,516	337

Source. As table 3.

London trade, for all its undoubted pre-eminence, was only part of a broadly based industry.[27] London operators rarely accounted for more than 10 per cent of service output in major towns; a much larger portion, about 20–25 per cent on average but subject to wide variations in particular cases, was committed to regional routes. Some towns, like Birmingham and Manchester, had well developed regional networks. The majority relied on a few services to two or three major centres, but routed so as to pass through all the important intervening. towns. In the 1780s Anderson's waggon from Sheffield to Bewdley, for example, carried traffic for Nottingham, Birmingham and all the other towns along the way.[28] By a mixture of through routes and end-on connections, a complex system of inter-provincial carrier routes was created. Figure 10 is an attempt, based on the evidence of twenty-one selected towns,[29] to sketch a reasonably representative version of the inter-provincial network during the 1780s and 1790s. As the map shows, services originating in Exeter or Salisbury met others from Birmingham in Bristol; Birmingham exchanged services with Liverpool and Manchester in the west and Leeds, Sheffield and York in the east, and from these places other services provided connections through the North-west and North-east to Glasgow and Edinburgh. At these points of interchange, traffic was handed on from one carrier to another and thus conceivably, though in fact most unlikely, could pass from one end of the country to the other in this way. More usually traffic would traverse part of the system, as when, in December 1768, John Wilson, a Leeds linen merchant, sent a parcel of blankets to the wife of one of his purchasing agents in Perth.

I have this day sent you per Pickersgill the Newcastle carrier the blankets ... I have paid him the carriage from Leeds to Edinburgh, as the carriers are apt to impose much when goods go through different carriers' hands. They will come from Newcastle to Edinburgh by Howie's waggon, of whom you may order your carrier at Perth to call for them.[30]

From the turn of the century inter-provincial services were strengthened and widened in most major towns, until railways began to bite into their traffic.

The local carriers

The London and inter-provincial services provided the basic framework of the national carrier system. Underpinning them, however, the feeder branches of the main lines so to speak, was an

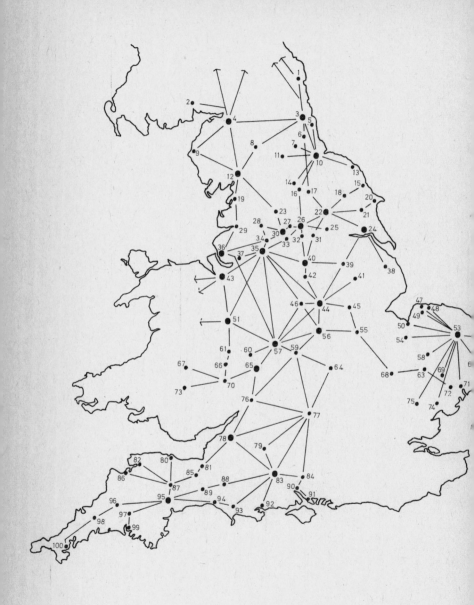

10   The inter-provincial road carrying network in the late eighteenth century. 1 Alnwick, 2 Dumfries, 3 Newcastle, 4 Carlisle, 5 Hartlepool, 6 Durham, 7 Bishop Auckland, 8 Brough, 9 Whitehaven, 10 Stockton, 11 Barnard Castle, 12 Kendal, 13 Whitby, 14 Leyburn, 15 Scarborough, 16 Masham, 17 Thirsk, 18 Malton, 19 Lancaster, 20 Bridlington, 21 Driffield, 22 York, 23 Skipton, 24 Hull, 25 Selby, 26 Leeds, 27 Bradford, 28 Burnley, 29 Preston, 30 Halifax, 31 Pontefract, 32 Wakefield, 33 Huddersfield, 34 Rochdale, 35 Manchester, 36 Liverpool, 37 Warrington, 38 Louth, 39 Gainsborough, 40 Sheffield, 41 Lincoln, 42 Chesterfield, 43 Chester, 44 Nottingham, 45 Grantham, 46 Derby, 47 Wells, 48 Fakenham, 49 Holt, 50 Kings Lynn, 51 Shrewsbury, 52 Yarmouth, 53 Norwich, 54 Downham Market, 55 Stamford, 56 Leicester, 57 Birmingham, 58 Thetford, 59 Coventry, 60 Bewdley, 61 Ludlow, 62 Southwold, 63 Bury St Edmunds, 64 Northampton, 65 Worcester, 66 Leominster, 67 Builth Wells, 68 Cambridge, 69 Stowmarket, 70 Hereford, 71 Woodbridge, 72 Ipswich, 73 Brecon, 74 Colchester, 75 Braintree, 76 Gloucester, 77 Oxford, 78 Bristol, 79 Devizes, 80 Minehead, 81 Bridgwater, 82 Barnstaple, 83 Salisbury, 84 Winchester, 85 Taunton, 86 Bideford, 87 Tiverton, 88 Shaftesbury, 89 Yeovil, 90 Southampton, 91 Portsmouth, 92 Poole, 93 Dorchester, 94 Bridport, 95 Exeter, 96 Launceston, 97 Tavistock, 98 Bodmin, 99 Plymouth, 100 Falmouth. *Source.* As fig. 11.

even greater profusion of local carrier services. A hint of the relationship is contained in fig. 10, in which greater detail, though still a
fraction of the whole, has been drawn in for Exeter, Norwich and
Stockton to illustrate how these local services extended the network
to smaller towns and villages. Every major centre marked on the map
was served by a range of local carriers, operating up to a distance of
twenty-five to thirty miles, and analysis of the aggregate trip data,
plotted in fig. 11, emphasises their preponderance. Short-distance
services of this kind, many of them timed to coincide with market
days, accounted, on average, for 65–70 per cent of all services
supplied in these centres. Industrialised towns, represented by
Birmingham in the diagram, had a higher proportion of longer-
distance services than the traditional market town such as Norwich.

   The local carriers' scale of operation was, of course, much more
limited, and simpler to organise, than that of their colleagues in the
London and inter-provincial trades. Many were part-timers, travelling to market once or twice a week and following other occupations
the rest of the time; others made it a full-time occupation by working to two or three different towns. Since they completed the round
trip in the course of a day, they needed no specialist premises in the
towns they served, and thus continued, unlike their bigger colleagues,
to be based on inn yards to the end of the period. Few would have
had more than a couple of vehicles and horses. Very much the 'one
man and a boy' end of the business, it was not unimportant, for all
that. Their traffic was no doubt predominantly the humdrum trade
of market towns but perhaps their dealings were more representative
of the pattern of economic activity. There has been little spatial
analysis of market size and structure in this period, but what evidence
there is points to a typically localised pattern of transactions; a radius
of twenty-five to thirty miles would capture most of them.[31] Examples of more elaborate supply networks are more eye-catching but
relate to a more restricted trade. For many people the local carrier was
their contact with the wider world and his services representative of
day-to-day affairs. And despite the greater complexity which the
industrial revolution brought to the economy, this factor grew rather
than declined. Directory evidence for the 1820s, 1830s and 1840s
demonstrates clearly that substantial expansion of such market services was a prominent feature of those decades, indicating a marked
strengthening of the transport links between market centres and their
hinterlands.[32] Thus roads carried a great deal of local traffic: the

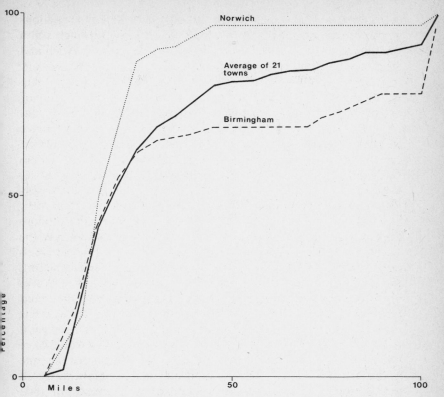

11   The distribution, by distance, of the carrier services of twenty-one provincial towns, c. 1790. Source. The carrier data were drawn from the following directories: Birmingham (Pye), 1785; Bristol (Matthews), 1793; Carlisle (Smith), 1795; Chester (Broster), 1797; Hull (Battle), 1791; Leeds (Ryley), 1798; Liverpool (Gore), 1796; Manchester (Scholes), 1794; Newcastle (Whitehead), 1790; Norwich (Chase), 1783; Sheffield (Robinson), 1797; Shrewsbury (Minshull), 1786; Worcester (Grundy), 1788, and the entries for Exeter, Halifax, Kendal, Leicester, Nottingham, Salisbury, Stockton and York in the *Universal British Directory*, II–IV, 1791–98.

promoters of the Leeds and Bradford railway, in 1830, emphasised
the point in order to assuage potential opposition from canal interests,
'as it is a fact, that more than *two-thirds* of the whole traffic, between
Leeds and Bradford, is already upon the Turnpike Road'.[33]

Road haulage and the economy

It remains to explain the place of road haulage, and the carrier, in the
growing economy of the industrial revolution. It is important to
reiterate that it is a question of looking not for particular types of
goods which uniquely went by road but for the sort of conditions
which road transport was best able to meet. The distinctive qualities
of road transport were many. It was accessible to all parts of the
country; it could follow the shortest, most direct routes; it was generally speedier than other modes and more reliable in bad weather; goods
could be more easily protected against damage. Certainly it was more
expensive, but for traffic needing any or a combination of these
qualities the price was worth paying. It was better to accept a lower
profit and rush goods in by land than to miss a market altogether.
Most heavy industrial and agricultural raw materials rarely posed such
needs. Coal, ores, stone, lime, manure, were not prominent road
traffics, except for limited local hauls.

Road carrying grew up providing several categories of service: a
personalised service to gentry and county families, a role largely gone
by the late eighteenth century; the conveyance of supplies for a variety
of retail traders, grocers, drapers, wine and spirit merchants and
druggists, a role which continued through to the 1830s; and the movement of industrial products, above all textiles. This last activity, when
extended to include agricultural produce, became the carrier's most
important contribution to the industrial revolution. Like the whole
topic of road goods transport, the subject requires a great deal of
further research, but the main lines of development can be sketched in.

Agricultural produce needed to reach the market before it deterio-
rated: the main requirement was speed of transit, which road transport
was well able to provide. The food supply of many urban centres
arrived at least in part by road, brought by farmers themselves or by
the local carriers' market-day services. In the early 1820s Edward
Baines remarked on the great number of carts then to be seen in the
Skipton market, 200 a week, he reckoned, where previously not a cart
was to be seen.[34] Some of the produce brought in gave rise to
remarkable organisation. In the 1790s eggs from as far afield as

Kendal and Penrith were brought by cart for sale in Manchester. Ten thousand to a cartload, they were packed in casks in layers of straw and, according to the reporter, 'few eggs [were] broken by the carriage'.[35] London was another market which relied in part on road haulage, including carrier services, for its food supply. Butter and meat were both frequently sent up by road from adjacent counties. In the early 1800s Buckinghamshire farmers could rely on an efficient carrier service. 'The only trouble which the dairyman has, is to carry his butter upon a horse to the nearest point where the carrier passes, to make his agreement with his butter factor, and monthly or otherwise to receive his money.'[36] In the 1830s both Smithfield and Newgate meat markets drew in supplies by road, conveyed in swift, lightweight vans.

Many manufactured items also went by road — textiles, dress goods, hats, light metalware, a mixture of the products of old and new industries in the industrial revolution. Much of this was traffic shared with water transport, depending on the circumstances. In the 1830s Leeds merchants sent most of their woollen cloth bound for Hull down the river, but over the Pennines to Manchester they insisted on sending by road because the canal routes were too slow. In the same years Stroud clothiers would not entrust their fine cloths to the waterways for fear of delay and damage in transit.[37] Admittedly these examples, like others which could be cited, involve relatively high-value products, but the point is that it was the needs of particular consignments of traffic rather than the nature of the product that determined which mode of transport was selected.

Rather than proceed further in general terms, it is more instructive to examine the choice that was made between transport modes in a couple of specific cases. One, a hat maker of Stockport, represents the traditional dress trades of the eighteenth century. The other, John Heywood & Son, quilting manufacturer, of Bolton, was engaged in the new cotton cloth industry. Small collections of business records, one for 1797–1804, the other for 1805–20, illustrate their activities.

Thomas Worsley supplied felt hats to the London wholesale hatter Miller Christy.[38] Worsley conducted his business in the classic merchant manufacturer style: operating from a warehouse in Stockport, he received orders from Christy, had them executed by the local outworkers he employed, collected the completed work, boxed it up and sent it off to London. The role of transport was to minimise the interval between the dispatch of the raw materials from London (wool, hair, hides, glue and dyestuffs) and their return to the capital as finished goods. Delay cost money. Worsley complained bitterly that materials delayed in transit by Pickford's 'could have [been] made into money long ago if they had come regularly to hand'.[39]

Efficient transport thus formed a necessary underpinning of the business. Coastal shipping, canal transport and road haulage were all employed, according to circumstances. As far as possible a steady flow of raw materials, ordered in relatively large unit loads, was maintained, usually shipped by coaster or, as in the case of the predominant cargo, wool — 'best Upland Kent lambs' wool' and 'good Surrey' — by canal. Not infrequently, however, small quantities of them were needed in a hurry or the water routes were subject to delay; on such occasions the traffic was switched to waggons. Although at times Worsley asked for all his wool to be sent by road, these seem to have been occasions when the canals were obstructed.

The wool dispatched by canal was packed in large wooden boxes. These served the double purpose of protecting the wool in transit and then serving admirably as containers in which the finished hats could be sent, undamaged, to London. Once completed, the hats had to be got there as quickly as possible; and the value added in the manufacturing process enabled them to absorb the cost of the fastest mode of transport, by road. Worsley kept a careful record of each box of hats sent off to London. A few went by canal, a few more by coach when extreme speed was called for, but the vast majority went by Pickford's waggon. Of 450 boxes dispatched in 1803, the last complete year for which the accounts survive, almost 80 per cent went by waggon. None was sent by canal.

Heywood's records are more limited, yet contain interesting insights.[40] The firm straddled the old and the new. Its product, cotton cloth, symbolised the new age of textiles but was woven by hand in the traditional way. In the letters which survive there are twice as many references to the use of road transport as there are to canals. It may have been, of course, that road transport caused more trouble and so gave rise to more correspondence, but such appears not to have been the case. Nor need it indicate the proportionate use of the two modes; the evidence is too thin for that. What does emerge, without, it is felt, reading too much into the evidence, is that when speed was required road transport was turned to. On 12 March 1806 John Heywood wrote to his London warehouse, Stirling Bros, one of several he employed, asking that all the goods they held for him be immediately returned to Bolton, 'by the first 5 days Waggon'. He had a buyer, but only if the goods arrived by 20 March. Two days later they were on their way, by Pickford's waggon.[41] Pickford's is the most frequently mentioned carrier, by road and canal, and, as a further sign of the search for speed, it is noteworthy that after the firm had introduced its fast vans between London and Manchester, in 1814, Heywood switched from waggon to van.

The import of this chapter can be briefly summarised. It has demonstrated, first, that the road transport industry, both passenger and goods, displayed a scale and complexity far in excess of that which conventional textbook treatments suggest. Secondly, by speeding the movement of goods, travellers and commercial information, it reduced barriers to trade and added to the efficiency and size of the market. External economies of this kind, allowing greater efficiency in the use of resources, were no less important than the direct cost reductions achieved by the industry or the more familiar technological advances in manufacturing processes. And finally, road transport revealed a potential which the railway was able to exploit more effectively. It is clear that personal travel was already a growth industry, such that the 'success' of railway passenger business becomes less of a surprise, while the special strengths of road goods transport — speed and reliability — could be supplied to a superior standard and at a lower cost. Much of this, however, lay in the future. Britain industrialised without the railway, and for much of the period even canals were of limited value. Chapter 2 concluded that the turnpikes were one of the pillars of the industrial revolution. To a considerable extent the country's economic growth rested firmly on an effective system of road transport.

Notes

We are grateful to the Social Science Research Council, who funded the research project from which the matter of the chapter has been drawn.

1   G. R. Hawke, *Railways and Economic Growth in England and Wales 1840–70*, Oxford, 1970, pp. 33–54.

2   D. E. C. Eversley, 'The home market and economic growth in England 1750–1780', in E. L. Jones and G. E. Mingay (eds.), *Land, Labour, and Population in the Industrial Revolution*; E. W. Gilboy, 'Demand as a factor in the industrial revolution', in A. H. Cole *et al.*, *Facts and Factors in Economic History*, Cambridge, Mass., 1932, reprinted in R. M. Hartwell (ed.), *The Causes of the Industrial Revolution*, London, 1967, pp. 121–38.

3   For a study of one such resort see J. Whyman, 'A Hanoverian watering place: Margate before the railway', in A. M. Everitt (ed.), *Perspectives in English Urban History*, London, 1973, pp. 138–60.

4   R. B. Westerfield, *Middlemen in English Business, particularly between 1660 and 1760*, New Haven, Conn., 1915, repr. Newton Abbot, 1968.

5   London's functions are surveyed by E. A. Wrigley, 'A simple model of London's importance in changing English society and economy, 1650–1750', *Past and Present*, XXXVII, 1967; F. J. Fisher, 'London as an "engine of economic growth"', in J. S. Bromley and E. H. Kossman, *Britain and the Netherlands*, IV, *Metropolis, Dominion and Province*, London, 1971.

6   Eversley, 'Home market', p. 216.

7   On the earlier background see J. Parkes, *Travel in England in the Seventeenth Century*, Oxford, 1925, chapter IV, pp. 52f.

8   Discussed in general in J. A. Chartres, 'The capital's provincial eyes: London's inns in the early eighteenth century', *London Journal*, III (1), 1977.

9   The approaches are discussed in J. A. Chartres, 'Road carrying in England in the seventeenth century: myth and reality', *Economic History Review*, 2nd ser., XXX (1), 1977; C. H. Wilson, 'Land carriage in the seventeenth century', and J. A. Chartres, 'On the road with Professor Wilson', *Economic History Review*, 2nd ser., XXXIII (1), 1980.

10   Several historians also fall into the same trap. While the railway certainly saw the long-distance coaches off pretty rapidly, this was only taking place from the end of the 1830s, and often led to the displacement of coaches to other areas, not to their total abandonment: see J. Copeland, *Roads and their Traffic, 1750–1850*, Newton Abbot, 1968, p. 108.

11   For a useful but rather disorganised history of the Brighton traffic see W. C. A. Blew, *Brighton and its Coaches*, London, 1894.

12   M. A. Richardson (ed.), *The Local Historian's Table Book*, Newcastle upon Tyne, 1841–46, II, p. 18.

13   F. M. L. Thompson, *Hampstead: Building a Borough, 1650–1964*, London, 1974, pp. 23–7.

14   For a general survey of the impact of bridge-building on the suburban character of south London see H. J. Dyos, 'The growth of a pre-Victorian suburb: south London, 1580–1836', *Town Planning Review*, XXV (1), 1954, pp. 59–78. On early provincial suburban networks, lagging far behind London, see, for example, G. C. Dickinson, 'The development of suburban road passenger transport in Leeds, 1840–95', *Journal of Transport History*, IV (4), 1960, pp. 214–23.

15   H. W. Hart, 'Sherman and the Bull and Mouth', *Journal of Transport History*, V (1), 1961, pp. 12–21.

16   P. S. Bagwell, *The Transport Revolution from 1770*, London, 1974, pp. 50–5.

17   Similar views to those expressed here will be found in T. C. Barker and C. I. Savage, *An Economic History of Transport in Britain*, 3rd edn., London, 1974; J. A. Chartres, *Internal Trade in England 1500–1700*, London, 1977; G. L. Turnbull, *Traffic and Transport: an Economic History of Pickfords*, London, 1979, especially chapters 1 and 4.

18   Pages 31–63.

19   Everitt, *Perspectives in English Urban History*, p. 14.

20   Chartres, 'Road carrying in England'; G. L. Turnbull, 'Provincial road carry-
      ing in England in the eighteenth century', *Journal of Transport History*, new
      ser., IV, 1977, pp. 17–39.

21   *Universal British Directory* (Barfoot and Wilkes), I, 1790, pp. 475ff.; Turnbull,
      Traffic and Transport, p. 28, and chapter 2 generally for the background to
      the London carrying trade.

22   *The Bury and Norwich Post*, 14 June 1837. We are grateful to Dr R. G. Wilson
      for this reference.

23   See table 3.

24   *Select Committee on Postage, P.P.*, 1837–38, XX, evidence of Daniel Deacon,
      q. 7267.

25   Historians have seriously neglected the extent to which railway promoters looked
      to road goods traffic as a potential source of revenue. The evidence can be read
      in many of the railway Bill select committee proceedings of the 1830s.

26   See the figures for 1715 in Chartres, 'Road carrying in England'.

27   Turnbull, 'Provincial road carrying'.

28   *Directory of Sheffield* (Gales and Martin), 1787, p. 80.

29   For details, see fig. 11 and the sources listed there.

30   J. Wilson to G. Swann, 23 December 1768. Wilson Mss, Leeds City Archives,
      W/3/3.

31   A. Everitt, 'The marketing of agricultural produce', in J. Thirsk (ed.), *The
      Agrarian History of England and Wales*, IV, *1500–1640*, Cambridge, 1967;
      J. A. Chartres, 'The marketing of agricultural produce', in J. Thirsk (ed.), *The
      Agrarian History of England and Wales*, V (forthcoming).

32   M. J. Freeman, 'The carrier system of south Hampshire, 1775–1851', *Journal
      of Transport History*, new ser., IV, 1977, pp. 61–85.

33   Advertisement for the Leeds & Bradford Railway, 1830, displayed in the
      Bradford Industrial Museum.

34   E. Baines, *History, Directory and Gazetteer of the County of York*, 1822, repr.
      Newton Abbot, 1969, I, p. 405.

35   J. Holt, *General View of the Agriculture of the County of Lancaster*, 1795, repr.
      Newton Abbot, 1969, p. 185.

36   W. Marshall, *The Review and Abstract of the County Reports to the Board of
      Agriculture*, 5, 1915, repr. Newton Abbot, n.d., p. 547, quoting Priest's report
      on Buckinghamshire, 1808.

37   These, and similar examples, are from the select committee proceedings on the
      relevant railway Bills.

38   Christy Mss, B/WW/3/32–5, B/P/2/34, Stockport Public Library.

39   Worsley to Christy, 6 February 1802, Christy Mss, B/WW/3/33.

40   Heywood Papers, Correspondence, ZHE/1–16, Bolton Central Reference
      Library.

41   Heywood to Stirling Bros, London, 12 March 1806; Loyd (Stirling Bros) to
      Heywood, 14 March 1806. Heywood Papers, ZHE/2.

4 CANALS AND RIVER NAVIGATIONS
Baron F. Duckham

'I have lately been viewing the artificial wonders of London and the natural wonders of the Peak,' recorded a correspondent of the *Annual Register* in 1763, 'but none of them gave me so much pleasure as the Duke of Bridgewater's navigation'. Popular economic history has traditionally seen in the opening of this short canal between Worsley colliery and Manchester in 1761 the birth of the canal age.[1] Although Professor Barker and others have corrected this view, it remains a highly convenient date.[2] The Bridgewater Canal undoubtedly fired the imagination of contemporaries, for as early as 1760 it was being confidently asserted that it would 'be the most extraordinary thing in the kingdom, if not in Europe'. It is therefore not surprising that in retrospect the example of the third Duke of Bridgewater, both in its technological achievement and economic success, appeared to mark a firm break with the past and herald an age in which man built his own waterways rather than simply improved those of nature. And the date of the canal's construction, 1759–61, fitted beautifully the notion that the industrial revolution only began in earnest from 1 January 1760! Yet despite the obvious solecism of regarding the Bridgewater Canal as a great leap forward, it was the first to be built under an Act of Parliament which specifically empowered its promoters 'to make a navigable Cut *or Canal*'.[3]

Promotion and chronology

It is reasonably certain that the short and quickly forgotten Exeter Canal of 1564–66 was the first true British deadwater canal with proper pound locks. Then, for over a century and a half, the precocity of this example was neglected and the cause of inland navigation furthered by river improvement schemes rather than canals.[4] The reasons are not far to seek. Most medieval and early modern centres of trade stood on or near navigable water, and the economic growth of the seventeenth and eighteenth centuries was never so explosive that it could not be met by improving and extending river navigation. There was in Britain no Colbert to involve the State in grandiose canal schemes, and private investment preferred in most cases projects that were strictly local and technologically simple. Between 1660 and 1750 at least forty rivers became subject for the first time to improvement Acts.[5] Until the more obvious river navigations had been 'perfected' there was little chance that capital would be diverted to the still more speculative construction of canals *ex nihilo*, though a few diminutive lockless cuts were occasionally dug by coalmasters and others. The endowment of nature was utilised as long as possible, with some inconvenient transhipment breaks being tolerated surprisingly far into the canal age. Despite the Don Navigation, Sheffield was not linked by canal to the river's effective head until 1819, and the canalisation of the Calder by-passed the important cloth town of Halifax until the canal connection of 1828.[6] The total mileage of river navigation available by *c*. 1750 cannot have been much less than 1,400 miles (fig. 12).

Ironically, it was in Ireland that the first eighteenth-century canal of any substance in the British Isles was built. Here State patronage provided the decisive step, for in 1729 the Dublin Parliament appointed 'Commissioners of Inland Navigation for Ireland' whose efforts eventually led to the opening of the Newry canal in March 1742. Though there was no direct economic connection between the Newry Navigation and the first canals of industrialising Lancashire, there was an important personal link. Thomas Steers, builder of Liverpool's first wet dock, was the engineer engaged to complete the Newry canal. His assistant and successor at Liverpool was Henry Berry, who provided the engineering expertise for Lancashire's own Sankey Brook Navigation, partly opened in 1757.[7] Originally conceived as merely 'river improvement', the Sankey Brook was actually constructed as a deadwater navigation. There is little doubt that its successful execution was one reason for the young Duke of Bridgewater's interest in canals — his own mineral-bearing estates lay quite near — nor that the Duke's engineer, James Brindley, learned from watching Berry. Whether we date the canal age from the Sankey Brook or the Worsley Canal, it is clear that a new dimension in the history of inland waterways in Britain was developing.

Between 1760 and 1769 there were twenty-nine Acts for inland navigation, at least sixteen of which were initial promotions.[8] From 1770 through to 1774 there were a further twenty-three Acts involving perhaps a dozen wholly or mainly new schemes. Thus in only fifteen years (1760—74 inclusive) there had been more parliamentary activity concerning inland waterways than in the previous fifty. Moreover the

12 River navigation, *c.* 1750

promotion schemes sanctioned by 1774 included projects for some long trunk canals, entirely different from any earlier authorisations. The Trent & Mersey Canal obtained its Act in 1766, the Forth & Clyde in 1768 and the Leeds & Liverpool in 1770. The fruits of some of these promotions were admittedly slow to ripen. Scotland's mighty Forth & Clyde Canal was not completed until 1790, while the Leeds & Liverpool had to wait until 1816 before it was finished. The overall achievement of these years was nonetheless remarkable. Birmingham received its first canal link in 1772, and the Trent, Mersey, Severn and Humber were figuratively united by 1777, though some of the routes were still circuitous in the extreme.

The motivation behind this promotional drive and flurry of investment has both simple and obscure facets. The objectives of the individual schemes are not in doubt. Josiah Wedgwood and his fellow potters had a clear interest in promoting reliable water carriage to Liverpool (and also Hull) for their fragile wares and securing cheaper supplies of coal, clay and other bulk shipments. Liverpool interests supported inland navigation largely to focus the flows of Cheshire salt and Lancashire coal through the port, where salt processing was becoming a lucrative business.[9] Edinburgh merchants, long jealous of Glasgow's mercantile prosperity, wanted a ready access to the Clyde, while in general it is undeniable that the example of Lancashire's early canals excited imitation. (The Quaker ironmaster Richard Reynolds — soon to become a prominent initiator of Shropshire canal schemes — had found the Bridgewater canals 'really amazing' when he had visited them in 1772.)[10] The surprising aspect of the canal age appears to be that it did not dawn sooner, particularly if there was a significant upturn in growth from the 1740s.[11]

One explanation of investment timing was that it was a function of the supply of capital and the cost of credit. Professor Ashton suggested the existence of a relationship between commercial and industrial investment on the one hand and the behaviour of long-term interest rates on the other. Thus, it can be argued, when interest rates were low, capital was cheaper to borrow, and potential investors were more willing to support transport improvement schemes where dividend prospects would appear more attractive than the poor, though safe, yields on Consols.[12] The proposition rested, however, on a number of assumptions, some rather doubtful. It ultimately assumed that a significant proportion of canal finance came from sources more interested in dividends than in the actual results of transport development. In actual fact research into canal promotion suggests that until the Canal Mania of the early 1790s the overwhelming majority of canal investors were local to the schemes in which they participated and often were 'interested' in their economic objectives. It seems unlikely that the interest rate was more than a somewhat vague predisposing factor. Moreover it is now well established that most holders of government funds lived in the Home Counties and that few resided in the main canal-building areas. Interest rates did not dictate when schemes were considered to be viable or desirable. In any case, the chronology of long-term interest rates (as measured by the average yield on 3 per cent Consols) correlates very imperfectly with the activity of canal promotion. It is true, as table 9 makes clear, that the yield on Consols was relatively high between 1775 and 1789 — a time of comparatively little waterway planning — and fairly low in the phases 1755–75 and 1790–94, when investment in navigations was active. But the years from 1730 to 1755 saw even lower levels of return on Consols without any sign of a canal boom. At no time before the

Table 9   Annual average yield on Consols, 1756–1800[a]

Year	%	Year	%	Year	%
1756	3.4	1771	3.5	1786	4.1
1757	3.4	1772	3.3	1787	4.1
1758	3.2	1773	3.5	1788	4.0
1759	3.6	1774	3.4	1789	3.9
1760	3.8	1775	3.4	1790	3.9
1761	3.9	1776	3.5	1791	3.6
1762	4.3	1777	3.8	1792	3.3
1763	3.4	1778	4.5	1793	4.0
1764	3.6	1779	4.9	1794	4.4
1765	3.4	1780	4.9	1795	4.5
1766	3.4	1781	5.2	1796	4.8
1767	3.4	1782	5.3	1797	5.9
1768	3.3	1783	4.8	1798	5.9
1769	3.5	1784	5.4	1799	5.1
1770	3.6	1785	4.8	1800	4.7

Note
a From their first issue and through this period the nominal rate of interest on Consols was 3 per cent.

Source. Mitchell and Deane, *Abstract of British Historical Statistics*, 1962, p. 455.

French wars began was the long-term interest rate so high that it could have deterred canal investment, nor so low that it might positively have excited it.[13]

A more likely explanation of investment timing lies in the pattern and pace of trade. Any consolidated increase in trade (whether internal or external, since both implied inland transit at some stage) at once demonstrated the need for more efficient conveyance of goods and reduced the risks of canal promotion. It was surely this, rather than interest rates, which rendered merely desirable projects worthy of implementation. The researches of Dr J. R. Ward have shown beyond reasonable doubt that the pace of economic growth was more intimately connected to the timing of waterway schemes than was any purely financial mechanism. Where inland navigation records permit the monitoring of toll receipts, such series provide a tentative and admittedly fragmentary index of the growth of trade. They appear on balance to support the view that periods of expansion heralded bouts of heavy investment in further waterway development.[14]

The view advanced here accounts for why, when trade growth slackened from the mid-1770s until the earlier 1780s, the number of waterway projects also fell. It does not make fully intelligible why the dawn of the canal age came only in the late 1750s, and not before (if we discount the Newry canal). Presumably it took until then for growth to press with sufficient insistence at the frontiers of the existing waterway provision that the need for wholly man-made waterways became evident. Nowhere would this be clearer than in those areas, like south Lancashire, where expanding urban demand for coal could no longer be met by transport on natural watercourses. It may, of course, also be the case that economic growth was still on a smaller scale around mid-century than the standard interpretation suggests[15] — in which event the absence of *any* entirely new river improvement schemes during the decade 1740–50 might be a straw in the wind. However, the number of projects during any decade of the century before 1765 is probably too small for us to draw tendentious conclusions from a turn in this figure or that, more especially when local conditions and decisions could so readily alter the total picture.

That the particular needs of the locality, rather than the abstract 'economy as a whole', formed the deciding factor, may be inferred from the fact that, of some fifty-two Acts for inland navigation between 1759 and 1774, the Midlands and North of England accounted for thirty-three, with the Scottish lowlands registering five more.

Thus the remainder of Britain shared only fourteen Acts — and almost all were for river improvement rather than for canals.[16] During the lean years of the American War of Independence new schemes for inland navigation were comparatively few (see table 10), averaging

Table 10   All Acts for inland navigation, 1760–1829 (inclusive)

Years	All Acts [a]	Initial promotions [b]	
1760–64	6	3	(1)
1765–69	23	13	(16)
1770–74	23	7	(12)
1775–79	13	5	(5)
1780–84	11	4	(2)
1785–89	11	6	(4)
1790–94	82	51	(52)
1795–99	44	9	(10)
1800–04	47	6	(8)
1805–09	44	3	(5)
1810–14	37	8	(12)
1815–19	30		(6)
1820–24	21		(2)
1825–29	35		(9)

Notes
a In most of these years the vast majority of Acts were for extending the powers of existing canal companies or navigation undertakers.
b In the case of river improvement, early schemes of a minor nature did not always necessitate an Act; therefore 'initial promotion' is a slightly flexible concept. The chief figures are from Ward and the bracketed totals are based on Priestley.

Source. Priestley, *Historical Account*, 1831, *passim*; Ward, *Finance of Canal Building*, 1974, p. 164 (for initial promotions of projects 1760–1814).

well under two a year. But under the impetus of trade expansion following the Peace of Paris in 1783, promotions revived and soon clustered in the major canal boom of 1790–94. Between 1790 and 1794 there were over eighty navigation Acts with perhaps as many as fifty-one representing authorisation for entirely new projects. Well might one Birmingham journalist humorously comment in February 1793, 'the Canal Bills so multiply, and petitions for and against them so increase, that they promise to be as tedious as the trial of Mr [Warren] Hastings'.[17]

A number of factors combined to produce the Canal Mania (see table 11). The rapid rise in foreign trade created a situation where pressure mounted for better carriage facilities. Very few trading

Table 11   Acts for inland navigations, 1789–97 (inclusive)

Year	All Acts	New promotions		Year	All Acts	New promotions	
		Canal	River			Canal	River
1789	2	2	0	1794	20	10	1
1790	8	1	2	1795	12	4	0
1791	11	6	3	1796	16	3	1
1792	8	6	2	1797	8	1	1
1793	31	18	3				

Source. Priestley, *Historical Account, passim.*

commodities began or ended their lives in the ports, and up-country producers were conscious not merely of dock and shipping charges but also of the costs and inconvenience of poor transport to and from tidal water. The yield on Consols was unattractive — the yearly average fell continuously between 1784 and 1792 — and although this in itself could not have inspired canal promotion it may at least have predisposed investors to seek alternative outlets for idle funds. There was also for a brief phase less likelihood that landed investors would sink capital in enclosure. The late 1780s witnessed ample harvests; consequently that sharp upward movement of wheat prices which was to prove such a stimulus to parliamentary enclosure had not yet become evident. Annual average wheat prices were only 49s 1d per quarter for the five years 1788–92 — as opposed to 61s 9d for 1793–97 or 84s 9d for 1798–1802. More relevant, perhaps, there seems to have been a mounting awareness of the profitability of several of the canals already in operation. Dividends on the widely noted Birmingham Canals exceeded 17 per cent by 1790, while on the Loughborough Navigation they reached 20 per cent. Though such figures were scarcely typical, a fairly general improvement in returns had occurred over the preceding decade. Even the now gouty Duke of Bridgewater found his huge navigation debts beginning to fall from 1786 as his canal profits rose. His biographer has no doubt that by 1792 the general public were attracted to canal investment by the example of such increased profitability.[18] In Yorkshire the proprietors of the flourishing Aire & Calder Navigation were able to divide £27,000 among themselves in profits in 1790, compared with £12,000 in 1780.[19] The behaviour of selected dividends is summarised in table 12.

Table 12   Dividends of selected navigations, c. 1780–91

Navigation	Year	Dividend	Year	Dividend (%)
Birmingham Canals	1780–82	13.9[a]	1789-91	17.5[a]
Coventry Canal	1789	3.0	1791	8.0
Don Navigation	1779–83	13.0[a, b]	1789–93	17.0[a, b]
Leeds & Liverpool Canal	1781	nil	1790	5.3
Loughborough Navigation	1780	5.0	1790	20.0
Trent & Mersey Navigation	1780	nil	1790	6.5[b]

Notes

a Arithmetical average of the (inclusive) years given.

b Reduced to a percentage from monetary amounts noted in the original; e.g. the Don Navigation had shares of £349 and dividends were quoted as a specific sum.

Source. Hadfield, *Canals of the East Midlands*, 1966, pp. 24, 39; *id., Canals of the West Midlands*, 1966, pp. 39, 68; *id., Canals of Yorkshire*, I, 1972, p. 75; Hadfield and Biddle, *Canals of North West England*, 1970, p. 79.

The Canal Mania, like most speculative booms, resulted in schemes ranging from the highly desirable to the economically suicidal or downright lunatic. Among the more useful additions to inland navigation were the ninety-three-mile long Grand Junction Canal and several important Welsh canals. The Grand Junction (England's only north–south canal of any consequence) rationalised the route between London and Birmingham, reducing the circuitous 269½ miles of 1789 to only 138½ miles by 1805. In Wales no canal promotion worthy of the name occurred until the eve of the mania. Then in 1790 the Glamorganshire Canal was authorised to penetrate the valley of the Taff, an example followed by the Neath Canal in 1793, and by the Swansea Canal in 1794. Nowhere did the investment of these years produce more solidly useful waterway mileage.[20] But several other canals were never to cheer the hearts or fill the purses of their backers, while a longish list of deeply rural canals were dismal failures. The Hereford & Gloucester Canal, for example, was authorised in 1791 to recruit £25,000 in share capital — 'with liberty to raise 30,000*l* more, if wanting'.[21] 'If wanting' proved to be something of a euphemism for a concern chronically short of funds. Most promoters never lived to see the canal connect the two cities in 1845, by which date railway development made all the effort fruitless. Some other mania waterways, like the Grand Western or the Salisbury & Southampton, were either never fully completed or entirely abandoned.[22]

The inflation of the French wars and the consequent difficulty of financing even some of the sound schemes gradually ushered in a disenchantment with canal promotion. Where John Phillips's *General History of Inland Navigation* had enjoyed three editions between 1792 and 1795, its fourth in 1803 was a miserable affair which seemed to symbolise the waning enthusiasm for canal investment.[23] Although there was a renewed flurry of Acts between 1810 and 1815, mainly for small agricultural canals or minor river improvements, perhaps prompted by the high agrarian profits towards the end of the Napoleonic wars, there was no second canal mania. Increasingly it was appreciated — not least by the canal companies themselves — that many extensions to transport facilities could be effected by laying waggonways rather than digging new or branch canals. After 1815 there were few, and after 1830 no major canals authorised (with two rather special exceptions).[24] As early as 1800 Thomas Telford had suggested that often a waggonway 'may be constructed in a much more expeditious manner than navigable canals; [and] it may be introduced into many districts where canals are wholly inapplicable'.[25] As regards expense of construction, John Grieve was claiming that an iron waggonway could be built for only £1,660 per mile, 'where no deep cutting, or high embankments, are required', but that the cost of providing a canal — presumably the lowest estimate — was £5,000 per mile.[26]

The mileage of inland waterway in England and Wales rose from 1,398½ in 1760 (almost entirely river navigation) to 3,875½ in 1830 and probably peaked at about 4,000 miles around 1850 (fig. 13). It seems unlikely that we need to add more than a further 215 miles for the whole of Scotland in 1830. Whatever the precise mileage, it represents a considerable engineering achievement.[27] Even modest projects could be productive of new constructional problems. Many of the techniques important for the railway age were first pioneered by canal engineers. Tunnels, cutting and embanking, a variety of bridges and aqueducts, not to speak of the miles of waggonways associated with canals, all taught skills not lost on those who built the railways. There is no space here to analyse the engineering

Broad Canal
Narrow Canal
River

Miles
Kilometres

0 30
0 40

N

Kendal

R. Riddle

Preston

Walton

LANCASTER

Burnley

Sowerby Bridge

Rochdale

Bury

IRWELL

LIVERPOOL

St. Helens

SANKEY

R. Mersey

BRIDGEWATER

WORSLEY

MANCHESTER

ROCHDALE

HUDDERSFIELD

CALDER & HEBBLE

Huddersfield

Bradford

LEEDS

Tadcaster

York

OUSE

Ripon

FOSS

New Malton

DERWENT

POCKLINGTON

Great Driffield

DRIFFIELD

Beverley

HULL

Goole

SELBY

AIRE

LEEDS & LIVERPOOL

LIVERPOOL

BRADFORD

LEEDS

Wakefield

BARNSLEY

Barnsley

DON

Doncaster

IDLE

TRENT

R. Humber

STAINFORTH & KEADBY

CAISTOR

Bishopsbridge

LOUTH

Louth

Horncastle

WITHAM

Lincoln

FOSSDYKE

Sleaford

GRANTHAM

Grantham

OAKHAM

Oakham

Bourne

WELLAND

Spalding

Wisbech

Kings Lynn

NAR

The Wash

Boston

BLACK SLUICE

Fossdyke

Thorpe Culvert

SHEFFIELD

Sheffield

CHESTERFIELD

Chesterfield

PEAK FOREST

MACCLESFIELD

Macclesfield

Leek

CAULDON

Uttoxeter

TRENT

MERSEY

Derby

EREWASH

CROMFORD

Nottingham

GRANTHAM

Moira

ASHBY

LOUGHBOROUGH

DERBY

TRENT

GRAND

Newcastle

B'HAM & LIVERPOOL JUNCTION

WEAVER

Chester

CHESTER

DEE

Holt

R. Dee

ELLESMERE

ELLESMERE

Llangollen

SHREWSBURY

Shrewsbury

SEVERN

WORCS

MONTGOMERYSHIRE

13 The principal waterways, c. 1830. From H. J. Dyos and D. H. Aldcroft, *British Transport*, Leicester University Press, 1969, pp. 104–5.

contribution of men such as Telford, Jessop, the Whitworths, Smeaton, the Rennies and many others. Yet the enormous advance in knowledge and confidence made by engineers in the first few decades of the canal age needs highlighting. James Brindley's engineering feats were soon the stock in trade of the average canal engineer. The cautious ponderousness of the first aqueducts gave way to the daring of Telford's Pontcysyllte, and an exaggerated respect for contours to a greater use of earthworks and flights of locks.

Such building programmes required not inconsiderable battalions of labourers, whose nickname of 'navigators' eventually gave a new word to the English language — navvy. The organisation of navvy gangs was increasingly delegated by a canal's consultative or design engineer to site engineers and contractors. Though most canals were built by a number of smallish contractors, there was by the evening of the canal age at least one firm of civil engineers who could undertake to build not merely a whole new waterway but any dock complexes and housing with which it might be accompanied. Joliffe & Banks, often associated with Rennie's works, were by 1826 the largest civil engineering organisation in Europe and had to their credit the ample Knottingley—Goole canal and the port and new town of Goole.[28] The impact of 'canal surgery' on the face of Britain over some seventy years was restrained and unobtrusive by the standards of railway or motorway development which came later, but its significance was nonetheless more than cosmetic.

The building of the last canals and the first railways had, however, few engineers in common, if we omit the obvious overlap of waterway and tramway engineers. This was partly in consequence of the decline in canal construction by the late 1820s, but more because the railway builders came largely from the north-east of England. Here the lively background of edge-rail waggonways and colliery steam engines provided just the right technology mix to supply men equipped to lay the new iron roads. What the designers of canals contributed was more subtle, but important for all that. It was they who had raised the status of their calling from rule-of-thumb millwright to that of true civil engineer, with a respect for scientific method and a regard for professional integrity. In 1771 a group of canal and harbour engineers had formed the loosely knit Society of Civil Engineers around the person of the ubiquitous John Smeaton, and in 1818–20 their successors established the modern Institution of Civil Engineers, whose first president, fittingly, was Thomas Telford. Of course, there were less than capable engineers too,[29] but in general Britain's canal builders bequeathed a transport system remarkable for sound workmanship and the quiet dignity of its architecture.

The investment and its nature

Inland waterways were financed by a variety of means. A few were paid for by individual landowners. The Marquess of Rockingham and subsequently the earls Fitzwilliam were outright owners of the Yorkshire Derwent Navigation (though the original finance had been advanced by a small syndicate), and the family paid for an extension of the waterway in 1813. Charlotte Bethell of Rise financed the Leven Canal in east Yorkshire, and Sir John Ramsden was sole proprietor of the navigation bearing his name in the West Riding.[30] The Gresley Canal in Staffordshire was built by Sir Nigel Gresley to carry coal from his mines to Newcastle under Lyme, and the Earl of Thanet connected his quarries near Skipton with the Leeds & Liverpool Canal by a short cut. Altogether as many as forty-three navigations may have been privately owned, though some were very minor in nature.[31] This would assuredly not describe the undertaking of the third Duke of Bridgewater, who created not so much a canal as a small waterway empire on the borders of Lancashire and Cheshire. In 1782 the debt on his concerns (presumably more than just his waterways) stood at almost £320,000, a tribute not only to his creditworthiness but also to his stubbornly held vision of a canal revolution.[32] But few men had the duke's resources, his way with bankers, or his will to innovate. 'Navigable cuts and canals,' wrote Adam Smith, '... are of great and general utility; while at the same time they frequently require a greater expence than suits the fortunes of private people.'[33]

Many river improvement schemes throughout the industrial revolution were financed by groups of local trustees or commissioners who were empowered to levy tolls and employ their revenue to maintain navigation. In some cases authorisation was also obtained to borrow specified sums of capital, usually on the security of these tolls. Several rivers, like the Yorkshire Ouse or the Thames, were subject to ancient, if often rather unsatisfactory, forms of conservancy.[34] All such organisations were generally supposed to be non-profit-making, and a persistent positive balance in the accounts was usually translated into further improvement or a reduction in tolls. Thus once the 'New' Driffield Navigation had paid off its debts it was able to announce massive toll reductions from 1 July 1823. Coal which had previously paid a due of 1*s*9*d* per chaldron was charged a mere ½*d*.[35] A few later canals, too, had legally restricted dividends, though the movement to limit profits never caught on generally. In several cases town corporations were effectively the conservancy agent and frequently found the waywardness of rivers taxed their navigation revenue quite severely.[36] In any case, not all river improvers thought, or were statutorily required to think, of the public good. The proprietors of the Aire & Calder continued to reap enormous profits, and only invested in major improvements (in the early 1770s and 1820s) when forced by traders' complaints and the threat of rival canals being promoted. Their organisation remained a charmed elite, not entirely broken by the first public issue of shares in 1884.[37]

The commonest means of financing canals proper was the joint stock company. Each undertaking was empowered to raise a stated sum by the issue of shares and a further amount of supplementary capital, should the need arise (it usually did), by borrowing. The concern's enabling Act also furnished a schedule of maximum tolls aimed to strike an appropriate balance between reasonable returns on capital and the public good. Since engineers' estimates tended to be very optimistic, a large number of companies was compelled by the burden of construction costs to petition Parliament for additional financial powers. Very few canals were in fact completed within their engineers' calculations, and the directors of the Pocklington Canal of 1818 actually left their gratitude on record that its builder had made it one of the rare exceptions.[38]

Virtually all the early canals, and probably a majority of the later ones, were overwhelmingly local in both promotion and finance. Smaller ventures were sometimes able to amass the necessary capital from among the promoters themselves. The Arun Navigation, for instance, was built by only thirty-one subscribers. Most canals were, of course, beyond the scope of such limited capital recruitment; yet in very many cases there was felt to be no necessity to attract wide investment from outside the locality. Promotion committees were normally closely integrated groups of local interests and worthies who sought stable financial commitment from men of known substance and probity. Like most other economic developments in eighteenth-century Britain, canals were a form of self-help which sprang from local initiatives and relied in the main on local resources. All the canals authorised before the 1790s, even fairly large concerns such as the Trent & Mersey, the Oxford Canal or the Leeds & Liverpool, had the largest proportion of their capital provided by the region through which they were cut. Admittedly the Trent & Mersey found some £56,000 in London, but the rest of the share and loan capital was mostly invested by Staffordshire and Cheshire.[39] The Leeds & Liverpool recruited most of its original capital — and as much as £300,000 had been expended by 1777 — in Lancashire and Yorkshire, especially from towns along the route. (Later the transfer of shares considerably altered this pattern, leading by 1800 to a 37 per cent holding by London and the Midlands together.)[40] In the case of smaller canals, such as the Stourbridge (authorised 1776) or the Erewash (1777), local financial involvement was to the almost total exclusion of any outside investment whatsoever.[41]

The absence of an appeal to wider reservoirs of capital and the desire by canal companies to rely on men with a financial stake in the region meant that canal shares were of large denomination, usually £100. Of a sample of 108 waterway promotion schemes, eighty-eight at least had initial issues in share certificates for £100 or more. Of the twenty remaining waterways, only one, the Scottish Bo'ness Canal of 1768, was earlier than the period of the Canal Mania, while twelve of them dated from the early nineteenth century.[42] Undoubtedly the greater competition for capital from around 1790 was one of the reasons for a slight 'democratising' of the canal share, as companies sometimes found that they had to cast their net deeper into the local social pool, or wider into financial waters beyond the region. Not only did initial issues in denominations below £100 become a little commoner, but several concerns, including some mighty names (for example, the Kennet & Avon, the Gloucester & Berkeley and the Thames & Severn) were compelled to lower the denomination of supplementary issues. The Kennet & Avon in fact took powers in 1809 to issue as much as £80,000 in £24 shares. Impecunious rural canals were particularly likely to have to resort to such practices: the Wiltshire & Berkshire at one stage even issued 10,000 shares at only £5 each, though it is true that this formed part of an amalgamation scheme.[43] In Scotland canal shares of small denomination were quite common almost from the first, a reflection not only, perhaps, of the country's relative poverty compared with England but also of its greater experience of sound joint stock banking and more careful garnering of capital.

The chief problem faced by many canals was less that of finding new categories of investor than of attracting continued investment at all. It can hardly be supposed that a generation which financed the wars against France between 1793 and 1815 was actually short of 'surplus' funds. The real difficulty lay in inducing supplementary subscriptions from a public rapidly becoming jaundiced by disappointing average returns. Dividend levels were the chief motive for, or deterrent of, secondary investment once the euphoric fever of initial promotion had passed. Wherever the prospects of fairly immediate profit languished, companies were forced to adopt a variety of blandishments. Thus, in addition to the traditional borrowing on toll security, canals raised capital by issuing annuities, promissory notes and a number of special bonds, some of which were essentially debentures or preference shares. This last type of bond, like those issued by the Regent's Canal in 1818 or the Gloucester & Berkeley after 1822, bore a fixed rate of interest which had to be paid before any return was declared on ordinary shares. Promissory notes gave a specified rate of interest for a definite period with automatic conversion into normal stock if the company failed to redeem them. Annuities were offered at the attractive rate of 10 per cent by the Worcester & Birmingham and Stratford on Avon canals in 1815, but their use was otherwise rare.[44] They represented a last desperate attempt to stave off bankruptcy, a state which a few canals only just escaped. Two German travellers noted as late as 1826 that many canals were 'far from being able to pay the interest on their cost of construction, and with more than forty the shares [had] only half their original value'.[45] Some canal stock sank as low as £5 for a £100 share, though in a very few cases (e.g. the Monkland and Barnsley canals) rich mineral traffic ultimately came to the rescue.

Nothing, however, did more to widen the geography of canal finance than the period of canal mania, 1790–94. Even though the early 1790s were propitious to mildly speculative investment, it is difficult to account for what actually happened. The canal boom developed into a wild frenzy of anything but mild speculation which fed for a time on its own considerable enthusiasm and caused men almost to fall over each other in their indecent haste to acquire canal stock.[46] Leicester and Birmingham established 'navigation share offices', and it was in the Midlands especially that canal fever reached its highest and unhealthiest temperatures. From Market Harborough in the north-east Midlands to Hereford and Gloucester in the south-west or Oxford in the south were to be found crowded meetings of canal promoters and a full coverage of events — and rumours — in the local press. South and mid-Wales shared in much of the excitement, as did Bristol and, to a lesser degree, Liverpool and Manchester. (Liverpool, however, did not emerge as a huge reservoir of capital in the way it was to do in the railway mania.)

The explanation of the Midlands' heavy involvement with the mania is not yet fully clear. Part of the answer lies in their landlocked situation and the obvious benefits which inland navigation might be expected to bring. Yet the enthusiasm associated with even agricultural canals suggests that much investment was hardly rooted in any careful analysis of likely profitability. Possibly in the west Midlands Welsh optimism was near enough to be infectious, and, as we have seen, Wales produced canal developments of real importance during these years. Ward is surely correct, too, in seeing towns and cities of relative economic stagnation (Bristol itself and many of the market towns of the rural Midlands) as being particularly anxious for *rentier* investment, since they lacked as many homespun opportunities for development as the industrial North. Bristol, smarting from the rivalry of Liverpool, was certainly keen to improve its communications with the interior, and the existence of a certain local patriotism behind subscriptions can by no means be discounted. But many new canal investors, outside the Black Country at least, seem to have represented the classic *rentier* position, not worrying overmuch about the economic advantages conferred by waterways provided they brought handsome dividends.

Altogether the mania of 1790−94 saw over £6 million authorised for canal and river projects.[47] It altered the nature of canal finance from being *almost entirely* local and 'interested', but it did not transform it into being *overwhelmingly* national and speculative. That would be a simplistic conclusion not supported by the evidence. Rather it bequeathed a situation in which the economic and financial motives of investors were more equally comingled and where local involvement was supplemented — not replaced — by geographically wider investment. Undoubtedly the mania was one agency that helped to wean investors away from a near-total dependence on government stock and so in the long run laid some of the foundations of railway finance. Yet the changes must not be dramatised. Canal and turnpike investment remained small beer indeed compared with the funds. And although the bigger canal companies were quoted in stock exchange lists from 1811 the holding of shares tended to be very stable and seldom gave rise to the kind of business calculated to guarantee a smile on the face of a stockbroker.[48] Indeed, there is nothing to suggest that the stock exchange took much notice of canals before about 1807. In a sense the experience of the canal age had to be repeated, though more rapidly and on a grander scale, with the railways; for here too local finance was behind the earliest promotions and a truly national share capital market did not exist before the 1840s.

Who provided the capital for Britain's canals? At first sight land-owners loom large as a source of investment. But the methodical study of canal finance by J. R. Ward, like that of river improvement by Professor Willan, demonstrates that the landed provision of capital (as opposed to participation in promotion) was more limited than the flourish of great names might incline us to believe. Not that many landowners actually set their face against canals, though there were a few, like Henry Baynes of Knostrop, who believed navigations had 'the impudence of highwaymen'.[49] Yet the great property owners were undoubtedly a force *for* canals rather than against them. Indeed, given the landed character of unreformed Parliaments and the power of both squire and peer locally, there would have been precious few canals without their acquiescence. Even where landowners did register marked involvement, part of their shareholding might represent a pay-ment of services rendered, particularly in providing land at a reason-able charge or smoothing the passage of a Bill. The privileges and duties of a deferential society, if nothing else, would have ensured that the landed interest had at least a token investment.

Dr Ward has analysed almost 29 per cent of the traceable capital raised for inland navigation schemes between 1755 and 1815, or roughly £5 million out of £17 million.[50] The percentage contributions of his classified groups are given in table 13. There are formidable dif-ficulties of identification, both in estimating true investment,[51] and in allocating subscribers to particular categories — any or all of which would not satisfy every economic historian.[52] At face value the table shows that in its seemingly widest sense the landed interest provided 24.3 per cent of the capital reviewed. Of course, it is by no means unlikely that some of the capital in other categories (e.g. 'clergymen', 'women' or even 'capitalists') was not also in some measure the fruit of land ownership. Equally we must remember that many landed gentlemen possessed sizeable commercial and industrial interests, and that strictly non-agricultural income may have financed some of their waterway investment. Yet, for all their shortcomings in detail, such classifications are surely a rough guide which may be followed with

Table 13 Sources of inland waterway capital, 1755–1815

Category[a]	% capital[b] provided
I Peers of the realm	5.4
II Landed gentlemen	17.3
III Yeomen, graziers, tenant farmers	1.6
IV Capitalists	21.4
V Manufacturers	14.7
VI Tradesmen	17.6
VII Professional men	10.0
VIII Clergymen	5.5
IX Women	6.5

Notes

a Discussion of the classification and its limitations is given in Ward, pp. 18–26.
b Based on 28.9 per cent of the capital known to have been raised for inland navigation schemes, 1755–1815.

Source. Ward, *Finance of Canal Building*, pp. 18, 74.

caution. We may accept, then, that landowners were not the backbone of the canal revolution, though their contribution remains respectable. Cases, like that of the Montgomeryshire Canal, where landed capital is known to have exceeded half the total expenditure are rare. A number of canals had landowner investment totalling over 40 per cent of the whole, but with notable exceptions, such as the Trent & Mersey, they were mainly second-generation waterways in deeply rural areas. And the high showing of landowners in the Trent & Mersey is partly accounted for by the single investment of £42,750 by Samuel Egerton of Tatton. Landowners as a class held most of their wealth in a very illiquid form and experienced many competing claims on their cash flow, ranging from investment in enclosure to the costs of fox hunting.[53] The desire to consolidate agricultural improvement by supporting transport developments was genuine enough, but the causes of self-interest and *noblesse oblige* alike could frequently be met by the weight of a name rather than the weight of a purse. By and large, landowner investment was understandably heaviest in those navigations which promised to confer local and fairly immediate benefits on their estates. Thus it tends to show up heavily in the so-called 'agricultural' waterways, like the Oakham Canal, or in a number of canals whose usefulness to mineral development — and therefore to royalty income — was obvious.

Like the river improvement schemes before them and the railways after them, canals were financed largely by a combination of mercantile, industrial and professional capital, with the first category the most important. In fact if we add together Ward's 'tradesmen' and 'capitalists' (chiefly merchants and bankers), then the broadly mercantile sector contributed 40 per cent of all capital raised in the sample examined (see table 13). The figures, however approximate, also confirm what one would expect *a priori*, namely that industrialists were not, as a separate group, particularly large providers of capital. Since much industrial expansion had to be financed by ploughing back capital, manufacturers also had prior demands on their capital, whilst merchants and tradesmen often had more disposable funds and less call on them for the creation of fixed capital in their own businesses. Moreover it would hardly be lost on this last sector that good physical communications lay at the very heart of all mercantile activity. The potential benefits of transport improvement to merchants in coal, corn, timber, wool, cotton, and so on provide ample motivation for investment, especially when the prospects for earning attractive returns are added. Mercantile groups — or very many of them — were also well established by the canal age, whereas industrial capitalists on a wide scale were still only an emerging class.

This analysis is not contradicted by the list of 'heroic' figures of the industrial revolution who invested in canals. Ironmasters such as the Darbys and Reynoldses were prominent in the creation of the Shropshire canals.[54] William and Richard Reynolds built small branch cuts, like the Wombridge and Ketley canals, and with other ironmasters (among them the famous John Wilkinson) formed the principal investors in the Shropshire Canal itself. Similarly Richard Crawshay personally contributed £9,600 — of £18,000 together with family and friends — to the original capital of £60,000 of another 'ironmasters' navigation', the Glamorganshire Canal, and lent £30,000 towards the completion of the Breconshire & Abergavenny.[55] Many captains of industry, however, made little more than token subscriptions. Despite acting as canal treasurer for a time, Josiah Wedgwood's contribution to the capital of the Trent & Mersey was only £1,000, while all the potters together subscribed only £15,000 out of an initial £130,000.[56] Richard Arkwright, though a keen promoter of the Cromford Canal, does not seem to have invested a major sum in it, and indeed manufacturers accounted for only about 10 per cent of the navigation's subscriptions. (On the other hand, he and

Samuel Oldknow were heavily committed to the Peak Forest Canal, and Arkwright took on the payment for the locks at Marple.)[57] In Scotland the Carron Company's involvement in the Forth & Clyde was little more than nominal.[58] The financial underwriting of waterway development by industrialists was at best patchy.

Bankers were inevitably linked to the financing of canals. A local bank was normally appointed treasurer of a canal company, and in addition bankers were involved in providing waterway proprietors with short-term credit. Yet the traditional reluctance of English bankers to 'lend long' finds some early substantiation in the behaviour of vulnerable country banks towards canals. The relationship was close rather than deep. Banks helped to 'place' shares, they negotiated loans and made advances, but they took little part in the provision of long-term capital. There are doubtless innumerable examples of banks investing in canals, but the sums were usually small.[59] The Brecon Old Bank bought stock worth a total of £7,800 in four of the principality's canals. Similarly William Praed, who had strong banking connections in Truro, invested an eventual £19,400 in the Grand Junction, while J. R. Pease, a member of the famous Hull banking house, had in 1816 £3,812 plus £2,020 in arrears in credit with the Driffield Navigation.[60] (However, it is frequently difficult to be sure whether a banker of this period is investing as a private citizen or on behalf of the bank as an institution.) Banks were, of course, important to needy canals in the provision of overdraft facilities. A particularly 'fortunate' company was the Kennet & Avon, whose overdraft was allowed to reach £60,000 in 1815 before being paid off the following year.[61] In Scotland the Royal Bank lent the Forth & Clyde £10,000 in 1801 and during the financial crisis of 1825–6 allowed the Union Canal to borrow £50,000. Both were essentially short-term aids, though the hard-pressed Caledonian Canal had an overdraft from at least 1827 to 1829 from the Bank of Scotland.[62]

Some injections of capital came from public funds. A handful of town corporations, including York and Beverley, maintained and periodically improved local river navigations, but the investment was seldom significant.[63] More important were the cheap loans made available to some canals under the Exchequer Bill loan facilities inaugurated by the Poor Employment Act of 1817. Between that year and 1828 over £600,000 was lent to a variety of waterways, including the Regent's Canal and the Gloucester & Berkeley.[64] Such assistance was probably vital to the completion of these two navigations, as was the £50,000 lent from the Scottish Forfeited Estates fund in 1784 to the Forth & Clyde Canal. Even more direct government support was accorded the Crinan and Caledonian canals, into which successive governments had — none too happily — poured over £1 million by 1848.[65] The only other example of naked State investment was that of the so-called Royal Military Canal (Shorncliffe to Cliff End, Winchelsea) of 1807, built to aid defensive measures in case of a French invasion.[66] State aid in no case sprang from a purely economic motive but was associated in differing degrees with either the post-Napoleonic 'premium against revolution' or with broadly strategic aims (which included the pacification of the Highlands).

The return on canal investment naturally varied widely. The dividends earned by a choice group of waterways could be most impressive, as table 14 shows. Besides the openly declared dividends there were also a few spectacular profits amassed by the proprietors of older navigations. By 1828, for example, the privileged and exclusive Aire & Calder Navigation had distributed some £2.25 millions among its investors.[67] However, in a famous calculation of 1825 the *Quarterly Review* analysed the profitability of eighty canal companies, representing

Table 14   **Peak dividends on a group of selected waterways**

Waterway	Year(s)	Dividend (%)
Loughborough Navigation	1827–29	154[a]
Trent & Mersey Canal	1822–33[b]	75
Birmingham Canal	1824–35	98
Monkland Canal	1817	72
Erewash	1826	74
Coventry Canal	1836	40
Leeds & Liverpool Canal	1843–46	34
Oxford Canal	1824–26	33⅓
Grand Junction Canal	1828–31	13

Notes

a The figure of 197 per cent is frequently quoted for 1824, but the above is the highest three-year average.

b The dividend of 75 per cent appears to have been paid throughout this period; certainly it was paid in both 1822 and 1833.

Source. Hadfield, *British Canals*, 1966, pp. 175–6; *id., Canals of the East Midlands*, 1966, pp. 66, 122, 143; *id., Canals of the West Midlands*, 1966, pp. 90–1, 170, 204; Lindsay, *Canals of Scotland*, 1968, p. 223.

a capital of roughly £13.2 million. It found that the ten most prosperous concerns (total capital £1.1 million) paid an average dividend of 27.6 per cent, but that the remaining seventy companies (total capital £12.1 million) paid rather less than 4 per cent, on average — and of this latter investment some £3.7 million yielded no dividend whatsoever. As an admittedly crude average, the return on the total capital of £13.2 million worked out at only 5.75 per cent.[68] The most lucrative undertakings combined comparatively low capitalisation per mile with heavy mineral traffic, though even quite costly canals could eventually produce handsome returns if shipments were large enough (see table 14). At the opposite pole lay those waterways mainly, though by no means exclusively, in the rural South, whose traffic density remained low. Of the canals yielding no dividend in 1825 one might mention the Thames & Medway, Wiltshire & Berkshire, Ashby de la Zouch, Grand Western, and the Huddersfield, the last reminding us that even some navigations of the industrial North were surplus to requirement.

Operational aspects

Despite their sometimes weighty capitalisation, canal companies were seldom large-scale businesses. There were several reasons for this. A navigation company provided a *way* — a *waterway* — and usually left the organisation of transit and warehousing largely or entirely to private interests. The staff of a typical canal company might amount to no more than fifty, consisting of a clerk or two, a few lock-keepers, a jobbing engineer (who sometimes doubled as canal agent) one or two carpenters and masons, and a variable number of toll collectors and wharfingers. Naturally the longer, many-locked canals demanded a larger staff under a professional manager to uphold efficient operation; but small bucolic concerns had a labour force which scarcely obtruded on double figures. There was no equivalent even on the greatest canals to the small army of employees needed to run only a modest-sized railway. Control was vested in an annual or bi-annual shareholders' meeting, but a large number of companies elected a committee to oversee day-to-day affairs. Nonetheless, not a few concerns were effectively run by part-time secretary, chairman and treasurer (with the help of a full-time agent) and found no call for any boardroom other than the lounge of a local inn. Some navigation proprietors still leased out the collection of tolls to a 'farmer', though such practice was commoner on rivers than canals and anyhow was tending to die out in waterway affairs during the late eighteenth century. (When the proprietors of the Aire & Calder took operations back into their own hands in 1774 their annual income immediately leapt from £8,500 to £40,232, so the growing suspicion of leasing tolls is not hard to understand!)[69] In any case, once the headaches of initial construction were over, many canal companies contrived to live a somewhat sketchy, almost shadowy, existence as collectors of tolls, maintainers of locks and towpath, and distributors of dividends.

Carriage services were usually operated by independent carriers. These exhibited an enormous variety, from the skipper-owner (the 'number one' of romantic canal literature) to fleets of all sizes owned by local merchants or large specialist carrier firms such as Pickford's.[70] In 1807, for example, the Malton merchant and banking firm of Fenton's were the chief carriers on the Yorkshire Derwent, but another thirty-seven vessels traded regularly on even this relatively modest navigation and a further fifteen occasionally.[71] Much is still to learn about canal carriers during the industrial revolution, but it is already clear that a large number of waterside firms — flour millers, coal merchants, collieries, ironworks and so on — operated their own barges, and that such transport enterprises were among the most common forms of vessel ownership. The humble 'number ones' enjoyed a limited and entirely subordinate role on most canals, and the chances of progressing from boatman to barge owner were remote. As Hanson has shown, the overwhelming majority of vessel owners in the North-west and Midlands were capitalists — usually firms with a high level of transport need themselves. In 1795 60 per cent of the boats in the five counties for which data exist were owned by interests running more than five vessels each, and only 10 per cent of all boats were owned by one man (or several men in the case of part ownership). And although a large number of independent carriers traded in the region, some 28 per cent of all boats were owned by only twelve firms, a figure which included three canal companies.[72]

The old myth that canal companies never acted as carriers until given the right to be common carriers under the Act of 1845 does not bear scrutiny. A small handful of canals, which included the Bridgewater Navigation, the Forth & Clyde, the Aire & Calder, the Herefordshire & Gloucestershire and the Thames & Severn, at least experimented with the provision of direct carriage. The Thames & Severn Canal, disappointed that so few carriers used their waterway, began transport services in 1788. By about 1800 the company employed some

250 persons in the carrying trade and operated a fleet of at least fifty vessels. Unfortunately the accountancy available to the canal was unsophisticated: the company eventually discovered that its venture was run at a loss and from 1805 virtually closed the business down.[73] The Aire & Calder appears to have done rather better, at least in the short term. Services between Hull and places on the two rivers were offered from the late eighteenth century, while in 1821 fly-boats began plying between Leeds and Selby, an operation which earned a profit of £3,522 in 1823. Yet even here competition with private carriers, with road transport and (after 1830) with the Leeds & Selby Railway persuaded the navigation to reduce its commitment.[74] In general, direct canal company carriage remained restrained in compass and never drew many inland waterways in the direction of big business. In any case, no canal company could rival the one specialist carrying firm, Pickford's, which alone could offer a really wide geographic coverage, namely an area bounded by Liverpool and Manchester in the northwest, by Derby and Leicester in the east, London in the south, and by Worcester and Bristol in the west. Their total number of canal vessels rose from ten boats in 1795 to 116 in 1838, a date by which they were beginning to think in terms of the new railways. Nonetheless, even when the Railway Clearing House was first set up in 1842, Pickford's canal carrying enterprises could still claim to cover a more extensive web of co-ordinated services than could the new railways.[75]

The overall lack of commercial sophistication of canals, their apparent inability to win a decisive say in the ultimate cost of water carriage, and their limited scale were all to be important factors in their falling relatively easy prey to the railways from the 1840s. Though canal companies could lower their tolls in an effort to fight competition, they could seldom determine the final carriage charge. This lack of control over freight charges and standards of service was thus a basic weakness which was masked before the railway age. Canal proprietors, too, were seldom moved to amalgamate their enterprises or form the type of alliances and agreements so common among railway companies. Though mergers and the leasing of one canal by another were not unknown, no navigation empires remotely comparable to the larger railways ever developed.[76] Built for the most part to serve strictly local ends, canals were individualistic and often quite parochial in their outlook. Their acts of imperialism, with a few exceptions, were fairly limited, and most remained substantially what they had always been — a business entity more suited to an industrialising rather than an industrialised society.

Parliament required main-line railways to observe a standard gauge from 1846, but no such legislation was ever applied to canals. In the heart of the English Midlands — where it was supposed that few estuarine river craft would penetrate — the so-called 'narrow' canals were constructed, whose lock width averaged 7 ft (see fig. 13). Naturally, canals of such modest dimensions could be excavated for a smaller capital outlay than those intended to cater for traditional river vessels — the wherries, flats, keels, and trows and sloops of tidal water.[77] Unfortunately an understandable parsimony guaranteed to narrow canals a popularity with promoters even where, from strict traffic considerations, there was a real argument for a 'broad' navigation (with a lock width usually just over 14 ft). Narrow canals severely curtailed potential loadings — a typical cargo was only 25 tons — while every break of gauge implied time-wasting and costly transhipment, with no hope of the emergence of a 'go-anywhere' canal barge. (A vessel's dimensions would have had to be as small as 6 ft 9 in. by 57 ft 6 in. for it to be able to pass without let or hindrance over the British canal network.) It cannot be denied that the narrow canals appeared at the time to make economic sense to relatively landlocked regions, but the legacy was to be an awkward one. And in addition to the basic broad/narrow divide some canals had bewildering combinations of lock sizes: sometimes broad locks on the main line and narrow ones on the branches or, more commonly, narrow locks on the more inland sections of the waterway. In fact it was by no means unknown for identical locks to vary in width on the same canal. Georgian measurement could be very approximate.

Even more troublesome was the heavy locked nature of the average canal. The Trent & Mersey had seventy-five locks in ninety-three miles, the Leeds & Liverpool ninety-two in 127 miles, the Grand Junction 102 in ninety-three and a half miles, the Worcester & Birmingham fifty-eight in thirty miles and, almost incredibly, the Huddersfield Canal had seventy-four locks in only twenty miles.[78] These simple statistics meant not only considerable transit delays (which became a severe embarrassment to canals after the coming of the railways) but also a chronic shortage of water, where summit pounds were not long enough to store sufficient 'lockage'. In dry spells some canals were unable to maintain a fully adequate depth for navigation, with the consequence that barges had to be light-loaded or goods transhipped. (Despite the provision of additional reservoirs the Huddersfield Canal was closed on several occasions by drought.)[79]

Duplicate locks were occasionally built to ease the worst congestion — the Grand Junction constructed duplicates on their lock staircase at Stoke Bruerne — but such expedients were no answer to water problems! Inclined planes and lifts offered a theoretical alternative to lock staircases; a few were built prior to 1830, and rather more afterwards, under the stimulus of rail competition. Time saving could be impressive. The renowned Hay inclined plane near Coalbrookdale could raise and lower a pair of small tub boats in four minutes, whereas an orthodox series of locks would have needed around three hours. But too frequently canals displayed a genuine interest in improving their facilities only when the threat of a rival waterway raised its head or, more likely, when railway promotion began. Until then many prosperous concerns shamelessly exploited their transport monopoly and resisted pleas for improvement, while unprofitable canals were unable to contemplate innovation. Experiments with steam towage or steam-propelled vessels were comparatively sparse before the railway age dawned, and even innovative companies discovered, as the Forth & Clyde had found in the famous *Charlotte Dundas* episode of 1801–03, that the wash of steamers badly damaged canal banks.[80]

Canal companies as a whole had accomplished little to speed up the transit of goods by 1830 except through the introduction of fly-boat services. The Birmingham Canal Navigations adopted a more businesslike attitude once railway promotion was in the air — even to the extent of receiving complaints about the excessive speed of its fly-boats. Other companies too supported fly-boats services. By the 1820s such vessels could complete the passage from Manchester to Liverpool (partly via the Leeds & Liverpool Canal) in sixteen hours. The best fly-boats required only two days between Birmingham and Lancashire, though most took three or four, as also did the stage boats from Birmingham to London. Slower craft, of course, needed two to three times as long for similar trips, being 'drawn by something like the skeleton of a horse, covered with skin', as William Hutton had observed back in 1783.[81] Assuredly some gains in speed over traditional river navigations (where towing by gangs of 'halers' was still sometimes practised) had been effected, but the average canal barge remained a slow form of communication. Regularity of flow for most bulk goods was, of course, a more important consideration than speed *per se*, but slow transit did mean that firms had to employ a greater proportion of their capital in buffer stocks than would have been the case if transport had been faster.

The waterways and the economy

Estimating the overall economic significance of canals is not easy. No scholar has yet 'Fogelised' the history of the inland waterway network; indeed, the patchy nature of the quantitative data available suggests that painstaking local studies into the regional impact of particular canals (rather than grandiose national surveys) will offer the best strategy for much future research.[82] Even where surviving statistics seem ample, formidable problems of double counting remain if one is attempting to arrive at any aggregate estimate of traffic. For instance, probably half to two-thirds of the merchandise conveyed on the Oxford Canal represented an interchange with the Grand Junction. Again, few, if any, canals built up their trade from virgin beginnings. Some was won from the roads, a proportion might be wrested from a neighbouring river navigation, and in certain areas at least a little traffic could be taken from the coasting trade. Bridlington felt it had been harmed by the development of the Driffield Navigation (which benefited Hull), while the upper Yorkshire Derwent Navigation probably abstracted some trade from Scarborough. Although countless ports gained from *local* canals extending their hinterland, the coasting trade frequently opposed cross-country canals (such as the Thames & Severn) whose line might siphon some trade away from the coastal routes.[83] That ancient trio of carrying agents — road, river and coasting vessel — rather than canals alone, demonstrably provided the essential bulk shipment for the initial 'take-off' of industrialisation.[84] Not till the 1790s was canal mileage really appreciable, a date by which most economic historians admit that significant growth was well in evidence. The actual mileage of both canal and river schemes completed between 1760 and 1790 was approximately 825,[85] but probably only three-quarters (at the most) of this represented genuine deadwater canals. Canals assuredly became a lifeline of the industrial revolution, but their emergence in that role was a little later than has sometimes been popularly thought. This thesis is, moreover, consistent with the importance we attached earlier to the expansion of traffic before the development of the extensive canal schemes of the 'mania' phase.

Of the special contribution of artificial waterways none is more impressive than their provision of a golden key with which to unlock the riches of the inland coalfields. By the beginning of the nineteenth century inland coal was often penetrating far beyond the point of its extraction. Staffordshire coal reached Reading via the Oxford Canal, where it met coal from the Forest of Dean brought by the Kennet & Avon. The fruits of the North Wales miner sold as far afield as Shrewsbury and Macclesfield, while Yorkshire coal was marketed in a vast area from Pickering in the north to Peterborough in the south. Wigan coalmasters found that the Leeds & Liverpool Canal enabled them to sell both in Ireland to the west and in the Yorkshire dales to the north-east. In 1815—16 (according to estimates made by the northern coalmasters) well over ten million tons of coal were carried by canals and waggonways.[86]

Locally the new supplies becoming available were of momentous account for many regions. The development of east Shropshire's iron trades, previously limited to the margins of the Severn, now depended increasingly on the spreading rash of canals and associated waggonways. In the Black Country generally the carriage of coal became enormous — perhaps as high as two million tons on the canals around Birmingham by 1845 — as foundry and forge grew up on sites adjacent to the new waterways. In south-west Yorkshire a dwindling supply of coal along the rivers Aire and Calder was eventually reversed by opening the Barnsley Canal, whose coal traffic rose from an annual average of only 5,000 tons in 1800—02 to 114,353 in 1820.[87] Several of the valleys of South Wales were successfully penetrated by canals and canal-owned waggonways, and exploitation of the ample coal reserves of the lower Rhondda, for example, followed the opening of the Glamorganshire Canal in 1798. Although canal development tapped only a modest portion of the Welsh valleys' enormous potential, ironmasters such as the Crawshays of Cyfartha could not have survived without artificial waterways, nor could the other works around Merthyr — Dowlais, Penydarren and Plymouth — or at Aberdare have been even contemplated. Indeed, Richard Crawshay was doubtless well satisfied that 'his' canal brought down to the sea lock in one barge the same tonnage as beforehand had needed twelve waggons, forty-eight horses, twelve men and twelve boys. By 1830 some 201,000 tons of coal and iron were carried on the Glamorganshire Canal alone, a figure which was to exceed half a million tons before the railway became king.[88] And finally (from among many instances which could be cited), the opening of the Chesterfield Canal led to at least a dozen major iron furnaces being established almost on its very banks, while the Erewash and Cromford canals made possible the building of several ironworks, including that of the famous Butterley Company. Thus the canal network of the east

Midlands played a major part in opening up the Derbyshire–Nottinghamshire coalfield and in assuring the burgeoning iron industry of a wider market.[89]

The easier conveyance of coal was, of course, the primary motive behind the creation of most canals, and cheaper fuel prices were among the first benefits of the canal age to be enjoyed by contemporaries. In cities like Manchester and Birmingham depot coal prices fell by roughly half on the opening of the first canals; Sir John Clapham, for one, believed that the severe urban fuel scarcity of the late eighteenth century would have restrained not merely economic growth but population expansion itself had not adequate means of bulk transportation been forthcoming.[90] Men had frequently talked in terms of coal *famine*, and even in cities reasonably close to tidal water — such as Edinburgh — the absence of canals ensuring links with developing new coalfields was felt to be a major factor behind high and damaging coal prices.[91] Not until 1822, when the Union Canal linked the Scottish capital to the Forth & Clyde Canal at Falkirk, did Edinburgh possess direct access to the coal of Lanarkshire and Stirlingshire. 'None can be more deeply convinced than we are,' wrote *The Scotsman* in 1824, 'of the benefits which have arisen to Edinburgh from this canal — especially by the supply which it has afforded of coals, and the great reduction of price which has resulted.'[92] Liverpool, whose processing of Cheshire salt had contributed to the city's voracious appetite for coal, had faced a fuel crisis as early as 1753. Largely owing to the opening of the Sankey Brook and other navigations it was receiving all the coal it required by the mid-1770s, and in 1791 was even able to export almost 80,000 tons.[93]

Small as well as great towns benefited from the canal carriage of coal. Driffield's New Navigation conveyed over 18,000 tons of coal into the heart of rural east Yorkshire in 1830, while in 1847 the county town, Beverley, received over 15,000 tons via its canalised beck. In such towns a whole list of industries depended on cheap imports of coal: lime-burning — so vital an ingredient of agricultural improvement — domestic ironfounding, smithies, brewing, not to speak of household requirements.[94] By 1830 there were few districts outside upland zones in Britain where a coalmerchant's waterside yard was more than half a dozen miles away. Even in mid-Wales Professor A. H. Dodd has pointed to the importance of cheaper canal-borne coal in the economy of Montgomeryshire and Merioneth. The Ellesmere Canal, in particular, allowed entrepreneurs like William Hazeldine of Shrewsbury to acquire coal mines and slate quarries, establish a foundry, erect lime kilns and open coal depots — all along the line of the waterway.[95]

On the other hand, local coal monopolies could sometimes be surprisingly difficult to break until quite late in the canal age. The opening of the Monkland Canal in 1793 did not entirely destroy the monopoly exercised by Glasgow coalmasters over the city's coal trade. In England's Great Northern Coalfield it was waggonways, not canals, that moved the coal from pit head to riverside. In 1826 some 3.6 million tons of coal were shipped coastwise from Newcastle and Sunderland combined — and although some would ultimately proceed up navigable rivers, the vast bulk would reach its destination with never a mile covered on an artificial waterway. Indeed, the powerful opposition of the North-east's coalmasters saw to it that legal and other obstacles were placed in the way of the canal carriage of inland coal into the greater London area. No significant quantities of coal ever reached the capital via the new artificial waterways during the whole industrial revolution. The northern coalmasters and their London agents comprised a formidable vested interest against canals, though it must be admitted that there was some justice in the frequent complaints of unfair competition laid against inland waterways. Until 1831 seaborne coal had to pay government duties while that conveyed by canal went free of exaction.[96]

The canal network was, of course, at its best in the movement of bulk goods of low unit value. Besides coal there was the regular carriage of large quantities of lime, manure and corn in agricultural regions; of sand, gravel, stones, bricks and timber for an age of unprecedented urban expansion; and of the product of some 300 or more blast furnaces by 1830. Road transport had naturally long supplemented the use of river and coastal routes to convey all these materials, but costs were high. In the 1780s it cost 3s 3d per ton to carry pig iron from the Severn at Bewdley to Wolverley Forge, hardly five miles away. The Staffordshire & Worcestershire Canal, which replaced these particular road carriers, charged tolls of only 1½d per ton mile for shipping iron under its Act of 1766, though naturally the canal carrier would charge a fee on top of this. In general, transport bills for the bulk trades fell by 50 — 70 per cent, though cost savings varied enormously. One must, however, remember that road carters offered a door-to-door service which canals, by their very nature, could never fully emulate. Too often, comparisons of road and waterway freights have overlooked the fact that many canal shipments spent a portion of their total journey in a humble road cart. It is true that the cost of land carriage from Liverpool to Manchester could, before 1760, be as high as 40*s* per ton, as compared with 6*s* 8*d* to 10*s* by river, or a later maximum of 6*s* by canal — but such figures clearly do not cover the *entire* cost to firms shipping by waterway unless their premises overhung the very navigation![97]

All improvements in inland transport benefited ports in a general sense, though not necessarily every port, for a few minor outlets were sometimes by-passed by canal development. Since ports depend on access to a wide hinterland it is obvious that inland water communication was vital before the coming of the railways. Ports without river and canal connections, unless they possessed a specialist entrepot trade or served an important local activity, were relegated to the role of mere harbours of refuge or refitting. The great ports of the industrial revolution, by contrast, enjoyed a prosperity very much bound up with the development of inland waterways. The rise of Liverpool rested not only on her overseas connections, but also on the improvement of the river Weaver and on a spreading web of Lancashire, Cheshire and even Yorkshire canals. Besides the tremendous trade in Cheshire salt (half a million tons were shipped annually down the Weaver by the 1840s), Liverpool's growing importance relied increasingly on canal links with Lancashire coal owners, Burslem potters, Staffordshire ironmasters and textile manufacturers throughout the north of England. Hull gained similarly from the truly enormous extension of the river navigations and canals of Yorkshire and the east Midlands. Interestingly, Dr Jackson has shown that virtually all the consignments shipped in or out of Hull spent a portion of their voyage on inland waterways — and he has concluded that such navigations were as necessary to the earlier phases of the industrial revolution as railways were to the later.[98]

The painful process of urbanisation was also made a little easier. The new urban masses may not have enjoyed a standard of living sufficient to raise their position above the controversy of historical debate, but they would have been colder, hungrier, worse clad and more poorly housed if canals had not been created. Besides the cargoes of coal and corn there were considerable quantities of sand, builders' lime, stone, slates, timber and bricks which passed over the miles of canalised water. Indeed, the cheaper movement of commodities representative of the three basic necessities of life was unquestionably the most vital service provided by the new waterways to the growth of towns.

In addition to helping the growth of the great commercial and industrial centres of the industrial revolution canals contributed in a modest way to the creation of new towns themselves, some almost *ex nihilo*. Professor J. D. Porteous and others have highlighted the building of five (mainly) tideway terminals of important canals: Stourport on the Severn (the most inland of Porteous's examples), Runcorn and Ellesmere Port on the Mersey, Grangemouth on the Forth, and Goole on the Yorkshire Ouse.[99] The last named, conceived and built by the Aire & Calder Navigation, became a foreign trade port in its own right, and in both scale and commercial impact was the most important of Britain's canal ports. But none had grown into a large town by 1830, and the absence of need for anything comparable with railway rolling stock works meant that even as company towns they lacked the drama of a Crewe or Swindon. Canal ports were no more than a late Georgian footnote to the industrial revolution. The real urban achievement of the canal age, as was suggested in the last paragraph, lay in the diffuse and inscrutable ways in which waterways aided the whole complex process of urbanisation generally.

Certain sections of canal also contributed to passenger and parcel transport between suitably situated towns or suburbs. The Regent's Canal in London and part of the Grand Junction carried large numbers of passengers between Paddington and Uxbridge, and the densely settled Glasgow basin witnessed an extraordinary flowering of such transport provision. By 1838 over 420,000 people were conveyed annually between Glasgow and Paisley in specially designed vessels pulled by horse teams which were changed every four miles. Liverpool had its own suburban passenger services to Crosby, Manchester was linked with Worsley and Bolton, Aberdeen with Inverurie, and so on. Regular inter-urban services were established in several regions, notably Glasgow to Edinburgh (197,710 passengers carried in 1836),[100] Liverpool to Manchester, and Preston to Lancaster, while many other canals ran packet boats. Yet the canal network as a whole was scarcely an attractive proposition for entrepreneurs of passenger transport. Sir George Head found more cheeses and fowls aboard than passengers when he travelled by barge between Chester and Ellesmere Port in 1835, and noted that 'it behoved each passenger to exercise some degree of watchfulness, to prevent his brains being beaten out by the arches of the numerous bridges across the canal'.[101] Though

Sir Archibald Geikie delighted in the comfort of barges (as opposed to coaches) and even declared that 'for mere luxury of transportation, such canal travel stands quite unrivalled',[102] the truth is that most inland waterways were simply too slow. There was more passenger transport on canals than is commonly recognised, but never any possibility of its competing with coaches on longer hauls.

Although canals most obviously underpinned the emerging 'brave new world' of industrial and urban growth, they brought considerable benefits too to the rural economy. Writers on agrarian improvement were deeply conscious of the dual role of waterways in providing for the essential imports of arable communities and helping them to dispose of their products. Arthur Young's fear that 'without ... a gread demand for coals, lime, etc. and the establishment of immense manufactures, canals [were] too precarious a speculation for the ready advancement of great subscriptions'[103] was only partially justified, for, as we have seen, a fair number of agricultural canals were built. Reporting for the new Board of Agriculture as early as 1794, Isaac Leatham could already comment approvingly on the complementary nature of trade developing between the agricultural East and industrial West Ridings of Yorkshire made possible by waterways. In vast areas of England canal trade consisted very largely of an interchange of agricultural and industrial commodities, a circumstance seen most easily on rural canals. The very number of such waterways is eloquent (if not financially convincing) testimony to the belief in their importance to farming. Inland navigation complemented enclosure and other agricultural improvement. Even so commercially unsuccessful a navigation as the Basingstoke Canal was felt locally to have made an enormous difference to the agriculture of the vicinity. Contemporaries pointed to the development of Bagshot Heath from a bleak waste to productive arable land consequent on the opening of the canal. Few transformations were perhaps so spectacular as this one, but there is no doubt that canal construction was a significant agency in providing capital-intensive and market-oriented farming with a wider geographic currency.

Overall, then, canals, along with navigable rivers, helped to sustain both the industrial and agricultural revolutions. They did this in company with the turnpike movement, extensions in the number and variety of road carriers' services and the improvement in ports and coastal shipping. Like these other transport media, they accelerated the trend towards a more national market and a closer integration of the regions, though this was a movement not wholly completed until the motorway age. Competition often existed among these media, but the picture which emerges from modern research is fundamentally one of transport being a 'whole garment' — not by any means seamless, to be sure, but nonetheless one of greater underlying unity than a study of any individual part suggests. Canals, roads and coastal transport coexisted in a way which became impossible among the transport media of both the age of the railway and that of the motor vehicle.

The demise of canals as an important element in Britain's transport system cannot be followed here. While it is true that inland waterways became the victims of a 'superior' form of transport — one which was faster, more flexible and more versatile — they were not helped by their own contradictions and their comparative institutional simplicity. Whatever their failings, canals served lowland Britain well during the most crucial two or three generations in its economic history. Their contribution cannot be satisfactorily quantified and has no doubt sometimes been overplayed by historians who underestimated the continuing importance of road and coastal carriage. But it would be both foolish and dangerous to belittle the economic significance of inland waterways during the industrial revolution. They shouldered the burden of the bulk trades in countless districts where no coasting vessel could penetrate, and they handled a sizeable proportion of general merchandise. Efficiency of conveyance naturally varied, but was generally of a much higher standard than the propagandist picture painted by railway promoters. Canals coped well with the demands of a rapidly industrialising economy and could have sustained it in a large measure of further growth had the coming of railways been delayed.[104] And if artificial waterways were not quite 'the greatest of all improvements' of the age, as John Phillips supposed,[105] nor were they the meanest.

Notes

1   *Annual Register*, 1763, p. 99. See also Hugh Malet, *Bridgewater: the Canal Duke, 1736–1803*, Manchester University Press, 1977, *passim*. The canal was opened to Stretford in 1761 and to Manchester in 1763. See H. Clegg, 'The third Duke of Bridgewater's canal works in Manchester', *Transactions of the Lancashire and Cheshire Antiquarian Society*, 65, 1955, pp. 91–103.

2   T. C. Barker, 'The beginnings of the Canal Age in the British Isles', in L. S. Pressnell (ed.), *Studies in the Industrial Revolution: Essays presented to T. S. Ashton*, University of London Press, 1960, pp. 1–22; *id.*, 'The Sankey Navigation', *Transactions of the Historic Society of Lancashire and Cheshire*, C, 1948, pp. 121–55; W. A. McCutcheon, *The Canals of the North of Ireland*, David & Charles, Dawlish, 1965.

3   *Annual Register*, 1760, p. 160; 32 Geo. III, c. 2, quoted in D. E. Owen, *Canals to Manchester*, Manchester University Press, 1980, p. 22.

4   W. B. Stephens, 'The Exeter Lighter Canal, 1566–1698', *Journal of Transport History*, III, 1957; T. S. Willan, *River Navigation in England*, Manchester University Press, 1936; A. W Skempton, 'Canals and river navigations before 1750', in Charles Singer *et al.* (eds.), *A History of Technology*, III, Cambridge, 1957.

5   Calculation based on the lists of navigations in J. Priestley, *Historical Account of the Navigable Rivers, Canals, and Railways throughout Great Britain*, London, 1831.

6   It is fair to concede that differences in level between town and river made the task in both cases comparatively expensive, though the point remains.

7   McCutcheon, *Canals of North of Ireland*, pp. 18ff.; Barker, 'Beginnings of the Canal Age', *loc. cit.*; Charles Hadfield and Gordon Biddle, *The Canals of North West England*, I, David & Charles, Newton Abbot, 1970, pp. 15–26.

8   Based on Priestley, *Historical Account, passim*. The resultant figures here (and elsewhere) differ slightly from those produced by J. R. Ward in his excellent monograph *The Finance of Canal Building in Eighteenth Century England*, Oxford University Press, London, 1974, but it is often a difficult matter to decide what constituted a 'new' scheme and sometimes (as in the case of combined Acts for drainage or harbour improvement) hard to decide what was mainly a waterway project. The differences are too minor to affect the analysis.

9   T. S. Willan, *The Navigation of the River Weaver in the Eighteenth Century*, Chetham Society, Manchester, 1951, T. C. Barker, 'Lancashire coal, Cheshire salt and the rise of Liverpool', *Transactions of the Historic Society of Lancashire and Cheshire*, CIII, 1951, pp. 83–101.

10   Arthur Raistrick, *Dynasty of Iron Founders: the Darbys and Coalbrookdale*, Longmans Green, London, 1953, p. 185.

11   Phyllis Deane and W. A. Cole, *British Economic Growth, 1688–1959: Trends and Structure*, Cambridge University Press, 1962, p. 61.

12   T. S. Ashton, *The Industrial Revolution*, Oxford, 1948, pp. 9–11, 58–9. See generally L. S. Pressnell, *Country Banking in the Industrial Revolution*, Oxford, 1956, and, more specifically, *id.*, 'The rate of interest in the eighteenth century', in Pressnell (ed.), *Studies in the Industrial Revolution*, pp. 178–219.

13   Full tables of the yield on Consols are available in B. R. Mitchell and Phyllis Deane, *Abstract of British Historical Statistics*, Cambridge, 1962, p. 455, (based for these years on T. S. Ashton, 'Some statistics of the industrial revolution', *Transactions of the Manchester Statistical Society*, 1947–48, and *id.*, *Economic Fluctuations in England, 1700–1800*, Oxford, 1959, p. 187).

14   Ward, *Finance of Canal Building*, pp. 165–9, 191–2.

15   A. J. Little, *Deceleration in the Eighteenth Century British Economy*, Croom Helm, London, 1976.

16   These and the following figures are based on Priestley, *Historical Account, passim*.

17   Quoted in S. R. Broadbridge, *The Birmingham Canal Navigations*, I, *1768–1846*, David & Charles, Newton Abbot, 1974, p. 87.

18   Malet, *Bridgewater*, p. 138.

19   Treasurer's Book, 1775–1816, Aire & Calder Navigation, British Transport Historical Records, ACN 4/36.

20   Charles Hadfield, *British Canals: an Illustrated History*, David & Charles, Newton Abbot, 2nd edn., 1966, pp. 120–1; Alan H. Faulkner, *The Grand Junction Canal*, David & Charles, Newton Abbot, 1973; Charles Hadfield, *The Canals of South Wales and the Border*, University of Wales, Cardiff, 1960; and Ian L. Wright, *Canals in Wales*, Bradford Barton, Truro, 1977.

21   John Phillips, *A General History of Inland Navigation, Foreign and Domestic* ..., 5th edn., London, 1805, p. 266.

22   Edwin Welch, *The Bankrupt Canal*, City of Southampton Papers, 5, Southampton, 1966.

23   W. H. Chaloner, 'John Phillips: surveyor and writer on canals', *Transport History*, V, 1972, pp. 168–72. Professor Chaloner remarks that the 3rd edition of 1795 had been 'a remarkably handsome volume'.

24   These were the Manchester Ship Canal, authorised in 1885 and quite outside the tradition of British inland waterways, and the New Junction Canal, opened in 1905, which really represented a rationalisation of the Aire & Calder network.

25   Thomas Telford, 'Report', in J. Plymley, *A General View of the Agriculture of Shropshire*, 1803.

26   John Grieve and James M'Laren, *Report on the Utility of a Bar-iron Railway from the City of Edinburgh to Dalkeith* ..., Edinburgh, 1824, pp. 4–5.

27   Charles Hadfield, *The Canal Age*, David & Charles, Newton Abbot, 1968, p. 208; Jean Lindsay, *The Canals of Scotland*, David & Charles, Newton Abbot, 1968, pp. 210–15, notes just under 200 miles of completed canal. There were, however, a number of small coal cuts, 'timber canals', etc., which would increase this mileage slightly. I am indebted to Mr Jack Howdle of Edinburgh for this information. See also Anthony Burton, *The Canal Builders*, Eyre Methuen, London, 1972; L. T. C. Rolt, *Thomas Telford*, Longmans, London, 1958; C. T. G. Boucher, *John Rennie, 1761–1821*, Manchester University Press, 1963; Robert Harris, *Canals and their Architecture*, Hugh Evelyn, London, 1969.

28   Baron F. Duckham, 'The founding of Goole: an early nineteenth-century canal port', *Industrial Archaeology*, IV, 1967; H. W. Dickinson, 'Joliffe & Banks, contractors', *Transactions of the Newcomen Society*, XII, 1931–32. Further references to Goole and other canal ports are given below in n. 99.

29   S. R. Broadbridge, 'John Pinkerton and the Birmingham canals', *Transport History*, IV, 1971, pp. 33–49.

30   Baron F. Duckham, 'The Fitzwilliams and the navigation of the Yorkshire Derwent', *Northern History*, II, 1967, pp. 45–61; Baron F. Duckham, *The Inland Waterways of East Yorkshire, 1700–1900*, East Yorkshire Local History Society, Hull, 1973, p. 34; Priestley, *Historical Account*, p. 567.

31   Priestley, *Historical Account*, pp. 349, 674–5; Phillips, *Inland Navigation*, p. 598.

32   Malet, *Bridgewater, passim*.

33   Adam Smith, *An Inquiry into the Nature and Causes of the Wealth of Nations*, 1776, ed. E. Cannan, Methuen University Paperback, 1961, II, p. 281.

34   Baron F. Duckham, *The Yorkshire Ouse: the History of a River Navigation*, David & Charles, Newton Abbot, 1967; F. S. Thacker, *The Thames Highway*, 2 vols, London, 1920, repr. David & Charles, Newton Abbot, 1969. The forms and manner of river improvement are well covered in Willan, *River Navigation, passim*.

35   Duckham, *Waterways of East Yorkshire*, p. 30.
36   See, for example, K. A. MacMahon, 'Beverley and its beck: borough finance and a town navigation, 1700–1835', *Transport History*, IV, 1971, pp. 121–43.
37   Duckham, 'Selby and the Aire & Calder Navigation, 1774–1826', *Journal of Transport History*, VII, 1965, pp. 87–95. The improvements were the Selby Canal, authorised in 1774 and opened in 1778, and the Knottingley–Goole Canal, authorised in 1820 and opened in 1826. The earlier history of the concern can be found in R. W. Unwin, 'The Aire & Calder Navigation, I, The beginning of the navigation', *Bradford Antiquary*, XLIII, 1964, pp. 53–87. See also Duckham, *Yorkshire Ouse*, p. 138.
38   Duckham, *Waterways of East Yorkshire*, p. 64.
39   Ward, *Finance of Canal Building*, pp. 28–9.
40   Priestley, *Historical Account*, p. 424; G. H. Evans, *British Corporation Finance, 1775–1850*, Baltimore, Ohio, 1936, p. 162.
41   Ward, *Finance of Canal Building*, pp. 37, 38–9.
42   Based on the digest of canal Acts in Priestley, *Historical Account, passim*.
43   Kenneth R. Clew, *The Kennet & Avon Canal*, David & Charles, Newton Abbot, 1968, p. 73; Priestley, *Historical Account*, p. 719.
44   Ward, *Finance of Canal Building*, pp. 48–9; Priestley, *Historical Account*, p. 734; Hadfield, *Canal Age*, p. 44.
45   C. von Oeynhausen and H. von Dechen, *Railways in England in 1826 and 1827*, Berlin, 1829, trans. E. A. Forward, ed. Charles E. Lee and K. R. Gilbert, Newcomen Society, Cambridge, 1971, p. 7.
46   For what follows I am indebted to Hadfield, *British Canals*, pp. 106–10, and Ward, *Finance of Canal Building*, pp. 86–96, 140–2.
47   Philip S. Bagwell, *The Transport Revolution from 1770*, Longman, London, 1974, p. 17.
48   E. V. Morgan and W. A. Thomas, *The Stock Exchange: its History and Function*, Elek, London, 1962, p. 100.
49   Henry Baynes to Viscount Irwin, 27 March 1774, Temple Newsam Mss, Leeds City Archives, TN/1A5/1/31.
50   Ward, *Finance of Canal Building, passim*.
51   For a review of some of the general problems in estimating capital formation see J. E. Ginarlis, 'Capital formation in road and canal transport', in J. P. P. Higgins and Sydney Pollard (eds.), *Aspects of Capital Formation in Great Britain, 1750–1850*, Methuen, London, 1971, pp. 121–30.
52   Similar problems also beset historians who have analysed the provision of railway capital. The degree of reliance one places on such analyses depends on how seriously one believes that contemporary descriptions in share registers of 'gentleman', 'esquire', 'merchant' can be taken, on whether they really tell us much, and on whether categories like 'capitalist', 'tradesman', etc., can be sufficiently distinguished from each other.
53   Ward, *Finance of Canal Building*, pp. 26–74; There is an excellent discussion of the role of landowners in canal finance on pp. 143–60.
54   Arthur Raistrick, *Dynasty of Ironfounders: the Darbys and Coalbrookdale*, Longman, London, 1953, pp. 182–92.
55   Charles Hadfield, *The Canals of the West Midlands*, David & Charles, Newton Abbot, 1966, p. 153; John P. Addis, *The Crawshay Dynasty: a Study in*

Industrial Organisation and Development, 1765–1867, University of Wales Press, Cardiff, 1957, pp. 16–17.

56   Hadfield, *Canal Age*, p. 42.

57   R. S. Fitton and A. P. Wadsworth, *The Strutts and the Arkwrights, 1758–1830*, Manchester University Press, 1958, pp. 222–3; Ward, *Finance of Canal Building*, p. 39.

58   R. H. Campbell, *Carron Company*, Oliver & Boyd, Edinburgh, 1961.

59   Pressnell, *Country Banking*, pp. 389–98.

60   Hadfield, *Canal Age*, p. 48; Duckham, *Waterways of East Yorkshire*, pp. 27–8.

61   Ward, *Finance of Canal Building*, p. 188. For this navigation generally see Clew, *The Kennet & Avon Canal*.

62   Lindsay, *Canals of Scotland*, pp. 35, 80, 160, 163. The Union canal's debt was later allotted among its shareholders.

63   Duckham, *Yorkshire Ouse*, p. 120; MacMahon, 'Beverley and its beck', pp. 121–43.

64   Hadfield, *Canal Age*, p. 47; *id., The Canals of Southern England*, London, 1955, pp. 184–7.

65   Henry Hamilton, *The Industrial Revolution in Scotland*, Oxford University Press, London, 1932, p. 233; Lindsay, *Canals of Scotland*, pp. 113–69.

66   Priestley, *Historical Account*, pp. 585–6.

67   W. W. Morrell, *History and Antiquities of Selby*, 1867, p. 174, quoted in Duckham, 'Selby and the Aire & Calder', p. 92; and in *id., Yorkshire Ouse*, p. 87.

68   Quoted in J. H. Clapham, *An Economic History of Modern Britain*, I, *The Early Railway Age, 1820–1850*, 2nd edn., Cambridge University Press, 1930, p. 82.

69   Duckham, *Yorkshire Ouse*, pp. 72–3.

70   G. L. Turnbull, 'Pickfords and the canal carrying trade, 1780–1850', *Transport History*, VI, 1973, pp. 5–29.

71   Duckham, 'Navigation of the Yorkshire Derwent', p. 57.

72   Harry Hanson, *The Canal Boatmen, 1760–1914*, Manchester University Press, 1975, pp. 16–19, 21–9. The five counties are: Lancashire, Cheshire, Staffordshire, Warwickshire and Gloucestershire.

73   Humphrey Household, *The Thames & Severn Canal*, David & Charles, Newton Abbot, 1969, pp. 91–115; Charles Hadfield, *The Canals of Yorkshire and North East England*, I, David & Charles, Newton Abbot, 1972, pp. 136–7.

74   Hadfield, *Canals of Yorkshire*, I, pp. 122, 136, 140, 157–7. Fly boats were operated on the stagecoach principle of changing the draught horses from time to time, thus offering a quicker, though more expensive, service.

75   G. L. Turnbull, 'Pickfords', *id., Traffic and Transport: an Economic History of Pickfords*, Allen & Unwin, London, 1979, chapter V.

76   Such groups as the Bridgewater, Aire & Calder and Birmingham Canal navigations may seem to be exceptions to this statement, but they were in reality small concerns when compared with such railway companies as the London & North Western, the Midland, North Eastern, Lancashire & Yorkshire and so on.

77   See, for example, Hugh McKnight, *Canal and River Craft in Pictures*, David & Charles, Newton Abbot, 1970; H. R. de Salis, *A Handbook of Inland Navigation for Manufacturers, Merchants, Traders and Others*, Blacklock, London, 1904. pp. 20–24.

78   See de Salis, *Handbook of Inland Navigation, passim*, and the appendices to the works of Charles Hadfield, already cited.

79   Hadfield and Biddle, *Canals of North West England*, II, p. 329.

80   Barrie Trinder, *The Hay Inclined Plane*, Ironbridge Gorge Museum Trust, 1978, p. 4. The *Charlotte Dundas*, named after a daughter of Lord Dundas, was built by William Symington to operate on the Forth & Clyde Canal. The canal directors rescinded their order for steamboats once they had witnessed the damage done by this vessel, and refused to re-examine the question of steam navigation until 1828. See Jean Lindsay, *Canals of Scotland*, pp. 35–6.

81   Broadbridge, *Birmingham Canal*, pp. 178–9; W. T. Jackman, *The Development of Transportation in Modern England*, Cambridge University Press, 1916, p. 450; Hadfield, *The Canals of the East Midlands*, David & Charles, Newton Abbot, 1966, pp. 122, 125; *id., Canals of North West England*, I, pp. 167, 176–7; II, p. 332; *id., Canal Age*, p. 73; Hutton, *History of Birmingham*, p. 268.

82   *Cf.* R. W. Fogel, *Railroads and American Economic Growth: Essays in Econometric History*, Johns Hopkins University Press, Baltimore, Md, 1964. Cost–benefit studies of certain navigations in their historical setting may well be possible. Unfortunately the first thesis in this area was not yet available at the time of writing.

83   Duckham, *Waterways of East Yorkshire*, p. 28; Jackman, *Development of Transportation*, p. 401.

84   The point remains valid in chronological terms even if one objects to concepts of 'take-off'. See D. Whitehead, 'The English industrial revolution as an example of growth', in R. M. Hartwell (ed.), *The Industrial Revolution*, Nuffield College Studies in Economic History, Oxford, 1970, pp. 3–27.

85   Hadfield, *Canal Age*, p. 208.

86   T. S. Ashton and J. Sykes, *The Coal Industry of the Eighteenth Century*, Manchester University Press, 1929, p. 237; Neil K. Buxton, *The Economic Development of the British Coal Industry*, Batsford, London 1979, p. 67.

87   Hadfield, *Canal Age*, p. 140; W. N. Slatcher, 'The Barnsley Canal: its first twenty years', *Transport History*, I, 1968, pp. 46–66; Hadfield, *Canals of Yorkshire*, I, p. 176.

88   E. D. Lewis, *The Rhondda Valleys*, Phoenix House, London, 1959, pp. 39–40; Addis, *Crawshay Dynasty*, p. 16; Ian L. Wright, *Canals in Wales*, Truro, 1977, p. 7.

89   Stanley Chapman, *The Early Factory Masters: the Transition to the Factory System in the Midlands Textile Industry*, David & Charles, Newton Abbot, 1967, pp. 149–51; P. J. Riden, 'The Butterley Company and railway construction, 1790–1830', *Transport History*, VI, 1973, pp. 30–52.

90   Hutton, *History of Birmingham*, p. 266; Clapham, *Early Railway Age*, p. 78.

91   John Hassan, 'The supply of coal to Edinburgh, 1790–1850', *Transport History*, V, 1972, pp. 125–51. For the general background see also Baron F. Duckham, *A History of the Scottish Coal Industry, 1700–1815*, David & Charles, Newton Abbot, 1970.

92   Quoted in Hassan, 'Supply of coal to Edinburgh', p. 132.

93   F. E. Hyde, *Liverpool and the Mersey: an Economic History of a Port, 1700–1970*, David & Charles, Newton Abbot, 1971, pp. 29–30; Barker, 'Lancashire coal', *loc. cit.*, pp. 83–101.

94   Duckham, *Waterways of East Yorkshire*, pp. 13, 30; MacMahon, 'Beverley and its beck', pp. 121–43.

95   A. H. Dodd, *The Industrial Revolution in North Wales*, University of Wales, Cardiff, 2nd edn., 1951, pp. 109, 193.

96   H. Hamilton, 'Combination in the west of Scotland coal trade', *Economic History*, II, 1930, and *id., The Industrial Revolution in Scotland*, pp. 193–204; Mitchell and Deane, *British Historical Statistics*, p. 111; Buxton, *Economic Development of the British Coal Industry*, pp. 42–3.

97   R. A. Lewis, 'Transport for eighteenth century ironworks', *Economica*, new ser., XVIII, 1951, pp. 278–84; Priestley, *Historical Account*, p. 618; Jackman, *Development of Transportation*, pp. 445–7.

98   Gordon Jackson, *Hull in the Eighteenth Century: a Study in Economic and Social History*, Oxford University Press, London, 1972, pp. 1–25.

99   J. D. Porteous, *Canal Ports: the Urban Achievement of the Canal Age*, Academic Press, London, 1977; *id., The Company Town of Goole: an Essay in Urban Genesis*, Hull University Occasional Papers in Geography, 12, Hull, 1970; Joyce Mankowska, *Goole: a Port in Green Fields*, York, 1973; Duckham, *Yorkshire Ouse*, chapter V; *id.*, 'Selby and the Aire & Calder Navigation'; *id.*, 'The founding of Goole', pp. 19–28.

100   Hadfield, *Canal Age*, pp. 88–104; Lindsay, *Canals of Scotland*, pp. 41–3.

101   Sir George Head, *A Home Tour through the Manufacturing Districts of England in the Summer of 1835*, London, 1836, pp. 61–2.

102   Quoted in Hadfield, *Canal Age*, p. 95.

103   Arthur Young, *General View of the Agriculture of the County of Norfolk*, London, 1804, p. 490.

104   See, for example, the arguments advanced by G. R. Hawke, *Railways and Economic Growth in England and Wales*, Oxford University Press, London, 1970.

105   Phillips, *Inland Navigation*, p. xi.

5 COASTAL SHIPPING
John Armstrong & Philip S. Bagwell

Before 1760

Whereas canal transport in Britain was virtually unknown before the industrial revolution, coastal shipping was an old established means of transport, long antedating the beginnings of modern industrialisation in the closing decades of the eighteenth century. It is therefore necessary to outline the nature of the earlier coastal trade, since it was from the sixteenth and seventeenth century foundations that the great expansion took place in the decades after 1760.

The regional variations of climate, topography and geology which are marked even in such a small area as the British Isles prompted the growth of the coastal trade in the two centuries before 1760 so that different kinds of farm produce, minerals and raw materials could be supplied to the regions where they were most in demand. Even allowing for the road waggon and the packhorse, it remains true that the carriage of *bulky* goods, over any but the shortest of distances, was most economic by water. Improvements in river navigation, though widespread, had obvious limitations. Thus the seas round Britain's shores were the most readily accessible and economical means of bulk transport.

London was the great magnet of the English coastal trade. With a population already over half a million at the end of the seventeenth century and with growing industries — ships, bricks, beer, soap, sugar and a wide range of metalwares — it was a centre not only of conspicuous consumption but also of *mass* consumption.[1] The capital accounted for 69 per cent of the total domestic trade of England and Wales in 1700.[2] Dominating that trade was the movement of coal from the North-east ports of Newcastle and Sunderland to meet the growing industrial needs of the capital and warm the houses of its citizens.

Between 1670 and 1750 London imported, coastwise, over 40 million tons of coal, an average of over half a million tons a year.[3] The voracious appetite for coal was a powerful influence on the size of ships engaged in the coastal trade. Growing traffic was met by increasing the capacity of collier brigs rather then by adding to their number. In 1606 the average cargo of coal brought up the Thames from the North-east was only 73 tons: by 1730 it was 312 tons. But in the first thirty years of the eighteenth century the number of ships in the east-coast collier fleet shrank from 1,400 to 1,000, of which 400 were supplying London.[4]

The rapidly growing population of the capital obtained a substantial proportion of its bread grain from the provincial ports. London's total import of corn rose from over half a million quarters in 1608 to nearly a million and a half in 1696. Not all this grain came round the coast; unknown quantities came by land or river transport. But in 1724 Daniel Defoe noted that the corn sold in the Bear Key market was 'provided in all the counties of England, near the Sea Coast, and shipped for London'.[5]

Londoners were also dependent on the coasting trade for much of their drink. In 1728 Faversham sent 353 ships to London, more than any other British port except Newcastle, Ipswich and Swansea.[6] The hops and barley they carried were used, with sea coal from Newcastle, to brew beer. Much of the wine and spirits consumed in the capital also came via the coastal trade, being reshipped from Bristol, Southampton and other ports. London exported coastwise a large quantity of groceries, such as tea, sugar and cheese, besides more exotic food and drink imports, and a great variety of manufactured goods.

During the eighteenth century the coasting trade of the provincial ports increased faster than that of London. In 1768 the eleventh edition of R. Baldwin's London directory listed 580 places in England and Wales to which goods could be sent by water, though the approach to some of these towns had to be partly by river or land. That the list was so long is indicative of the role of coastal shipping in bringing commodities as near to the consumer as possible, minimising the role of the more expensive land-based part of the total journey. Eighteenth-century customs returns demonstrate the remarkable expansion of the coastwise traffic. The tonnage engaged in this trade rose from 92,929 in 1709 to 154,640 in 1760.[7]

The heaviest concentration in the coasting trade was on the eastern side of England. This is explained partly by differences in geographical and topographical conditions, for the east-coast shipping lanes, though plagued by storms and hazardous shoals, often formed the most direct line of communication between important commercial centres. The Lleyn peninsula and Pembrokeshire in Wales and the

Cornish peninsula ensured that sea lanes between ports of the western side of the kingdom and between western and southern ports were perilous and time-consuming. A second reason for the greater importance of the east coast was the exchange of Newcastle coal for East Anglian farm produce. In 1700 Great Yarmouth and Kings Lynn together took 15 per cent of Newcastle's coal shipments coastwise (the second largest share after the 70 per cent sent to London). Improved navigation on the Yare and the Fenland rivers helped the two East Anglian ports to become great entrepots for the dispatch of large quantities of agricultural produce to the industrialising North-east. Nevertheless the western and southern ports carried on important specialised trades which included cheese from Chester to London; tin and copper from Truro, Penryn and Penzance; hilling stones from Padstow, and timber and salt from Southampton — to mention only a few examples.

The great entrepot ports — London, Exeter, Plymouth, Bristol, Chester and Liverpool — drew in a great deal of general merchandise from their hinterlands and redistributed it round the coast. The result was that 'a great many of the records of coasting trade cargoes [read] as if a general shop had been bodily transported on board ship for conveyance to a more profitable district'.[8]

Thus coastal shipping played an indispensable part in the growth of Britain's internal trade in the two centuries before 1760. Industries whose early growth depended heavily on the coastal trade included iron, tin, copper and lead processing; the leather trades, brick-making and the building trades, the manufacture of alum and dyes, and cloth-making.[9] Without the coastal trade the expansion of markets in London and other sea-based cities and towns — the most populous urban centres before 1760 — would have been appreciably slower. Through the extension of the network of coastal trading links and the development of exchange which took place in those years the foundations were laid for the more rapid industrialisation which followed.

The growth of coastal shipping

The growth of coastal shipping during the industrial revolution is summarised in table 15. Before offering any detailed interpretation of these statistics, however, a number of reservations must be expressed. Firstly, the Musgrave manuscript (British Museum Add. Ms 11255), covering the period up to 1782, does not include the tonnage of coasters registered in London, the dogmatic assertion being made

Table 15 Tonnage of ships engaged in the coastal trade of England and Wales, 1760–80, Great Britain, 1781–83, 1785 and 1790, and the United Kingdom, 1824–30, counting each ship once only in each year

Year	Tonnage	Year	Tonnage
1760	154,640	1777	238,731
1761	150,791	1778	245,580
1762	157,362	1779	247,926
1763	169,909	1780	243,744
1764	182,850	1781	275,089
1765	199,941	1782	284,431
1766	209,106	1783	270,074
1767	197,079	–	
1768	205,572	1785	293,019
1769	211,894	–	
1770	211,031	1790	332,962
1771	221,895	1824	833,416
1772	222,398	1825	853,906
1773	214,977	1826	863,959
1774	221,351	1827	744,182
1775	218,683	1828	810,101
1776	228,349	1829	812,148
		1830	829,238

Note. No returns are available for the years 1791–1823 inclusive.

Source. British Museum, Add. Ms 11255; P.R.O., Customs 17/7, 17/8, 17/9 and 17/12; *P.P.*, 1830, XLI, p. 51; CCLXXVIII, p. 118; 1847–48, XXI, p. 346; 1849, LII, p. 177.

that 'no coasters belong to this port'. The registration returns of 1789, on the other hand, show 26,839 tons of coasters belonging to London. Thus the tonnage of coasters for 1760 needs to be increased by between 15,000 and 20,000 tons to allow for the inclusion of the London ships.[10] Secondly, the figures for 1781 and subsequent years include Scottish coastal shipping as well as that of England and Wales. Thirdly, P.R.O. Customs 17/12 (for 1790) includes repeated voyages, as do the parliamentary returns for the years 1824–30. To obtain a degree of comparability with the earlier statistics, therefore, the tonnages shown in the official figures for the years 1790 and 1824–30 have been divided by eleven, the average number of round trips made by coasting vessels annually.[11] Steamships, especially steam packets on regular passenger routes, made more voyages in the course of a year. However, since in 1826 steamship tonnage entries coastwise represented less than 5 per cent of all entries and in 1830 had still only risen to 10 per cent, the estimate of eleven round trips a year is reasonable.[12] A fourth problem arises from a change in the measurement of shipping tonnage over the period 1760–1830. Until 1773 government records were of tons burden, i.e. the carrying capacity of ships. Between 1773 and 1786 'measured tonnage', i.e. the tonnage measured by rules which shipwrights had developed, was increasingly, but not exclusively, used. After the compulsory registration of ships by Act of Parliament (26 Geo. III, c. 60) in 1786 all government shipping statistics were expressed in terms of measured tonnage. While some ships after 1786 carried less than their measured tonnage, the all-important collier brigs usually carried far more. At the 1786 registration Scarborough owned 152 ships of 24,887 tons measure; this was said to be 'on an accurate calculation equal to 35,000 tons burden'.[13] Therefore the recorded figures after 1773 understate the tons burden of ships engaged coastwise and make the growth rate of coastal shipping look less impressive than would have been the case had tons burden, rather than measured tonnage, been retained as the basis of calculation. A further problem is that coastwise shipping tonnages are shown to drop substantially in 1827. This was because an accumulated error had arisen through ships not being removed from the register when they were broken up or lost. To allow for this past negligence the tonnage of ships on the register was reduced by 13 per cent.[14] Finally, even though both countries were ruled from Westminster from the beginning of 1801 and all tariff barriers between them were removed, it must be noted that Anglo-Irish trade was not treated as part of the coasting trade until after 10 October 1823 (3 Geo. IV, c. 72). The statistics include shipping employed exclusively between British and Irish ports from 1824, and as a pointer to its importance, in 1824, with repeated voyages included, 810,422 tons of shipping were engaged in the trade between Great Britain and Ireland. Allowing an average of twenty voyages a year (since the average voyage was shorter than that made by English coasters and a bigger proportion of the voyages were of the 'liner' rather than the 'tramp' variety) we arrive at a figure of 40,000 tons. This is included in the total figure for 1824.[15]

There remains the question of the impact of the Seven Years War (1756–63), the War of American Independence (1776–83) and the French revolutionary and Napoleonic wars (1793–1815) on the British coasting trade. There is little evidence that the first two of these conflicts seriously interrupted the expansion of coastwise shipping. On the other hand, the activity of enemy vessels and privateers seriously harassed the shipping of the east and south-coast ports in the years 1793–1815. Convoys were organised but were often inadequately protected.[16] The entrepot trade of the southern ports was reduced in consequence of the interruption of the Mediterranean trade, although there were compensations in the rapid expansion of the trade across the Irish Sea and the Severn estuary.[17] Since no statistics are available for the period of the French wars, it is impossible to determine whether the growth of coastal shipping on Britain's western shores outweighed the disruption caused to coastwise trade in the east and south. However, the information available for the years 1824–30 reveals a healthy expansion of coastal shipping by comparison with the situation in 1790.

With the above reservations in mind, we can now proceed to examine the trends revealed in the table. In the seventy years after 1760, it emerges that the tonnage of ships engaged in the coastal trade grew at least fourfold. The most rapid development took place in 1761–66, when the growth rate was 7.7 per cent per annum. The explanation of this peak period of growth lies not only in the diversification of manufactures but also in the expansion of overseas trade through an increased variety of goods exported and the wider spread of markets. The increased tonnage of coastal shipping was employed in marshalling goods for export and in distributing a greater volume of imports round the coasts, as well as supplying the growing centres of manufacture with raw materials such as coal, iron, copper, tin, china clay, etc. In the years 1761–65 the value of imports to England and Wales rose by 5.7 per cent per annum, a powerful stimulus to the growth of coastal shipping.[18] Taking the longer time span from 1760 to 1782 inclusive, the annual rate of growth of coastal shipping averaged 2.9 per cent. In the even longer thirty-eight-year period from 1790 to 1824 growth rates quickened to an average of over 5 per cent a year. For the remaining six years of our period it is difficult to give a meaningful growth rate because of the scaling down of tonnages recorded in 1827 to allow for ships scrapped or lost at sea but not removed from the records. However, from the new start of 1827 there was an average increase in tonnage of 3.8 per cent per annum for the ensuing three years. Taking the entire span of years from 1760 to 1830, it is clear that coastal shipping tonnages rose at a faster rate than the general level of economic activity.[19]

Table 16 indicates for selected years the relative importance of coastal tonnage compared with that engaged in the foreign and colonial trade. The figures for 1760, 1770 and 1780 are based on

Table 16   **Tonnage engaged in coastal shipping, as against foreign and colonial (%)**

Year	%
Excluding repeated voyages	
1760	37
1770	37
1780	47
Including repeated voyages	
1824	78
1830	75

Source. B.M. Add. Mss, 11255; *P.P.*, 1833, XLI, p. 51.

actual tonnage engaged in each of the trades, counting each ship only once in each year. The outstanding characteristic from 1760 to 1770 is the constancy of the proportion of coastal tonnage, at around 37.5 per cent of total tonnage, indicating that about a third of total shipping tonnage was engaged in the coastal trade. By 1780, however, the coastal proportion had risen to about 47 per cent, as vessels normally engaged in the deep-water trades were switched to the coastal trade when the outbreak of the War of American Independence, involving France on the American side, cut off some trade routes and made others significantly more risky on account of privateers and enemy warships. Overseas trade was also less regular, owing to the need to form convoys with Royal Navy protection. Once the war was over, the coastal tonnage in fact reverted to its earlier level.

The figures for 1824 and 1830 are calculated on a different basis: the tonnage of ships entering United Kingdom ports, including repeated voyages. The coastal proportion is so large, over 75 per cent, because coastal ships tended to make shorter and more frequent voyages than those engaged in the foreign or colonial trades, and so entered port more frequently. The percentages in fact understate the coastal tonnage, since they include only coastal ships carrying cargoes, whereas the foreign and colonial tonnage includes ships entering in ballast. Evidence from 1832 suggests that if ships from foreign ports carrying cargoes only were to have been counted, this would push the coastal proportion up by another 2 per cent.

The regional distribution of coastal trade

Table 17, showing the ten leading ports in the coastal trade, makes clear the remarkable preponderance of the east-coast ports in the coastal shipping of the period 1760–80. In the years 1760, 1765, 1770 and 1775 the east coast provided all but three, and in 1780 all but two, of the ports included. Dominating the east-coast trade were the four ports of Newcastle, Sunderland, Scarborough and Whitby, which together provided 51.6 per cent of the coastal shipping tonnage of England and Wales in 1780, and in 1765 and 1770 were responsible for nearly as great a proportion — 49.7 and 47.0 per cent respectively. The continued presence of Kings Lynn and Great Yarmouth in the tables underlines the importance at this time of inland waterway links with coastal ports, the rich agricultural hinterland of East Anglia being linked with the two ports by the Great Ouse, Yare and Bure, which fed farm produce outwards to London and the industrialising North-east, receiving coal and general merchandise in exchange. Hull's importance was also secured partly through the improvement in inland waterways.[20] Its coastal trade outwards was predominantly in oats, wheat, butter, cheese and potatoes, initially channelled to the port by the river Hull and its tributaries.[21]

Had commerce with Ireland been treated as part of the coastal trade of the eighteenth century, Bristol and Liverpool would have ousted ports such as Weymouth and St Ives from the tables and offset the heavy predominance of the east coast, but it was not until 1824 that the Anglo-Irish trade was included in the statistics. In the 1760s Gloucester was more important for the distribution, coastwise, of the produce of the Severn valley than was Bristol. Of the south-coast ports Weymouth, with its shipments of Portland stone to the capital and its substantial entrepot trade in wines and sugar, earns a place in the table.

After the 1780s there is a sixty-year gap before the appearance of the next comprehensive set of statistics of coastal shipping for individual ports. Despite this drawback it is worth abstracting information about the ten most important ports in coastal shipping from returns for the year ending 31 December 1841, since these provide the most reliable information available on how the relative importance of the

Table 17 The ten leading ports in the coastal trade of England and Wales, 1760–80, London excepted, measured by the tonnage of coastal shipping belonging to each port, and the proportion of their coastal shipping tonnage to their total tonnage

Port	Coastal tonnage	Overseas trade tonnage	Total tonnage	Coastal tonnage proportion
1760				
1. Newcastle	26,618	5,265	31,883	83.5
2. Sunderland	21,060	10,010	31,070	67.8
3. Scarborough	12,060	22,820	34,880	34.6
4. Whitby	10,740	3,470	14,210	75.6
5. Great Yarmouth	7,140	3,480	10,620	67.2
6. Hull	5,494	5,670	11,164	49.2
7. Kings Lynn	5,480	2,010	7,490	73.2
8. Poole	4,462	4,068	8,530	52.3
9. Lymington	4,211	–	4,211	100.0
10. Harwich	4,210	–	4,210	100.0
1765				
1. Newcastle	48,830	4,794	53,624	91.0
2. Sunderland	29,544	13,598	43,142	68.5
3. Scarborough	12,360	24,340	36,700	33.7
4. Whitby	8,696	1,460	10,156	85.6
5. Kings Lynn	6,980	2,490	9,470	73.7
6. Hull	6,760	9,071	15,831	42.7
7. Great Yarmouth	6,140	3,020	9,160	67.0
8. St Ives	5,278	300	5,578	94.6
9. Gloucester	4,110	398	4,508	91.2
10. Weymouth	4,040	956	4,990	81.0
1770				
1. Newcastle	49,990	5,380	55,370	90.3
2. Sunderland	30,576	10,753	41,329	74.0
3. Scarborough	12,100	22,100	34,200	35.4
4. St Ives	8,800	160	8,960	98.2
5. Kings Lynn	7,620	1,890	9,510	80.1
6. Hull	6,249	9,552	15,801	39.5
7. Whitby	5,578	3,500	9,078	61.4
8. Great Yarmouth	5,520	3,840	9,360	59.0
9. Weymouth	4,760	1,240	6,000	79.3
10. Lymington	4,612	–	4,612	100.0

Port	Coastal tonnage	Overseas trade tonnage	Total tonnage	Coastal tonnage proportion
1775				
1. Newcastle	56,720	7,645	64,365	88.1
2. Sunderland	33,402	12,959	46,361	72.0
3. Scarborough	13,300	20,000	33,300	39.9
4. Whitby	7,000	5,879	12,879	54.4
5. Kings Lynn	6,780	3,640	10,420	65.0
6. Great Yarmouth	6,480	2,460	8,940	72.5
7. Hull	6,420	10,975	17,395	36.9
8. Beaumaris	5,273	1,060	6,333	83.3
9. Cardigan	4,911	–	4,911	100.0
10. St Ives	4,483	60	4,543	98.6
1780				
1. Newcastle	70,220	7,720	77,940	90.1
2. Sunderland	35,636	12,572	48,208	74.0
3. Scarborough	12,200	18,400	30,600	39.9
4. Hull	8,916	9,820	18,736	47.6
5. Maldon	7,876	682	8,558	92.0
6. Whitby	7,420	3,549	10,969	67.6
7. Kings Lynn	6,700	4,624	11,324	59.2
8. Great Yarmouth	6,040	2,900	8,940	67.6
9. Cardigan	5,923	–	5,923	100.0
10. Beaumaris	5,549	488	6,037	91.9

Note. Fishing vessels not included.

Source. B.M., Add. Ms 11255.

different ports had changed since the early years of the industrial revolution. The statistics of this return, shown in table 18, are separate from those of the eighteenth century, since they include repeated voyages of ships. Any attempt to determine an average number of voyages per ship would be misleading, because of the greatly enhanced proportion of steam shipping by comparison with the 1820s and the great discrepancy between the average number of voyages per year of vessels powered by sail and by steam.

The table reveals a remarkable contrast with the position in 1760–80. Instead of an overwhelming dominance of east-coast ports, west and east-coast ports are equally represented, though the predominance of tonnage remains within the Newcastle–London axis. The appearance in the table of three of the west-coast ports — Whitehaven, Liverpool and Bristol — is due primarily to their important trade links with Ireland, from 1824 regarded as a part of the coastal trade. The other two western ports — Newport and Swansea — grew into prominence with the opening up of the South Wales coalfield and the progress of the industrial revolution in that region. Whitehaven's export of iron ore coastwise to South Wales helped this development. In 1841 Newcastle's shipping was much more equally divided between meeting home and export demand for coal than it had been sixty years earlier, whereas Stockton's dedication to the coastwise coal trade in the 1840s was as complete as Newcastle's had been in the 1770s. In the case of one port in the table, Hull, overseas trade exceeded the coastal trade; at the other end of the spectrum, coastal shipping was so important for Stockton, Swansea, Newport and Bristol that it accounted for over 80 per cent of their clearances. However, Bristol's coastal shipping figures are heavily weighted by the frequent and regular service of steam packet-boats to Irish ports. The lowly position occupied by Hull arises in part from the rivalry of up-river Goole, where a new dock was constructed in 1826, ahead of Hull's much needed Junction dock, not completed until three years later. Goole's rise 'set a lasting check to the coastwise trade at Hull' because it was better placed to distribute the textile and metallurgical goods of the industrialising Pennine valleys.[22]

Bulk freight

In the eighteenth and nineteenth centuries, as in the twentieth, British coasters concentrated on the carriage of bulk goods. Within this general category coal was outstandingly important. Tables 19 and 20

Table 18 The ten leading ports in the coastwise trade of England and Wales in 1841; tonnage entered inwards and cleared outwards, including repeated voyages

Port	Coastal shipping tonnage	Foreign and colonial trade tonnages			Total British-owned tonnage (A + B)	Grand total, all ships (A + D)	Coastal shipping as proportion of British-owned ships	Coastal shipping as proportion of all shipping
		British-owned	Foreign-owned	Total				
	A	B	C	D	E	F	A/E × 100	A/F × 100
1. London	4,110,543	3,042,097	609,500	3,651,597	7,152,640	7,762,140	57.5	53.0
2. Newcastle	2,268,560	1,665,954	288,409	1,954,363	3,934,514	4,222,923	57.7	53.7
3. Liverpool	1,931,859	1,291,305	587,911	1,879,216	3,223,164	3,811,075	60.0	50.7
4. Stockton	1,088,113	66,364	62,368	128,732	1,154,477	1,216,845	94.3	89.4
5. Sunderland	737,435	366,560	102,543	469,103	1,103,995	1,206,538	66.8	61.1
6. Swansea	636,256	80,491	16,131	96,622	716,747	732,878	88.8	86.8
7. Bristol	568,399	121,216	17,083	138,299	689,615	706,698	82.4	80.4
8. Newport	548,344	40,018	24,937	64,955	588,362	613,299	93.2	89.4
9. Whitehaven	445,539	50,492	335	50,827	496,031	496,366	89.8	89.8
10. Hull	369,326	384,275	133,139	517,414	753,601	886,740	51.0	41.6

Source: *P.P.*, 1843, LII, pp. 382–3.

Table 19　Coal carried coastwise, 1779–84

Year	Coal entering London coast-wise (tons) A	Coal entering outports coast wise (tons) B	Total Great Britain (A + B) (tons) C	Coal entering Irish ports (tons) D	Total UK (C + D) (000 tons) E	Coal entering London as proportion of total $\frac{A}{E} \times 100$ F
1779	750,975	720,143	1,471,118			
1780	837,675	519,500	1,357,175	211,570	1,569	53
1781	830,025	654,733	1,484,758	223,402	1,708	49
1782	842,775	770,934	1,613,709	217,901	1,832	46
1783	886,125	822,046	1,708,171	241,332	1,949	45
1784	924,375	797,107	1,721,482	259,097	1,981	47

Source. T. S. Ashton and J. Sykes, *The Coal Industry of the Eighteenth Century*, 1929, appendix E; *P.P.*, 1786, X, pp. 139–40; 1785, VI, p. 81.

Table 20　Coal carried coastwise, 1818–29

Year	Coal entering London coastwise ('000 tons)	Coal entering outports coastwise ('000 tons)	Total Great Britain ('000 tons)	London as % of total
1818	1,535	2,453	3,988	38.5
1819	1,492	2,748	4,240	35.2
1820	1,684	2,825	4,509	37.3
1821	1,647	2,611	4,258	38.7
1822	1,575	2,823	4,398	35.8
1823	1,828	3,137	4,965	36.8
1824	1,870	2,989	4,859	38.5
1825	1,814	3,114	4,928	36.8
1826	1,986	3,336	5,322	37.3
1827	1,882	3,041	4,923	38.2
1828	1,961	3,126	5,087	38.5
1829	2,019	3,643	5,662	35.7

Source. Column 1: Ashton and Sykes, *The Coal Industry of the Eighteenth Century*, appendix E. Column 3: 1818: *P.P.*, 1819, XVI, pp. 216–17; 1819: *P.P.*, 1821, XVII, p. 90; 1820–28: J. R. McCulloch, *A Dictionary of Commerce and Commercial Navigation*, 1839, p. 298.

illustrate the growth of the trade in the two periods 1779−84 and 1818−29. By dividing the 1779−84 and 1824−29 figures by 11 (to take account of repeated voyages), and allowing for a capacity of 1.35 tons of coal for every registered ton of shipping (see p. 146), we find that in the earlier period approximately 40 per cent of coastal shipping capacity and in the later period some 42 per cent was devoted to the carriage of coal. Thus the coal trade was the largest single activity of coastal shipping during the industrial revolution. The tonnage of coal shipped coastwise from the north-east ports alone exceeded the whole volume of English and Welsh imports in practically every year of the eighteenth century.[23]

Sea coals came to London in greater quantity than to any other port. Column F of table 19 shows that in the early 1780s between 45 and 53 per cent of all coal carried coastwise was destined for the capital. In the years 1818−29, as shown in table 20, London's share of the coastal trade in coal fell to between 35 per cent and 39 per cent, showing that demand was increasing at a faster rate in the outports — the more important of which acted as feeders of raw materials to the growing industrial areas — than it was in London. The industrial revolution was essentially a provincial phenomenon.

Throughout the whole period of the industrial revolution the coal trade was flourishing. The growth rate of coal tonnages carried coastwise between 1779 and 1784 was 3.3 per cent for Great Britain. Between 1784 and 1818 it was 3.0 per cent and between 1818 and 1829 3.8 per cent for the United Kingdom. Apart from questions of growth, the significance of the huge *volume* of coastwise trade in coal should not be overlooked.

Second only in importance to the coal trade was the trade in grain, which is summarised for the two periods 1780−86 and 1819−27 in tables 21 and 22. A comparison of the two totals of all grain shipments shows a nearly threefold increase over four decades, with shipments of barley increasing at above-average and those of oats at below-average rates. The difference may be explained in part by a larger proportion of oats being sent by canal.

Tables 23 and 24 show the ten most important ports sending grain coastwise in the two periods 1781−86 and 1819−27, while table 25 lists the ten leading ports receiving grain by coast in the years 1819−27. No figures are available for grain received by individual ports in 1781−86. The tables make clear some leading features of this important trade. In both periods the suppliers are small ports linked by

Table 21   Coastwise carriage of grain, 1780–86

	Tons per annum average				Percentage		
	Total	Top ten ports	Top five ports	Top three ports	Top ten ports	Top five ports	Top three ports
Wheat	62,974	41,097	25,702	17,527	65.3	40.8	27.8
Barley	32,294	15,654	11,461	7,876	48.5	35.5	24.4
Oats	57,789	42,430	35,120	31,035	73.4	60.8	53.7
Malt	13,659	9,361	7,937	6,325	68.5	58.1	46.3
All	166,716	108,542	80,220	40,818	65.1	48.1	24.5

Source. P.P., 1788, XXII, pp. 568 and 571. Information for each year given in quarters. These have been converted into tons, one quarter being equivalent to 480 lb wheat, 376 lb barley, 304 lb oats and 260 lb malt.

Table 22   Coastwise carriage of grain, 1819–27

	Tons per annum average				Percentage		
	Total	Top ten ports	Top five ports	Top three ports	Top ten ports	Top five ports	Top three ports
Wheat	169,663	98,824	63,045	43,138	58.2	37.2	25.4
Barley	126,505	79,334	58,151	47,092	62.7	46.0	37.2
Oats	110,565	77,742	61,494	48,625	70.3	55.6	44.0
Malt	39,585	33,017	27,869	23,733	83.4	70.4	59.9
All	446,318	288,917	210,559	109,006	64,7	47.2	24.4

Source. 1819–23: *P.P.*, 1824, XVII, pp. 108–31. 1824–27: *P.P.*, 1828, XVIII, pp. 330–45.

inland waterway to rich agricultural hinterlands. The two exceptions are Hull and London, both populous urban areas which were entrepots for the redistribution of grain received partly from abroad. In addition London possessed the most important grain market in the kingdom. The pull of the capital's huge market is reflected in the fact that all but one of the leading suppliers in the 1780s and all ten in the 1820s were east-coast ports with more direct and generally shorter lines

Table 23 **The top ten ports sending grain coastwise, 1781–86 (Great Britain; tons per annum average)**

Port	Wheat	Oats	Barley	Malt	Total
Hull	3,823	11,005	203	18	15,049
Boston	379	14,268	67	6	14,720
Berwick	3,751	5,762	1,532	4	11,049
Harwich	3,997	447	1,615	3,542	9,601
Colchester	5,456	452	2,197	1,372	9,477
Maldon	6,433	1,518	564	517	9,032
Leigh	5,638	541	208	1	6,388
Faversham	4,178	367	483	199	5,227
Sandwich	2,725	79	1,242	627	4,673
Bridgwater	917	107	1,970	1,411	4,405

Source. P.P., 1788, XXII, pp. 568 and 571.

Table 24 **Top ten ports sending grain coastwise, 1819–27 (Great Britain; tons per annum average)**

Port	Wheat	Oats	Barley	Malt	Total
Great Yarmouth	5,343	362	22,457	9,112	37,274
Boston	8,584	28,075	175	27	36,861
Kings Lynn	16,134	1,739	15,541	1,457	34,871
Berwick	13,228	9,897	4,715	5	27,845
London	10,246	8,286	3,898	1,520	23,950
Ipswich	4,226	961	3,704	10,995	19,021
Wisbech	13,776	4,289	434	9	18,508
Hull	850	10,653	614	45	12,162
Wells	2,385	41	9,094	290	11,810
Harwich	6,692	238	1,118	3,626	11,674

Source. 1819–23: *P.P.*, 1824, XVII, pp. 108–31. 1824–27: *P.P.*, 1828, XVIII, pp. 330–345.

of communication to the principal centre of demand than ports on the south and west coasts. Furthermore the principal grain-growing counties were (and are) on the eastern side of England. The domination of the east-coast ports over the grain trade was even more pronounced in the 1820s than it had been forty years earlier.

Table 25   Top ten ports receiving grain coastwise, 1819–27 (Great Britain; tons per annum average)

Port	Wheat	Oats	Barley	Malt	Total
London	76,933	66,259	36,875	26,577	206,644
Hull	30,922	2,187	20,649	220	53,978
Leith	9,021	4,450	18,628	407	22,506
Liverpool	6,211	3,517	4,732	5,002	19,462
Grangemouth	4,672	2,635	9,566	175	17,048
Bristol	3,714	5,162	6,213	519	15,608
Newcastle	3,778	772	4,431	474	9,455
Glasgow	3,316	1,211	1,504	144	6,175
Rochester	1,669	2,152	836	688	5,345
Portsmouth	2,993	386	1,059	887	5,325

Source. As for table 22.

Although a great number of small ports did some coastwise business in corn, the trade was concentrated in relatively few outlets. Table 21 shows that the top three ports were responsible for roughly a quarter and the top ten for about two-thirds of the total; it is clear from table 22 that a similar pattern of concentration of suppliers was characteristic of the 1820s. There was specialisation as well as concentration. Thus in the 1780s Boston was the leading supplier of oats; the Essex ports of Maldon, Leigh and Colchester, with Faversham in Kent, sent the largest quantities of wheat, while Harwich despatched nearly as much malt as all the other nine leading ports in the trade. Forty years later Boston was still the biggest supplier of oats; Yarmouth provided most barley; both Ipswich and Yarmouth supplanted Harwich in deliveries of malt, and Kings Lynn and Wisbech had become more important suppliers of wheat than the Essex ports.

Looking at the receiving end of the trade, it is clear from table 25 that the big centres of population on the coast dominated the market. If Leith is treated as a port for Edinburgh, then all ten leading importers, with the exception of Grangemouth and Rochester, were major towns or cities with huge populations to feed. The need to provision the navy (Chatham being hard by Rochester) helps to explain one of the exceptions. Portsmouth, of course, was also a naval centre. The top ten ports receiving grain coastwise took well over four-fifths of the total grain imports coastwise.

We may summarise the nature of the trade by stating that supplies came from medium-to-small-sized ports on the east coast and were distributed to a few large centres of population, principally Glasgow, Liverpool and Bristol in the west and London, Hull, Newcastle and Edinburgh on the east. A widely dispersed supply was concentrated, via inland and coastal navigation, to a few large markets.

Other food supplies which figured prominently in the coastal trade were livestock, salted meat, fish, dairy produce, sugar and many other types of groceries. The great contributor of supplies of livestock was Ireland, as shown in table 26, which from 1820 to 1825 inclusive sent

Table 26   Numbers of livestock shipped from Ireland to Great Britain, 1815–25

Year	Horses	Cattle	Sheep	Swine	Total
1815	1,283	33,809	26,502	127,570	189,164
1816	801	31,752	34,483	83,618	150,654
1817	848	45,301	29,460	24,193	99,802
1818	2,142	58,165	25,152	23,960	109,419
1819	2,994	52,175	19,710	61,759	136,638
1820	2,552	39,014	24,159	99,107	164,832
1821	2,392	26,725	25,310	104,501	158,928
1822	1,089	34,659	35,685	65,037	136,470
1823	2,277	46,351	55,158	82,789	186,575
1824	2,081	62,314	61,137	73,027	198,559
1825	3,130	63,519	72,161	65,919	204,729

Source. P.P., 1833, V, p. 64.

an average of 175,015 head annually to other ports in the UK but mostly to England. The greatest expansion in this traffic was in sheep and lambs, increasing steadily in number from 24,159 in 1820 to 72,161 in 1825.[24] On the establishment of regular steamer services with Bristol in the 1820s the economy of the city of Cork was radically changed; live beasts replaced processed meat in the holds of the ships and the leather and glue trades of the city went into a sharp decline.[25] About the same time Aberdeen's shipments of live cattle to ports on the east coast, and especially London, began to increase in importance.[26]

The demands of the building industry gave rise to an entire range of coastal shipping cargoes. Timber from the Baltic was transhipped into coasters at Hull; numerous small ports in Suffolk and Essex supplied London with bricks; stately homes and public buildings depended on Portland stone from Weymouth and Poole, and slates carried round Lands End from Aberystwyth and Aberdovey were used for roofing. However, it was not until the repeal in 1831 of the *ad valorem* tax on slates carried coastwise that they replaced tiles in the construction of humbler dwellings, and Portmadoc enjoyed a generation of prosperity as the chief port in this specialist trade.

The economics of coastal freight

Goods were sent by coaster rather than by land because it was decidedly cheaper. Even under the most favourable conditions coal doubled in price when carried overland a dozen miles. Water carriage was cheap partly because the capacity of a canal barge or coasting vessel was so very much greater than that of a waggon. No land carrier could cope with more than a tiny fraction of the 200–300 tons of coal a collier brig could stow in its hold by the late eighteenth century. Before the opening of the Bridgewater Canal in 1761 the cost of transporting a ton of coal the ten miles from Worsley to Manchester was 10s.[27] The maximum charge by canal was fixed at 2s 6d, or 3d per ton mile. Shipment by coastal vessel was often even cheaper than by canal, because the coaster could benefit from economies of scale. The cost per ton of coal from Sunderland to London by sea was 7s 1d per ton, or, assuming a journey of 270 miles, less than ½d per ton mile.[28] Even though at times charges rose to twice this rate, sea carriage was still decisively cheaper than land or, even where the route was a direct one, canal carriage.

The charges for commodities other than bulk ones showed a similar differential. For example, to send a consignment of files from Warrington to Glasgow in 1800 cost 23s by road but only 4s by sea.[29] As was made clear in chapter 1, however, cheapness of transport might not be the guiding criterion in such commodity movement. Speed or reliability of delivery could be more important in the case of such items as precision tools, with a high value in relation to their bulk or weight: some consignments of this nature even went by stagecoach.

In the 1820s and 1830s coastal shipping still had a decisive cost advantage over land carriage where speed and reliability of delivery was not all-important or the voyage by coaster not too circuitous. With the advent of the steamboat, though, delivery times were sometimes nearly as quick and as dependable as by land. In 1832 a steamboat beat the stagecoach in bringing newspapers from London to Plymouth with news of the passing of the Reform Bill.[30] In 1826 the *Prince Frederick*, the first steamboat to ply regularly between Hull and London, charged $2\frac{3}{4}d$ a ton mile for the conveyance of heavy goods to the capital, the average passage time being thirty-two hours. The Royal Mail coach took eighteen and a half hours, but was only suitable for small consignments; other forms of road transport had difficulty in matching the journey times of the steamer.[31]

Where river or canal transport was able to complement the work of the coasters the cost advantages of water carriage were especially great. As late as the early 1840s the Norwich firm of Towler Campian & Co., which employed a thousand workers, obtained its worsted yarn from Hull and Yarmouth, whence a small river steamer shipped the yarn to the factory. Charges averaged a penny a ton mile.[32] So attractive were freight rates by coaster that tradesmen in the industrial Midlands found it worth their while to send goods by seemingly unlikely and roundabout routes to take advantage of them. In 1836 B. Redfern, a general merchant, of Birmingham, who dealt mainly with firms in Edinburgh, 'sent South to go Northwards about', despatching his goods by canal to London before they were transhipped out to the Edinburgh steamboat. Alternatively he used the inland waterway to Hull, whence coasters carried his wares northwards. He had even sent his consignments by canal to Liverpool, thence by coaster to Glasgow and finally by canal to Edinburgh, but had found this route, at £4 10*s* a ton, dearer than via London or Hull, though cheaper than by land carrier.

Canal freights, which included the twin elements of tolls and carrier's charges, were generally higher than charges by coastal sailing vessel. At least on the south coast, where competition on the water was less keen than it was on the east coast or across the Irish Sea, charges by coastal steamboats, at $2d$ to $4d$ a ton mile, approximated more closely those of canals. However, inland waterway transport was more frequently complementary to, rather than competitive with, coastal shipping. As at Gloucester, Topsham, Shoreham, Yarmouth, Kings Lynn, Hull and many other places, the coasters fed the river barges and canal boats with traffic and in return were fed by them.

Passenger traffic

Coastwise passenger traffic was growing in importance even before
the age of the steam packets. Appreciable numbers of travellers opted
for the sailing coasters rather than the coaches to reach their destination. Their main reason was that it was cheaper than going by road.
In the 1790s, for example, the well appointed hoys which carried
passengers from the Bear Quay in the Pool of London to Margate
charged only 2s 6d for the single journey. Travelling the seventy-two
miles by coach, the 'inside' passenger paid four times as much.[33] An
estimated 18,000 people took the hoy to various Kentish resorts in
1792.[34]

In 1750 the north-eastern port of Berwick had no vessels that could
take the much prized local salmon to London. By the end of the
century there were no fewer than twenty-one locally owned fast sailing smacks engaged in this profitable trade. Their speed soon attracted
passengers as well. In 1802, impressed by the success of the Berwick
vessels, a group of Leith merchants established the Edinburgh & Leith
Shipping Company to serve the coast route, while seven years later the
London & Edinburgh Shipping Company was providing yet more
smacks to accommodate passengers, as well as goods, making the 420
mile journey to London.[35] The single fare, in the early years of the
century, was as low as £4, comparing favourably with the cost of the
journey by road, which, when incidental expenses were included, came
to as much as £13.[36]

Nevertheless the unpredictability of journey times set severe limits
on the expansion of passenger travel in the days of sail. When John
Wesley visited the Isle of Wight on 10 July 1753 he reached Cowes
from Southampton in three hours; but a report presented to the
Postmasters General in February 1820 noted that there were plenty of
instances of a passage not being effected 'within 4, 5 or 6 hours' with
consequent uncertainties about the time of arrival of the mail.[37]
There was no certainty of a Dubliner being able to keep an appointment in London when sailing times from Howth (near the Irish capital)
to Holyhead varied from less than eight hours to over fifty.[38] Not
surprisingly, on the most important Irish Sea route, between Holyhead
and Dublin, only 14,577 people made the crossing in either direction
during the course of 1814.[39] On the most popular of all coastal
passenger routes, London to Margate, an estimated 23,000 people
made the journey by sailing vessel in 1815; but some 400,000 made
the same journey by steamer fifteen years later.[40]

The launching of Henry Bell's 28 ton 4 h.p. steamship *Comet* on the Clyde on 24 July 1812 was as important for the development of coastal passenger transport as was the triumph of the Stephensons' *Rocket* at the Rainhill trials in 1829 for the railway. The success of the steamboat was 'instantaneous and complete'. What had been an experimental means of water transport had 'changed overnight into an assured commercial venture'.[41]

The subsequent development of steam navigation in British coastal waters passed through three stages before the establishment of a basic network of railways by the middle years of the nineteenth century brought about some change in the role of steamships in coastal shipping. Until the early 1820s progress was mainly, though not exlusively, confined to the extension of passenger services in estuarine waters. The 1820s saw the development of longer-distance coastal and cross-Channel services during the spring, summer and autumn seasons. By the 1830s improvements in marine engines and ship design made regular sailings possible throughout the year, even on the most exposed passages. Table 27 illustrates the growth in the steamship

Table 27 Number of steam vessels, with tonnage and number of men that belonged to the several ports of the UK, 1814–28 inclusive

Year	Vessels	Tons	Men	Year	Vessels	Tons	Men
1814	11	542	65	1822	129	11,007	924
1815	25	1,558	150	1823	151	13,104	1,112
1816	34	2,064	201	1824	168	14,708	1,276
1817	42	2,382	233	1825	213	18,730	1,630
1818	53	3,807	305	1826	285	26,904	2,278
1819	60	4,155	369	1827	318	30,239	2,566
1820	78	5,086	478	1828	338	30,912	2,708
1821	121	8,003	712				

Source. P.P., 1829, XVII, p. 191.

fleet, almost all of whose vessels were employed exclusively in coastal waters. It was the proliferation of steam packet services implicit in table 28 that, in the words of a contemporary, 'excited the locomotive propensities of the English people in a most remarkable degree'.[42] Certainly in the late 'teens and early '20s of the century there was a rapid growth of services from the main estuarine ports, the

Table 28 Passenger journeys by steamboat

Packet stations	Date	No. of passengers
London–Margate	1821	27,291
	1825	71,469
	1833	390,000
London–Gravesend	1831	120,000
	1833	290,000
	1835	670,000
	1842	1,141,000
London–Southend	1834	7,000
London–Dover	1836	12,480
Holyhead–Dublin	1829	54,000[a]
Bristol–Exeter	1836	12,000
London–Edinburgh	1821–31[b]	100,000[c]
	1843	18,000

Notes

a   City of Dublin Steam Packet Company services only.

b   Inclusive.

c   London & Edinburgh Steam Packet Company services only.

Source. London–Margate: W. Camden, *The Steam Packet Boat Book*, p. 36; H. Humpherus, *History of the Origin and Progress of the Company of Watermen and Lightermen of the River Thames*, III, p. 207. London–Gravesend: Porter, *Progress of the Nation*, 1838, II, p. 318; Humpherus, *op. cit.*, p. 283. London–Southend: H.L.R.O., S.C. on Southend Pier Bill, 1835, evidence of T. Ingram, waterman, of Southend. London–Dover: H.L.R.O., S.C. on South Eastern Railway Bill, 1836, XXXVI, p. 15, statement of number of passengers travelling by steamboat. Holyhead–Dublin: S.C. on the State of the Poor in Ireland, *P.P.*, 1830, VII, p. 27. Bristol–Exeter: H.L.R.O., S.C. on Bristol & Exeter Railway Bill, 1836, evidence of W. Charman, employee of the Stamp Office. London–Edinburgh: S.C. on Steam Navigation, *P.P.*, 1831, VIII, appendix 6, p. 163; H.L.R.O., S.C. on North British Railway Bill, 1844, evidence of W. Marshall, Leith.

Tyne Steam Packet plying from Newcastle to Shields in 1814,[43] and along the coast, with 400 ton, 100 h.p. vessels in service between London and Edinburgh by 1821.[44] A close examination of developments in the different regions of the UK bears out the truth of G. R. Porter's comment that scarcely any two ports of consequence could be pointed out between which steam communication was not maintained in the early 1830s 'as well for the conveyance of passengers as for the transmission of goods'.[45]

The new steam packets carried goods as well as passengers, but for technological and economic reasons the goods were generally of high value and small bulk (though steamships on the Cork – Bristol run did take large consignments of agricultural produce and livestock). The simple side-lever engines installed in the early steamboats were much akin to the Watt beam engines seen in pumping stations on land. They consumed a great deal of fuel, and a large part of the hold was taken up with bunker coal, leaving relatively little space for cargo. The direct-action engines which gradually displaced them in the 1820s were more efficient, but screw colliers began their slow displacement of collier sailing brigs only in the 1850s. During the first two decades of operation, at least, coastal steamships were generally confined to such cargoes as groceries, general merchandise and books rather than bulky commodities like coal, grain or building materials.

Finance and ownership

It was as true in 1830 as in 1760 that the typical British coaster was financed by interested parties living in the locality of the ship's port of registration. The pattern of ownership in 1825, from a sample of 315 ships registered in nine ports and with a total tonnage of 31,782, is summarised in table 29. The sample shows that 42.4 per cent of the owners (i.e. of those with a sixty-fourth share or more) lived in the port of registration. A further 47.7 per cent lived within twenty miles of it. Allowing for the 3.3 per cent of owners whose place of residence cannot be traced, this leaves less than 7 per cent as real outsiders, remote from their investment.

The occupations of the owners were mainly such as benefited directly from the services provided by coastal shipping. Nearly a third were merchants or manufacturers involved in selling or processing the cargoes carried coastwise. More than a tenth were master mariners or mariners, often men employed in the ships in which they had a direct financial interest. Those associated with the organisation of shipping, such as wharfingers or shipping agents, held 9 per cent of the shares. The direct interest of the 6 per cent of the owners who were shipbuilders is manifest. Landed interests — landowners, farmers and those simply labelled 'Esquire' — were weakly represented, with only 5.6 per cent of the ownership, though in Beaumaris, with its agricultural hinterland, they owned nearly 14 per cent of the shipping tonnage. In the professions, bankers owned as many shares as all the other professions taken together. The widows, spinsters and

Table 29 Place of residence and occupation of owners of coastal vessels, 1825

	Tons	%
Place of residence		
Within the port of the ship's registration	13,479	42.4
Within a twenty-mile radius of the port of registration	15,168	47.7
Outside a twenty-mile radius of the port of registration	2,102	6.6
Not given, not traced	1,033	3.3
Occupation		
Merchants and manufacturers	10,115	31.8
Mariners	6,827	21.5
No specific source of income (widow, spinster, gentlemen, MP)	3,794	11.9
Ship owners	2,904	9.1
Service sector (e.g. shipping agent, wharfinger, etc.)	2,859	9.0
Shipbuilders (not included under manufacturers)	1,877	5.9
Landed interest (farmer, yeoman, 'Esquire')	1,772	5.6
Professions (attorney, surveyor, surgeon)	469	1.5
Bankers (not included in the above)	491	1.5
Not given, unclear or ambiguous	674	2.2

Source. Stratified sample of 315 ships of a total of 31,782 tons from the shipping registers for Beaumaris, Bideford, Bristol, Cardiff, Glasgow, Gloucester, Ipswich, Newcastle and Sunderland. Reports of sailings included in the mercantile press and the local newspapers were also used.

gentlemen who held 12 per cent of the shares were those most likely to have invested in coastal shipping simply for a financial return rather than from any other business interest.

A few examples from many in the ships' registers reveal the extent to which coastal shipping was an enterprise sponsored by members of the local community rather than by distant and otherwise un-involved investors. The 212 ton Newcastle brig *Formora*, built in 1794, had ten different owners, all resident on Tyneside. The largest block of shares — sixteen — was held by Joseph Shahan, a master mariner. The other shareholders included three wharfingers, two agents, another master mariner, a sailmaker and two widows. In 1830 eight shares of the 125 ton Cardiff sloop *Diligence* were owned by a local victualler and a further eight by William Bird, the leading bookseller of the city; three master mariners held two shares each, and other shares were held by a sailmaker, a saddler, an accountant, a shipbuilder, all of Cardiff, and a widow, a blacksmith and a mariner, from near-by Newport. All but five shares in the 170 ton steamer *Ailsa Craig*, launched at Yarmouth in 1825, were owned by merchants, thirteen of whom lived in Yarmouth, four in Norwich and one in Stoke, in Norfolk. The odd five were owned by a master mariner of Yarmouth. The ship pursued a regular liner trade with London, serving well the primary interests of her owners.[46] Many of the mariners registered as owners were master of the ship in which they held shares. Such men might be called the self-employed of the coastal trade.

In a different category were the large companies designed to exploit the Anglo-Irish trade or the most lucrative long-distance coastal routes such as Edinburgh and London or Glasgow and Liverpool. Preeminent among them was the City of Dublin Steam Packet Company, established on 13 September 1823 by Charles Wye Williams and twenty-nine other leading merchants and gentlemen of Dublin or its neighbourhood. By way of calls on subscribers and mergers with rival concerns the capital of the company was increased from its original £24,000 to £174,000 by 1828. The shareholders were held together by a deed of co-partnership, the law at the time making a joint-stock company difficult to establish and denying shareholders limited liability.[47] In 1826 individual ship-owners of Liverpool and Cork decided to merge their holdings into a new concern, the St George Steam Packet Company, which for the next two years was the principal rival of the Dublin company. Eventually, the astute Williams persuaded the shareholders of the two companies to sign an agreement for pooling receipts from the Irish Sea passenger traffic.[48]

As ship-owning was perhaps the riskiest form of business in Britain during the industrial revolution, an adequate system of marine insurance was all-important. Until the passing of the Marine Insurance Act, 1824 (5 Geo. IV, c. CXIV), two large chartered companies, the Royal Exchange Assurance and the London Assurance, together with the underwriters at Lloyd's, were widely believed to enjoy a monopoly of the business. But the Royal Exchange Assurance charged high premiums and refused to insure sums below £10,000, while the London Assurance concentrated on vessels trading overseas. Thus the field was left open for the rise of local mutual insurance clubs in the ports.

The disaster of early 1800, when sixty-nine out of seventy-one vessels bound from the Tyne for London were wrecked or captured by French privateers and 500 sailors were taken prisoner, was one of the worst of many such misfortunes. The perils of the east-coast passage prompted the lead which Tyneside set the rest of the country in establishing marine insurance clubs. The first was set up in North Shields in 1778, but it was the risks occurring in the 'years of war' (1793–1815) that brought about a proliferation. The Equitable Association of South Shields, formed in May 1797, was run on a premium basis, where insurers deposited an initial premium per voyage and were liable to further calls if members' claims exceeded the amount paid in over a stipulated period of time. By 1816 there were nine such associations on Tyneside. Separate clubs, such as the Nautical & Impartial of South Shields, had also been created for the insurance of cargo and freight.[49] Outside the North-east, with its hundreds of vessels based on the Tyne, owners were slower to establish their own insurance clubs, since their fleets were smaller. It was not until the 1850s that the first ones were founded in west Wales.[50] There is some evidence that the larger concerns by-passed both the big London insurance companies and any local organisations, instead making their own arrangements for covering losses. In the first two years of its existence the City of Dublin Steam Packet Company insured its vessels for £10,000 each. By 1826, when the fleet had increased substantially, it decided to place a premium, half-yearly, in a 'reserve insurance fund' of its own, saving the shareholders over £6,000 a year.[51] Ten years later the Aberdeen Steam Navigation Company also determined to make its own insurance arrangements.[52]

Coastal shipping and the economy

Coastal shipping's most important contribution to the industrial revolution was in the extension of the market. In *The Wealth of Nations* (1776) Adam Smith wrote:

As by means of water carriage a more extensive market is opened to every sort of industry than what land-carriage alone can afford it, so it is upon the sea coast, and along the banks of navigable rivers that industry of every kind naturally begins to sub-divide and improve itself.[53]

Coal mining offers the outstanding example of an industry heavily dependent on coastal shipping for the extension of its market.

The growth of coastwise coal shipments from nearly 1½ million tons in 1779 to over 5½ million in 1829 greatly stimulated the opening up of new collieries, with all the ancillary equipment, such as winding and pumping engines, railways and waterside staithes needed for their operation. John Constable's water colour of 'Coal brigs on Brighton beach'[54] reminds us that it was not only by massive deliveries in the Pool of London but also through the despatch of brigs to countless places round the coasts that the market for coal was extended. An indirect advantage of the growth of the coal trade was that return freights were remarkably cheap, since vessels would otherwise have had to return in ballast. The preponderance of tonnage carried southwards from Newcastle was so great that return freight rates from London to the Tyne were as low as 3*s* a ton. This boosted the demand for general merchandise and manufactured goods despatched northwards from the capital.[55]

The rapid expansion of the iron industry would have been inconceivable but for the growth of markets for its products. The role of coastal shipping in making that growth possible is best illustrated by the case of South Wales. In 1796 there were no vessels trading regularly between Cardiff and London, an average of no more than eight voyages a year being made in either direction. By 1829, however, the local Cardiff directory noted a 'very considerable' and regularly conducted trade with both London and Bristol, no less than 60,000 tons of the best manufactured iron besides 20,000 boxes of tinplate being shipped coastwise each year.[56]

But for the facilities offered by water transport, the development of the gas industry in the early nineteenth century would have been confined to the coalfields. In the twenty years following June 1826 one London concern alone, the Gas Light & Coke Company, used the services of 580 collier brigs for single voyages or longer periods.[57] Numerous other towns accessible by coaster owed better lighting of their streets and factories to cheap seaborne coal.

Other mining industries besides coal depended on coastal shipping for expansion. This was particularly true of Cornish tin and copper. In the early years of the nineteenth century the mining district served by Portreath on the north coast of Cornwall was the most highly industrialised in the West of England. A common sight in the port itself was a huge dump of copper ore awaiting shipment for smelting at Neath and Swansea, and an even larger dump of coal awaiting carriage to the mines and towns of the hinterland.[58] Vast quantities of tin were sent coastwise from Falmouth and Truro for smelting into tinplate at Pontypool or Kidwelly. The outbreak of the War of American Independence in 1776 deprived Etruria of its supplies of fine-quality china clay from Virginia, Florida and South Carolina. The American exporters' loss was the Cornishmen's opportunity. Shipment coastwise from Cornwall via the Mersey multiplied ten times between 1776 and 1826. To reduce the cost of freight Josiah Wedgwood, with three others, acquired the sloop *Hendra* in 1803 to carry their own china clay direct to Etruria.[59]

The unprecedented growth of London, the new industrial towns and the major seaside resorts was dependent on coastwise imports of vast quantities of the raw materials of the building trade. Before the rapid development of Portmadoc after 1819 as the principal exporter of slates, Caernarvon enjoyed the lion's share of this profitable trade, which in 1790 brought £50,000 worth of business to the town. In the following decade nearly 2,000 shipments were despatched coastwise from the port.[60]

Coastal shipping facilitated the much wider exchange of agricultural produce for general merchandise. In the days when Ireland was linked with Great Britain by sailing vessels the shipment of cargoes to England was known as the 'back' trade, since their total value was lower than in the opposite direction. Following the advent of steam in the 1820s, shipments from Britain to Ireland began to be regarded as back trade, so greatly had the volume and value of the farm produce sent eastwards increased. The wealthy Dublin ship owner Charles Wye Williams commented in 1830 that the small Irish dealers who in the days of sail rarely travelled farther than their nearest market town were now, by virtue of the steamboat, making frequent visits to the industrial towns of England, where they sold large quantities of eggs, poultry and butter before returning with general merchandise purchased in exchange. In consequence of this quickening of activity retail shops were opening up in Irish villages and small towns hitherto ill served in this respect, or not served at all.[61]

The farmers of East Anglia too experienced an extension of their markets when they used the services of the steamboats that called at Colchester, Great Yarmouth, Kings Lynn or Boston on their way to the Thames or the Tyne. The market boats of the Severn estuary served a similar purpose in bringing the farm produce of Somerset and the Severn valley to the population of industrial South Wales and Bristol. Through the agency of hundreds of coastal vessels the productivity of farming was improved and a rapidly growing urban population was being fed, a development which helped to sustain the momentum of industrialisation.

The coastal steamship services which spread so rapidly in the 1820s helped to reduce the overhead costs of retail and wholesale trade, and even of branches of manufacture, such as ironfounding and tin and copper smelting, where high-value raw materials could bear steamboat freight charges. The reliability and speed of steamboats compared with sailing ships meant that less warehouse space was needed and the turnover of working capital was quicker. Wye Williams found that 'it was not necessary in Dublin or any other port in Ireland to have a large stock of goods on hand'. Traders could have 'from any of the manufacturing towns in England within two or three days even the smallest quantity of any description of goods'.[62] Similarly, regular steamboat communication with Liverpool was a boon to the shopkeepers of North Wales even though it undermined the prosperity of the local fairs.[63]

Although coal factors did not share in the blessings of more regular coastwise supplies until the second half of the century, marginal improvement in the regularity of sailings was achieved through the use of steam tugs on the Tyne. On 18 June 1819, when there was a build-up of sixty-seven laden colliers in the harbour at Blyth owing to a persistent southern wind, some of the more enterprising ship owners hired a steam tug which towed three of the laden vessels to sea. When the tug returned the ship owners went on board and 'spent the afternoon in great conviviality'.[64]

The authors of a directory of Cumberland and Westmorland in 1829 remarked on the value to business of regular steamship services from the Cumbrian coast to Liverpool:

Few places have reaped greater advantage from the facilities offered by steam navigation than Whitehaven; until its introduction, the man of business was occupied two entire days at a heavy expense in travelling by the stage-coaches from Whitehaven to Liverpool; whereas by steam he now goes on board the packet in the evening where he can in moderate weather sleep as comfortably as in his own bed and be landed at Liverpool in the morning.[65]

The building and maintenance of no fewer than 350 steamships, almost all of them employed in the coastal service, provided a decisive stimulus to marine engineering. In 1825 no less than forty-four steam vessels were under construction in Liverpool and London alone.[66] Early steam packet services, particularly those on the Clyde and on the London–Greenwich, London–Margate and Bristol–Cork stations, were highly competitive. The urge to produce more efficient marine engines was irresistible. In the decade of the 1820s seventy different improvements were patented. The 'spin-off' effects of the work of the pioneers were substantial. When the time was ripe, from about 1840 onwards, for the extension of steam communication to more distant lands — with the alluring prospect of a greater volume of international exchange — the knowledge and experience of steamship operation gained earlier in coastal waters proved invaluable.

It is often assumed that it was only the railways that drew traffic from the stagecoaches and forced them off the road. But wherever they plied more or less parallel to the stagecoach routes it was the steamboats that first brought alarm and despondency to the coaching interests. Kent was a case in point. J. Wheatley, a stagecoach proprietor in Greenwich, told a parliamentary select committee in 1837 that his business had been very adversely affected by the proliferation of steamboats on the London–Greenwich route. He complained of the unfairness of the tax system, under which he paid licence duty based on seating capacity for every coach he put on the road, irrespective of the number of passengers, where the steamboat proprietors paid nothing.

William Wimberley, of Doncaster, who kept the accounts of several coach proprietors operating on the Great North Road, told an equally gloomy story. The 'increase of navigation by steam' had drawn away his clients' traffic. He was obliged, though, to concede that if travel on the 'great lines' of the coaches had diminished, on the 'collateral lines' it had increased. People 'flocked by the scores' from Sheffield through Doncaster to Hull, whence they completed their journey north or south by steamboat.[67] His experience was typical. In fact we may summarise the impact of coastal steamships on coach travel by saying that coach services on routes parallel to the steamships suffered heavy loss of traffic but that 'feeder' traffic to the ports increased.

Coastal shipping interests sometimes opposed canal projects because they feared loss of traffic.[68] The apprehension was generally ill founded. It was expected that the Basingstoke Canal, opened in 1796, would draw coastal traffic away from the ports of Sussex, Hampshire and the Isle of Wight, particularly in view of the wartime depredations of privateers. The brief spell of peace in 1803 returned security to the coasting trade, and the company feared that this might 'induce many customers of the canal to prefer that mode of sending their goods as being cheaper than by the canal'. Indeed it was found that 'a considerable quantity of the goods consigned to the Isle of Wight, Jersey, Guernsey, etc. which used to go up the canal to Basingstoke, and thence by Waggons to Southampton, are now sent directly from the Thames in vessels trading to those islands'.[69]

Where ports were linked with navigable waterways, as in the case of Hull, Kings Lynn, Yarmouth, Gloucester, Cardiff or Liverpool — to mention only a few outstanding examples — the shipping records indicate unmistakably that inland waterway improvements were a stimulus to the growth of coastal traffic rather than an impediment to it. Moreover, in large areas of the country geography precluded the development of a canal system. The south-west of England, for example, moved straight from the coasting vessels, the country road and the packhorse to the railway age.[70] Certainly in 1830 coastal shipping appeared secure in the immediate future from the challenge of any other form of transport.

Notes

The authors wish to thank the Social Science Research Council and the Leverhulme Trust for helping to finance the research on which this chapter is based.

1   F. J. Fisher, 'The development of London as a centre of conspicuous consumption in the sixteenth and seventeenth centuries', *Transactions of the Royal Historical Society*, 4th ser., 30, 1948, pp. 37–50.

2   H. J. Dyos and D. H. Aldcroft, *British Transport*, Leicester University Press, 1969, p. 44.

3   T. S. Willan, *The English Coasting Trade, 1600–1750*, Manchester University Press, 1938, p. 61.

4   *Ibid.*, pp. 12–14.

5   D. Defoe, *A Tour through the whole Island of England and Wales*, Everyman edn., Dent, London, 1928, I, p. 397.

6   W. Maitland, *The History of London*, London, 1772, II, chapter 5.

7   British Museum Add. Ms 11255; P.R.O., Customs 17/1–6.

8   Willan, *Coasting Trade*, p. 51.

9   *Ibid.*, p. 190.

10   R. Davis, *The Rise of the English Shipping Industry*, David & Charles, Newton Abbot, 1962, p. 404.

11   S.C. on Commerce, Manufactures and Shipping, *P.P.*, 1833, VI, q. 7428, evidence of Robert Anderson, representing the ship owners of South Shields.

12   Accounts and Papers, House of Lords, *P.P.*, 1830, CCLXXVIII, p. 118; 1847–48, XXI, p. 346. House of Commons, *P.P.*, 1849, LII, p. 177.

13   Davis, *Shipping Industry*, p. 35.

14   *Ibid.*, p. 396.
15   G. R. Porter, *The Progress of the Nation*, London, 1851, p. 345.
16   J. Grant, *Old and New Edinburgh*, London, 1883, III, p. 211, cites a number of instances of French privateers' harassment of east-coast shipping in 1804–05.
17   R. Warner, *A Tour through Cornwall in the Autumn of 1808*, London, 1809, pp. 87–140. The author contrasts the depression of the county's southern ports, a result of 'the continuance of the war and the shutting up of Mediterranean ports', with the 'busy scene of commercial bustle' at Hale on the north coast, prospering from the growing domestic industrial demand for copper. G. R. Porter, *The Progress of the Nation*, 1851, p. 342, shows that the value of Anglo-Irish trade increased between 1801 and 1813 by over 7 per cent per annum for imports into Ireland, and nearly 3.5 per cent per annum for exports from Ireland, in real terms.
18   P. Deane, 'The industrial revolution in Great Britain', in C. M. Cipolla (ed.), *The Fontana Economic History of Europe*, I, *The Emergence of Industrial Societies*, Fontana, London and Glasgow, 1973, p. 169. B. R. Mitchell and P. Deane, *Abstract of British Historical Statistics*, Cambridge University Press, 1962, p. 280.
19   W. A. Cole, 'The measurement of industrial growth', *Economic History Review*, XI, 1958, pp. 309–15.
20   B. F. Duckham, *The Inland Waterways of East Yorkshire, 1700–1900*, East Yorkshire Local History Society, York, 1973, p. 305.
21   G. Jackson, *The Trade and Shipping of Eighteenth Century Hull*, East Yorkshire Local History Society, York, 1975, pp. 32–8.
22   W. G. East, 'The port of Kingston-upon-Hull during the industrial revolution', *Economica*, XI, 1931.
23   Davis, *Shipping Industry*, p. 209.
24   *P.P.*, 1833, V, p. 630. G. O. Tuathaigh, *Ireland before the Famine, 1798–1848*, Gill & Macmillan, Dublin, 1972, p. 136.
25   Cork Incorporated Chamber of Commerce and Shipping, *Cork: its Trade and Commerce*, Cork, 1919, p. 444.
26   J. MacDonald (ed.), *Cattle and Cattle Breeders*, Edinburgh, 1886, p. 72.
27   T. C. Barker and C. I. Savage, *An Economic History of Transport in Britain*, Hutchinson, London, 1974, pp. 37–8.
28   E. E. Allen, 'On the comparative cost of transit by steam and sailing colliers and on the different modes of ballasting', *Proceedings of the Institution of Civil Engineers*, XIV, 1854–55, p. 318.
29   T. S. Ashton, *An Eighteenth Century Industrialist: Peter Stubs of Warrington, 1756–1806*, Manchester University Press, 1939, p. 89.
30   G. Farr, *West Country Passenger Steamers*, Stephenson, Prescot, 1967, p. 166.
31   W. Parson (ed.), *Directory, Guide and Annals of Kingston upon Hull*, 1826, p. 53. A. Bates, *Directory of Stage Coach Services*, David & Charles, Newton Abbot, 1969, p. 79.
32   H.L.R.O., Commons S.C. on the Norwich and Brandon Railway Bill, evidence of Messrs A. Towler and G. P. Bidder.
33   *The Kentish Traveller's Companion*, Canterbury, 1799, p. 160.
34   *The Kentish Companion*, Canterbury, 1792, p. 160.

35 J. Fuller, *The History of Berwick upon Tweed*, Edinburgh, 1799, p. 398. Anon, *Tales, Traditions and Antiquities of Leith*, Leith, 1865, p. 366.

36 *London and Leith Smack and Steam Yacht Guide*, Edinburgh, 1824, p. viii.

37 J. Wesley, *Journal*, Everyman edn., Dent, London, 1906, II, p. 263. P.O. Records, Post 42/106, No. 47 of 14 February 1820.

38 P.O. Records, *Irish Packet Delays*, P.O. 133C, 1818.

39 E. Watson, *The Royal Mail to Ireland*, Edward Arnold, London, 1917, p. 108.

40 W. Camden, *The Steam Boat Pocket Book: a descriptive guide from London Bridge to Gravesend, Southend, the Nore, Herne Bay, Margate and Ramsgate*, London (n.d., but probably early 1830s), p. 34.

41 J. Guthrie, *A History of Marine Engineering*, Hutchinson, London, 1971, p. 37.

42 G. R. Porter, *The Progress of the Nation*, London, 1838, Part 3, p. 48.

43 S. Middlebrook, *Newcastle on Tyne: its Growth and Achievement*, Kemsley House, Newcastle, 1968, p. 184.

44 *Edinburgh Evening Courant*, 14 and 25 June 1821.

45 Porter, *Progress of the Nation*, Part 3, p. 49.

46 Ownership details taken from ships' registers at the custom houses of Newcastle, Cardiff and Great Yarmouth.

47 Articles of Agreement, City of Dublin Steam Packet Company, 13 September 1823, Irish P.R.O., 1070/88. Deed of Settlement, City of Dublin Steam Packet Company, 1828, Irish P.R.O., D 5925.

48 W. J. Barry, *History of the Port of Cork Steam Navigation Company*, Cork, 1915, p. 5. P.O. Records, Pkt 54D, 1828.

49 G. B. Hodgson, *The Borough of South Shields*, Newcastle on Tyne, 1903, pp. 296–305.

50 M. E. Hughes, 'The Historical Geography of the Seafaring Industry of the Coast of Cardigan Bay in the Nineteenth Century', unpublished M.A. thesis, University of Wales, 1962.

51 P.O. Records, Pkt 549D, 1828.

52 Aberdeen Steam Navigation Company, Minute of meeting 21 March 1836, Ms 2479/1.

53 A. Smith, *An Inquiry into the Nature and Causes of the Wealth of Nations* (1904 edn.), Grant Richards, London, I, p. 20.

54 In the Cecil Higgins Art Gallery, Bedford.

55 H.L.R.O., S.C. Newcastle and Berwick Railway Bill, 1845, evidence of C. Allhausan, merchant of Newcastle for twenty years.

56 *Directory and Guide to the Town and Castle of Cardiff, 1796*, Cardiff, 1796, p. 14.

57 S. Everard, *History of the Gas, Light and Coke Company*, Ernest Benn, London, 1949, p. 78.

58 R. Pearse, *The Ports and Harbours of Cornwall*, Warne, St Austell, 1963, p. 121.

59 R. M. Barton, *A History of the Cornish China Clay Industry*, Truro, 1966, pp. 24, 39; *V.C.H. Cornwall*, I, 1906, p. 577.

60 A. H. Dodd, *The Industrial Revolution in North Wales*, University of Wales Press, Cardiff, 1951, p. 121; M. Hughes, *Immortal Sails*, Stephenson, Prescot, 1969, p. ix.

61 S.C. on the State of the Poor in Ireland, *P.P.*, 1830, VII, qq. 3128–50, evidence of C. W. Williams.

62   *Ibid.*, answer to q. 3130.
63   Dodd, *North Wales*, p. 130.
64   Blyth Harbour Commission, *Port of Blyth*, 1954, p. 20.
65   Quoted in L. A. Williams, *Road Transport in Cumbria in the Nineteenth Century*, Allen & Unwin, London, 1975, p. 134.
66   R. A. Fletcher, *Steamships and their Story*, Sidgwick & Jackson, London, 1910, p. 75.
67   S.C. on Taxation of Internal Communication, *P.P.*, 1837, XX, qq. 285, 314, 321, 454–9.
68   C. Hadfield, *British Canals*, Phoenix House, London, 1950, p. 35.
69   C. Hadfield, *The Canals of Southern England*, Phoenix House, London, 1955, p. 79–81.
70   *Ibid.*, p. 19.

6 THE PORTS
Gordon Jackson

The role of trade in the industrial revolution is generally recognised. By contrast, the contribution of the ports is generally neglected (beyond passing references to Liverpool and Hull), while the existence of a specific 'port industry', facilitating the flow of industrial goods, raw materials and foodstuffs, is scarcely noticed and frequently ignored. Yet the trade of most ports grew in vigorous fashion in the quarter-century after 1783, and many reacted by completely transforming their facilities for handling ships and goods. Although there had been ports from time immemorial, it is fair to say that the 'modern' port was created, in England, to answer the needs of industrial growth at the end of the eighteenth century. Conversely, it is doubtful, to say the least, whether economic growth of this order could have been sustained without the massive application of capital and recent technical innovations to the removal of physical obstacles inhibiting the speedy receipt and despatch of shipping. The growth of trade and the renewal of the ports were, in no small measure, interdependent. But before turning to the changes which occurred in both trade and ports it is important to note a number of points which affect our understanding of the history of ports. They can best be summed up in two fundamental questions: what was a port, and what do we mean by trade?

Problems of definition

The port as a legal entity

The necessity of easy communications between landing places and hinterland, and the wide spread of markets for imports and sources of exports, had, from the earliest times, encouraged the evolution of port functions wherever a viable water site appeared to command a private hinterland, and ports were originally stretches of coastline subject to a specified customs officer rather than specified places. However, while every part of the coastline continued to be part of some port or other for revenue purposes, the proliferation of landing places in response to regional or local incentives was eventually brought to a halt not by the exhaustion of sites but by the deliberate action of the Crown, eager to safeguard its ancient right to levy duties and regulate shipping by confining trade to places which could be adequately and cheaply supervised. Definitive legislation in 1559 set out not merely the port towns through which all trade must pass but also, with the exception of Hull, the exact locations within them — the Legal Quays — where all goods must be landed or loaded.[1] Ports were therefore legally defined places, and though some were appointed after 1559 the list soon ossified.[2] The overseas commerce of the industrial revolution was consequently channelled through some seventy-four English port towns appointed in a more leisurely age for trade flows and goods that did not necessarily bear much relationship to those for which ports were now required, and for hinterlands whose economies had changed markedly over time. No new ports were created for general trade purposes during the industrial revolution until Grimsby was appointed at the turn of the century (though a number of new 'ports' began the coastal shipping of minerals, in which the customs took little interest). Moreover in the case of London, and probably other places, expanding trade was handled at Legal Quays which were actually smaller than they had been before 1559,[3] and in no port do they appear to have been extended. While certain low-duty goods could thus be landed at Sufferance Quays, there were constant problems over the inadequacy of quay space. Some of the more ludicrous congestion during the early stages of the industrial revolution can be understood only in the context of these legal constraints, which ignored the needs of commerce in their urge to protect the Revenue. On the other hand, the fact that a place was legally a port did not guarantee its prosperity, and, as we shall see, many if not most ports were by-passed in the great eighteenth-century trade boom. Any generalisation about ports must therefore take into account their vast range: some were giants and some were dead. In particular it is worth remembering that there were many places which were not major ports serving the industrial regions, but which never-theless played a vital role in the development of transport.

Coastal versus foreign trade

The second problem involves the definition of 'trade'. In common parlance the word now usually implies overseas connections, but almost until the present century the foreign variety, romantic and vastly profitable though it might be, was only part of the story.

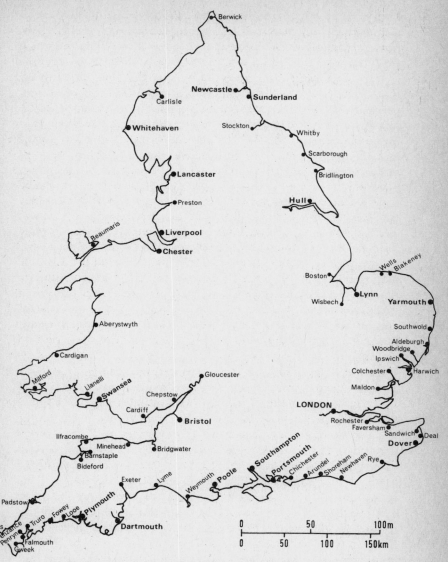

14 The English and Welsh ports, *c.* 1770, distinguishing (in heavy type) those with more than 10,000 tons of shipping per annum entering from foreign parts

Both before and after the industrial revolution some ports were equally indebted — and many were more indebted — for their business to that interchange of goods between the various parts of England which (with home consumption) was the very basis of economic life (see chapter 5). Although recent work has shown that internal transport by road and river was by no means as difficult in the pre-industrial period as was once thought[4] (and it certainly seems unreasonable to talk of strong trade flows through ports without acknowledging that the goods concerned must have had some way of moving around the hinterland), it is difficult to envisage the long-distance movement of bulky goods in a poor society without some part of the journey taking place on the cheaper coastal run, which might with some justice be regarded as an extension of the river system.[5] Coastal trade was classed as essentially different from foreign trade only because it was legally defined and regulated for Revenue purposes and because transhipment between river craft and ship was often — though not always — involved. In serving this particular part of economic life the trade of most ports was conducted not with foreign but with neighbouring ports, and represented the exchange of goods between places whose small private hinterlands were not easily connected by inland transport. Despite this general interchange of products, the chief trade of most places was with London, whose voracious appetite for food and fuel was the supreme influence on the prosperity of many provincial ports and a most important encouragement to the production of agricultural surpluses or coal in their hinterlands.

At the same time London was incomparably the largest consumer of foreign products, having displayed a marked tendency from the late seventeenth century to attract to itself the imports and exports of much of the country. Since these goods were distributed or collected via the coastal trade, it was not necessary, in practice, for Bristol to have direct connections with Hamburg, or Hull with Ireland, for them to obtain goods from those places: they could be obtained coastwise with less effort or financial and mercantile involvement, and in this respect London was already performing for Britain the entrepot function which Britain was later to perform for Europe. It is an important point, which goes a long way towards explaining the fairly rigid regional specialisation of ports which will be outlined below: they could specialise in the certain knowledge that general needs could be served by the coastal trade.

If there are good reasons for questioning the rigid distinction between internal and coastal traffic in their contribution to the national economy, there must equally be some dubiety surrounding the distinction between coastal and foreign trade in their effect on the development of ports. For while customs officers and modern economists may perceive a substantive difference between the two, the fact remains that both sorts of shipping are — ton for ton — equally demanding of harbour room. Some of the problems facing ports during the industrial revolution were caused less by the peculiar needs of the exotic trades than by the sheer volume of mundane coastal traffic. Nevertheless there were very real differences between the two trades in the demands they made on ports and in the treatment they received within them. Foreign-going vessels were usually larger, requiring deeper water and larger quays; they took longer to load and unload because cargoes were difficult to assemble or despatch (though the purpose of the warehouse was partly to avoid excessive delays); they commonly rested longer between voyages than coasters, which built up a large tonnage by rapid turn-round of fewer ships; and they were more commonly laid up in the winter, especially when engaged in trade with northern Europe. Moreover, because foreign cargoes were often more valuable, there was a greater problem of security, and a tendency to delay (and confusion in harbours) caused by the slow operation of the customs service and the need to pass foreign trade over the Legal Quays.[6]

It was precisely because of the higher value of foreign goods, and the great wealth generated by individuals and communities in foreign trade, that they (both communities and individuals) saw themselves as links with foreign countries rather than as part of the internal trading system, in which wharfingers rather than merchants were involved. Coastal trade, whatever its economic importance, was never regarded as anything other than inferior to 'real' trade — the sort that involved the merchants, made the money, gained the prestige and, incidentally, paid the bulk of the port dues and the whole of the customs. Unfortunately any accurate assessment of the relative demands on harbour room from coastal and foreign trade is impossible at the moment, and would require a vast amount of labour for a possibly unsatisfactory result. Suffice it to say that coastal trade, though faster-moving than foreign trade, was exceedingly important in many places, but that the ports which played the major part in the development of the industrial revolution were those engaged extensively in foreign trade.

The importance of volume rather than value

The third point to be borne in mind when considering ports concerns the measurement of trade. Traditionally it has been the value of trade which has attracted the attention of economists, but for a variety of reasons the values attached to goods in the eighteenth century are rough estimates at best and pure fiction at worst. Recent calculations by the late Ralph Davis have done a great deal to present something more nearly resembling an accurate growth pattern for the major trades, and these will be outlined below.[7] Nevertheless it should be stressed that the value of trade which is of such great interest to the historian of the economy can be positively misleading to the historian of transport. Without too much exaggeration it could be argued that the demands made by goods for facilities, and their contribution to the prosperity of ports, were inversely proportional to their unit value. It was bulk that counted. Bullion could be shipped from almost any south-coast pier in a reasonable state of repair, but the importation of timber and wine and the exportation of coal and cottons demanded acres of specialised and costly works. This point is especially important in considering ports in the early nineteenth century, when the rapidly declining price of cotton goods gave the appearance of stagnation: the dock system at Liverpool was choked by the volume of cotton, not by its value. It was, of course, a lucky port whose bulky goods were also valuable, but, if the choice had to be made, the wise place would have gone for volume rather than value, because that was the line of greatest potential growth — though merchants would no doubt have preferred goods with the greatest value, since they earned the profits without requiring the expensive works which pushed up handling charges.

The expansion of trade

The commercial revolution and changing trade flows

In practice ports did not usually choose which goods they would handle and which they would not. These things were decided for them by the impersonal laws that directed the economy and the physical laws which, with the occasional intervention of man, fashioned the ports. The eighteenth century witnessed the interaction of these two forces as shifts in demand at home and abroad stimulated different ports in different ways and at different times, and as refinements within the ports themselves eased and encouraged the flow of goods

and bestowed the competitive advantage on those places which became
the major ones. Many of the larger ports encountered similar problems
which, in as much as their physical circumstances allowed, they
tackled in roughly similar ways, but the most impressive feature of
the ports as a whole in the first half of the eighteenth century is their
progressive diversity rather than their uniformity.

This diversity rested, ultimately, on the variety of new activities
arising in their hinterlands. Most early modern ports had been roughly
similar in character, dealing with a narrow range of goods and to be
found chiefly on the south and south-east coasts opposite the Conti-
nent and within easy reach of London and the bulk of the population.
Almost seventy per cent of English ports had grown up south of the
line from Severn to Wash, a reflection of the original economic importance of that division of the country which was already diminishing
long before the industrial revolution began. Although the South-west
still produced its minerals, and the South-east its provisons, the decline
of the wool trade and the migration of the textile industry had seriously
upset the prosperity of many of those small harbours and inhibited
the extensive remedial work which alone could have prevented the
silting up of their havens or the building up of their sand bars. The
expansion of trade after the Restoration, now commonly called the
commercial revolution, further accelerated this fall — and rise — of
ports, and it is worth noting the salient features of that revolution,
which shifted the balance between the ports and produced the new
trade flows that were of paramount importance in serving — or
stimulating — the industrial revolution.

The first, and in many ways the most important, change in overseas
trade had been the ending of the long growth in the export of woollens
to western Europe.[8] Towards the end of the seventeenth century the
spreading art of cloth-making had threatened the continuance of international trade at its old level as countries increasingly served their own
markets. So far as English trade was concerned, a temporary reprieve
was gained by diverting exports from central Europe to the Baltic and
the Mediterranean, a move which alone cast serious doubt over the
future of many of the ports of the South-east. At the same time a
shortfall in domestic wool production, and a growing self-reliance in
linen manufacture, encouraged the importation of textile raw
materials and dyestuffs, and this was, from the point of view of the
ports in general and the northern ports in particular, a promising
innovation. The traffic flowing through them was greater than in the

past because, whereas England had originally produced her own wool, the export of textiles now tended to be more than evenly balanced in volume by the importation of materials. This movement towards import substitution — in many spheres besides textiles — was well under way in the early eighteenth century: the importation of linens fell by almost a third during the first three-quarters of the century, while all other manufactured imports fell by almost three-quarters. By contrast the importation of raw materials in general rose by almost 90 per cent, and miscellaneous foodstuffs by 30 per cent.[9] These figures are technically value figures, but because they were based on official valuations they are more properly an index of the volume of goods passing through the ports, and represent growth of a magnitude that could not fail to produce major changes in the ports through which it passed.

England enjoyed commercial revolution rather than commercial stagnation because the advances in the export of textiles to the Baltic and Mediterranean — which might have been expected to slow down in their turn — had been followed shortly by a sudden and massive growth in the new re-export trades. To her small population and meagre resources England had added a colonial empire of (as yet) small size but large capacity for producing the sort of luxury consumer goods that were highly prized in Europe, the chief undoubtedly being sugar and tobacco, for which Britain — since Glasgow too was soon heavily involved — became the international storehouse. Moreover, because the productivity of both people and capital was so much greater in America than in England, the wealth of the colonies was growing faster than that of any other part of the European world; and since neither American farmers nor West Indian planters had the skill or incentive to engage in industrial pursuits, a vast new and protected market opened up, first to supplement and then partially to replace the stale European market for manufactured goods, this time to the great advantage of the western ports.

One further overseas trade demands attention for its effect on the prosperity of English commerce in general and on the relative prosperity of the ports in particular. The expanding trade with India and the Far East, while not a serious generator of exports, was soon providing light textiles, coffee, tea and other goods which found a ready market in Europe and, to some extent, in America, where one commodity at least is enshrined in mythology in the 'Boston Tea Party'. Nevertheless, that rapid rise in colonial re-exports which occurred in the late seventeenth and early eighteenth centuries could not continue unabated, and while the total value of this trade continued to rise, its place as the principal dynamic in trade was eventually taken by the export of miscellaneous manufactures from both old and new industries, even before cotton textiles became yet another revolutionary element.

The impact of political constraints

Quite apart from any inherent advantages in trading methods or goods, there were three political constraints which acted in favour of the trade of English ports, although their importance can never be accurately measured. The first was the reinforcement, in the second half of the seventeenth century and continuously throughout the eighteenth, of the system of protection for trade and shipping called the 'Old Colonial System'. Under it, all the trade of colonial territories was forced to go through English or Scottish ports rather than direct between colony and foreign country, with the result that the trade of some ports was built up quite independently of the needs of their hinterland. They managed, through the commercial services they offered, to interpose themselves as entrepots in this protected colonial trade. The second constraint had the opposite effect of greatly diminishing the position of the south-coast ports by disrupting trade with France. The eighteenth century was a period of intense hostility between the two countries, and even when they were not at war discriminatory duties hampered legal trade, even if they provided smugglers with their much-publicised livelihood. The third constraint was the exclusive nature of trade with Ireland, which was reserved, like colonial trade, to Britain, though paradoxically Ireland appeared in the customs records as a foreign country. Irish trade was exceedingly important because of the linens and provisions it provided, and because it consumed a vast range of manufactures which could find in an undeveloped Ireland — as in the colonies — a market which was increasingly denied by the industrial self-sufficiency of the more advanced countries of Europe. Thus it is important to remember, when discussing trade and ports, that a considerable portion of the 'foreign' trade of some places was with Ireland and that it had the appearance of coastal rather than truly foreign trade long before it was officially reclassified after the Union of 1801.

The great trade boom

These various developments in trade, when expressed in terms of constant official prices which provide an index of volume, add up to an overall growth in national commerce which, when fluctuations are averaged out, was almost continuous throughout the eighteenth century. And while providing the context for the industrial revolution, it also illustrates the extent to which the ports were involved in long-term expansion antedating the traditional 'take-off' of industrialisation. (Table 30.) Although it would be extremely unwise to regard these

Table 30   Index of trade volume, 1700–99 (ten-yearly averages)

	Imports	Exports	Re-exports
1700–09	100	100	100
1710–19	115	106	125
1720–29	143	110	166
1730–39	157	131	189
1740–49	153	146	211
1750–59	176	195	207
1760–69	228	224	265
1770–79	255	206	303
1780–89	289	227	248
1790–99	430	371	541

Source. Calculated from customs figures printed in E. B. Schumpeter, *English Overseas Trade Statistics, 1697–1808*, 1960, pp.15–16.

figures as anything more than approximate representations of reality, the trend is unmistakable. Imports appear to have grown fairly rapidly in the 1720s, and then stagnated before beginning a long-term growth around the middle of the century. Exports, fairly steady during the first quarter of the century, moved to a higher plane in the second quarter and again in the third. Re-exports rose rapidly in the first quarter and again in the 1760s. But the most distinctive feature is, of course, the boom in all trades following the American revolutionary war. The manufacture of cotton yarn and textiles most certainly expanded at a remarkable rate, to account for around a fifth of exports, by value, at the end of the century and over 40 per cent by 1804–06,[10] and inevitably stimulating a whole range of supporting trades. Unfortunately the recent recalculation of trade values during the industrial revolution undertaken by Ralph Davis does not give adequate guidance on volumes to the port historian, and these obviously more accurate figures must be rejected, for our purpose, in favour of the continuing series of official values. These show only the slightest increase in the volume of imports during the first quarter of the nineteenth century, followed by a 50 per cent rise in the mid-1820s and a 25 per cent rise in the mid-1830s. Re-exports remained fairly steady throughout the thirty years, while exports, in marked contrast, grew very steadily and experienced a 146 per cent increase in volume between *c.* 1800 and *c.* 1830, with a sharper rise coming in the late 1830s.[11]

Average figures do not, of course, reflect the true impact of the growing volume of trade on the ports. Short-run spurts, especially after the eighteenth-century wars (in 1748, 1763 and 1783), could have a devastating impact on port operations which is completely masked if boom years are eliminated: major ports have, after all, to equip themselves for something approaching maximum rather than average usage. Moreover it is important to note that the national figures cover the whole spectrum of trade goods, and in consequence do not represent a true volume in terms of cubic capacity demands on shipping and harbour room, and requirements for specialised facilities. For instance, an increase in the importation of diamonds from the East Indies would be included in the total value of trade; but a far more telling factor in port development was the increasing value of timber, with its far greater volume-to-value ratio. A breakdown of some of the bulkier items shows that the quantity (as opposed to value) of bar iron rose by a factor of 2 between 1724–26 and 1799–1801, hemp by 4.5, timber by 4.6, sugar by 4.7, flax by 6.4, tea by 27.3, rum by 40.2 and corn by 86.2.[12] The largest part of this increase was, as might be expected, in the last two decades of the century. By contrast a number of the bulkier trades were fairly stagnant during the first quarter of the nineteenth century, especially timber and corn. The only notable signs of progress among the major imports were in flax and raw silk, wool and cotton, the latter reflecting the massive growth in the export of cottons which was the chief bright spot in a relatively uninspiring period of trade history.[13]

The uneven distribution of trade among ports

Increases in volume of the order quoted above would have been serious enough had they been distributed evenly round all the ports, but as noted earlier, the majority did not have widespread hinterlands demanding imported raw materials in bulk or producing large volumes of manufactures; nor did they have great concentrations of population to be fed, clothed, housed or pampered with imported luxuries. Indeed, the majority of the 70 per cent of ports located south of the line from Severn to Wash had no effective hinterland at all. What occurred, therefore, was the channelling of trade through a small number of ports with very special — because very extensive — hinterlands. An analysis of the shipping belonging to all seventy-four listed ports on the eve of the industrial 'take-off', in 1772, reveals that 59 per cent of them had less than 500 tons actively engaged in foreign trade, and that 22 per cent had no ships at all in the foreign trade.[14] Only seven ports had more than 10,000 tons, and these between them accounted for no less than 276,556 tons, or 81.7 per cent of the national total. The situation was little different in 1785, the last year when this sort of statistic was recorded. Although tonnages in general had moved upwards by 37 per cent to carry the expanded trade, there were still 65 per cent of the ports with less than 1,000 tons of foreign-going shipping, and 20 per cent with none. At the other end of the scale there were now nine ports with more than 10,000 tons, and between them they accounted for 401,632 tons, or 86.5 per cent of the total. (Table 31.)

It is not enough simply to say that major ports developed where the hinterland was suitable for industrial development, for extended industrialisation would have been impossible in most cases without access to a port. For example, the old adage that Sheffield steel goods were made where coal, millstone grit and water power coincided may be perfectly true, but it should also be remembered that imported bar iron was a vital ingredient of good-quality steel in the eighteenth century. A similar argument might be used for most new industries, including — *par excellence* — cotton, which relied on the ports for the whole of its raw material and a fair proportion of its sales. There were, however, only a very limited number of ports possessing river communications adequate for the cheap transportation of bulky raw materials, and it was these places, sited on the chief river estuaries, that catered for the advances in trade experienced during both the commercial revolution and the industrial revolution. Perhaps one might go further and suggest that the pattern developed during the former was a major factor in determining the geographical location of the latter. The emergence of the cotton industry in the North was

Table 31   English ports, classified by the amount of foreign-going tonnage belonging to them, 1772 and 1785

Range of tonnage	1772				1785			
	Ports			% of total	Ports			% of total
	No.	%	Tonnage		No.	%	Tonnage	
0	16	21.6	0	0	15	20.3	0	0
1–500	28	37.8	6,559	1.9	25	33.8	5,796	1.2
501–1,000	6	8.1	3,972	1.2	9	12.2	5,465	1.2
1,001–2,000	7	9.5	9,176	2.7	8	10.8	10,463	2.3
2,001–5,000	7	9.5	21,560	6.4	3	4.1	8,841	1.9
5,001–10,000	3	4.1	20,520	6.1	5	6.8	32,197	6.9
10,000 +	7	9.5	276,556	81.7	9	12.2	401,632	86.5
Total	74		338,343*a*		74		464,394	

Note

a There is a slight discrepancy between the sum of the ports and the total as recorded in the source, viz. 338,403.

Source. Calculated from tables in P.R.O., Customs 17/1 and 17/9.

certainly the most notable feature of industrialisation, but it did not mark the beginning of economic activity north of the Trent: that had been gathering momentum at least since 1660. It was, therefore, of crucial importance that the north of the country not only possessed adequate supplies of certain raw materials and soft water which doubled as water power but was intersected by the best natural transport system in the country: the rivers flowing into the Humber and Mersey estuaries. As an element in the process of industrialisation the southern ports were useless except where they shipped materials such as copper or clay for use in the North.

The evolution of the river and canal system is discussed in chapter 4, and all that need be done here is to emphasise its importance in the growth of the major ports, and the intimate and interacting relationship between those ports and inland navigations, as much as with external navigations. Beginning with the improvement of river systems in the late seventeenth and early eighteenth centuries, which opened up the Don, Derwent, Ouse, Aire, Calder and Trent, and followed by the construction of feeder navigations such as the Soar, Erewash and Ure, Hull became easily accessible from most of central and northern England.[15] While Liverpool was less favourably served by natural waterways, the first canal in England, the Sankey Brook, was built to connect that port with the St Helens coalfield, so providing it with valuable exports and enabling it to spread its influence in the colonies and Ireland. In 1773, meanwhile, the Bridgewater canal acquired its dockside terminus (Duke's Dock), linking Liverpool and Manchester.[16] Then in the following year the Leeds–Liverpool canal was begun (though not completed until 1816), and by the end of the decade Liverpool and Hull were linked by the Grand Trunk canal, allowing them partial access to each other's hinterland. The hundreds of miles of the canal network that followed were linked with the great trunk system based on the Mersey–Humber–Severn–Thames axes. The importance of the canals (in this regard) is not that they connected industrial areas with the sea but that they linked them with existing major ports capable of handling and organising both foreign and coastal trade.

It was not simply the case that the centre of export production and import consumption was gravitating northwards with the drift of population and industry. The industrial revolution also brought about changes in the direction and composition of trade which added to or detracted from the obvious geographical advantages of ports *vis-à-vis* foreign countries, and enhanced the disparity between them. It involved, moreover, a rapid divergence in the size as well as the number of ships frequenting the various ports, leaving some quite adequately served by existing facilities while creating congestion and calling for improvements in others. The north-east ports were chiefly involved in the export of coal and the import of raw materials from northern Europe, where the long haul, often in inclement weather, encouraged large ships which also enjoyed economies of scale where bulky cargoes were concerned. However, while most ports, wherever situated and of whatever size, received small shipments of timber — usually in small foreign ships — from Scandinavia, the western ports, together with London, enjoyed a virtual monopoly of the transatlantic trades. Although London, Liverpool, Bristol and Whitehaven (because of its coal trade) were undoubtedly the leading places, a substantial number of ships were to be found passing back and forth between North America (especially the Canadian provinces) and Lancaster, Chester, Swansea, Bideford, Dartmouth, Exeter, Falmouth, Plymouth, Poole, Portsmouth and Southampton. Indeed, the Newfoundland trade, traditionally pursued by fishing interests in the South-west, was completely dominated by Bristol, Dartmouth, Exeter and Poole. These transatlantic traders were often — though not universally — large vessels, but the average tonnage of shipping in the western ports as a whole was drastically reduced by their heavy involvement with their second principal interest: trade with Ireland, which, in 1790, accounted for around a third of the tonnage entering and clearing at Liverpool, around a fifth at Bristol, over four-fifths at Chester, and no less than 98 per cent of the huge tonnage of the export trade (230,562 tons) of Whitehaven.[17] Of the eastern ports, only Newcastle and Hull had any transatlantic trade worth noting in the eighteenth and early nineteenth centuries, and none of them was actively engaged in trade with Ireland. The southern ports of Portsmouth, Southampton and Poole did play some part in long-distance foreign trade, but the remaining ports on the south coast, and those on the south-east, were extremely circumscribed in their activities. A flood of small vessels traded with France, Spain and Portugal and Dover became one of the lesser major ports in consequence; but, since the majority of them were involved chiefly with France, their activity waxed and waned for reasons beyond their control. Finally, the ports of East Anglia were engaged chiefly in trade with Holland, though Lynn and Yarmouth had contacts with most of the countries of Europe, and again ships were generally of fairly small size in consequence.

Thus, allowing for inevitable exceptions and necessary qualifications, the pattern of trade shows the majority of ports trading chiefly — and some exclusively — with those foreign countries to which they were nearest or which provided a major commodity — such as timber — that was universally demanded and transhipped with difficulty. The western ports did not generally trade eastwards or the eastern ports westwards, though naturally a ship was more likely to find its way from Devon to Europe than from East Anglia to America. However, the relationship between port, hinterland and foreign partners was not always a simple one. While almost any port could handle a direct shipment or two of goods for consumption in its immediate hinterland, large cargoes of bulky or more valuable goods were either disseminated throughout a wide hinterland or destined for re-exportation via the foreign or coastal trades. In these circumstances it mattered little where goods were first landed, and there was every incentive for merchants to break bulk in the places most readily accessible by sea and most suitable for long-distance internal distribution.

Shipping from smaller ports then gathered their crumbs at the great ports' quays.

The role of the major ports

Of the major trading centres London was clearly the chief. On the one hand she had her huge population, an excellent harbour and a favourable location for trading with all parts of the world and most ports in the country. On the other hand, she also enjoyed a unique legal position. The great desire of the Crown to regulate trade, and a corresponding petition from aspiring monopolists, had led to a situation in which, until 1813, all trade to the east of the Cape of Good Hope and west of Cape Horn was restricted to vessels of the East India Company and to the port of London. This concentration of exotic goods from India and the Far East, augmented by others from the West Indies, the Levant and Africa, was the basis of a great national emporium which secured for the capital the lion's share of both foreign and coastal trade.

The position of the East India Company in London was unique, but a roughly similar situation developed in other trades and in other ports because of the dynamic function of the merchant in the early stages of the industrial revolution. The initiation and encouragement of novel trades with undeveloped countries demanded 'connection', credit and a range of mercantile skills on a far higher plane than most of the small ports could offer. As the demand for sugar, tobacco, rum, timber, linen yarn, iron and cotton grew it was the English (or Scottish) merchant who went out in search of it, who funded development costs, gave advances against shipment, provided the ships, insured the cargoes and settled the international payments. Until well into the nineteenth century the import trades, at least, remained firmly in the hands of the great merchants; and the great merchants remained firmly in the great ports. The lines of communication were not abstractions drawn up to illustrate trade flows, but the working connections of long-established commercial centres on whose expansion and diversification the growth of the late eighteenth century was dependent. It actually mattered that merchants had connections with plantations or iron mines; that one could dispose easily of tinplate or buttons while another had access to pit props or hemp.

Nor should the influence of the ship owner be forgotten. While many places owned a few ships, the emergence of the ship owner independent of the merchant at the end of the eighteenth century tended to concentrate shipping in the larger ports where cargoes were easier to obtain (regular 'liners' were already running in some trades) and where accommodation was superior to that obtaining in the minor ports.

The extent to which trade ran through the major ports, and especially the northern ports, is clearly shown by an analysis of shipping frequenting some seventy ports in 1789−91.[18] London alone accounted still for 37 per cent of that entering and 27 per cent clearing, and the North-west and North-east together accounted for 40 and 51 per cent. The *average* tonnage entering and clearing the major ports in these regions (77,000 and 105,000) exceeded the *total* entering and clearing East Anglia, the South-east, South or Welsh ports, and only the south-west region — with Bristol making up much of its total — could compete. By comparison the average tonnage clearing from the minor ports ranged from 4,494 at the Welsh ports to no more than 330 at the south-eastern ports; the range of average tonnages entering fell between those two. While obviously these averages hide places — such as Portsmouth, Southampton and Poole — with greater activity, the fact remains that the vast majority of ports had failed to acquire a share in the mounting prosperity of English trade. so, for that matter, had Bristol, second at the beginning of the century and well down the list of major ports at the end of it, whose relative decline is one of the most notable features of mercantile history in this period. London, of course, also experienced a declining share of trade as the northern ports developed, but in her case the fact was obscured by the huge (and increasing) volume of her shipping and her large share of the more valuable trades, which, at official values, amounted to 52 per cent of national exports and 63 per cent of imports as late as 1780.[19]

Although the smaller places had little foreign trade, most of them redressed the balance to some extent by their involvement in the coastal trade. Over the country as a whole the tonnage of vessels entering from foreign parts in 1789−91 was only slightly over half of those entering coastwise, and the tonnage clearing was no more than 40 per cent, largely because of the immense importance of the coastal coal trade. The smaller places in particular had a very much bigger coastal than foreign trade: the *average* tonnage entering coastwise in the Welsh ports was greater than the *total* entering from foreign parts, and though the discrepancy was less pronounced in other regions the ratio between foreign and coastal trade ranged from 1 : 1.4 in the

North-east to 1 : 8 in East Anglia. In only one region — the North-west — was this relationship reversed: Liverpool was too isolated to sustain an extensive coastal trade, especially since Bristol and London, with equally good transatlantic connections, dominated the south-west and south coasts. In this respect there was a striking difference between Liverpool and Hull, which, with its excellent position in the middle of the east coast, was able to conduct a flourishing coastal distribution trade in the products of its hinterland and foreign trade, in return for materials, food and luxuries secured elsewhere on the coast or brought from abroad into London.[20]

The provision of port facilities

The pressure of expanding trade on existing facilities

Trade expansion, protracted as it was, had been troubling as well as pleasing merchants since the late seventeenth century. Despite extensive dredging and expensive pier-building, the ports which accommodated the expansion of trade during the commercial revolution were essentially primitive in character. By later standards their trade was slight, their ships small and their water site precarious. All that had been necessary when ports were established was a decent anchorage sheltered from the sea, preferably with a relatively steep shore on which a wooden or stone quay could easily be constructed. They followed two basic patterns. On rocky coasts with high cliffs the cove port was common, supplementing by simple artifice the advantages of natural features. However, the high cost of building and maintaining breakwaters and piers — often on exposed coasts — limited their number and their size. More significantly, perhaps, the obstacles to carriage in their immediate hinterland frustrated their merchants and hampered their growth. The manhandling of smuggled goods over sheer cliffs and steep roads is good fiction, and was doubtless profitable with highly taxed goods of great value and small bulk; but such athletic feats were no basis for a traffic in peas or pantiles. Ports of this sort were more commonly harbours of refuge, or centres for the leisurely — and seasonal — shipment of agricultural produce, than permanent hives of commerce; none was to be counted among the great ports of the industrial revolution, though they might, of course, be suitable for mineral shipment. By contrast, the best place for a port was inside a river mouth which provided shelter from storms, safety from attack and suitable banks for the erection of

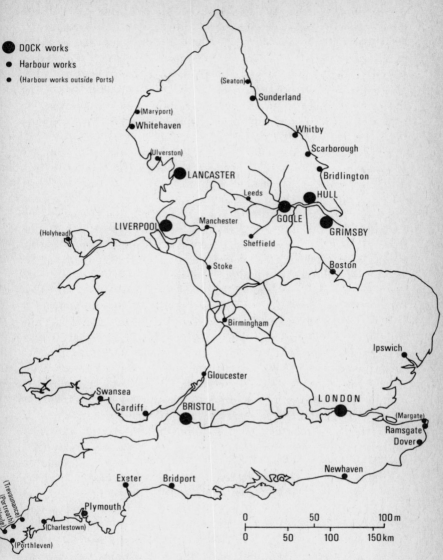

DOCK works

● Harbour works

• (Harbour works outside Ports)

(Seaton)
Sunderland
(Maryport)
Whitehaven
Whitby
Scarborough
(Ulverston)
LANCASTER
Bridlington
Leeds
HULL
(Holyhead)
LIVERPOOL
Manchester
GOOLE
Sheffield
GRIMSBY
Stoke
Boston
Birmingham
Ipswich
Gloucester
Swansea
Cardiff
BRISTOL
LONDON
(Margate)
Ramsgate
Dover
Newhaven
Exeter
Bridport
(Trevaunance)
(Portreath)
(Hayle)
Plymouth
(Charlestown)
(Porthleven)

0	50	100 m
0	50	100	150 km

15   English and Welsh Ports *c.* 1830, showing dock and major harbour works, and
principal canal linkages.

wharves and warehouses; ports with the greatest chance of success were those where the advantages of a safe harbour on the one hand were augmented by those deriving from lengthy internal river communications on the other, or where a better than average position and commercial structure encouraged a major entrepot function. Given adequate access to landward and seaward, a very considerable amount of traffic could in fact pass through an unimproved harbour, though obviously there was an intimate relationship between a port's advantages in terms of internal communications and water site and the type of goods which might profitably pass through it. The extent to which they dealt in wine, wool and corn tends to obscure the extent to which ports specialised from an early date in the goods demanded or produced in their hinterland and entered into trade at the point where improvements in the transport linkages (among other things) made their movement profitable. Apart from the decayed ports, it is doubtful if factors within the ports themselves were of much weight in this regard until the middle of the eighteenth century, when changes in the size of ships and the volume and composition of trade raised problems which in many places called forth the engineer to improve on the inadequacies of previously under-utilised natural harbours.

These problems arose at different times in different places as new trades demanded new facilities, and at the same time the growth of seasonal trades involving the periodic laying up of ships caused special problems, particularly in London and Hull, leading to the construction of the Howland 'dock' on the Thames at the beginning of the century and to proposals for similar works at Hull — and Bristol — in the 1750s.[21] But influences in favour of harbour improvements generally faced the same questions: who should organise the work, and who pay for it? In most of the ancient ports the town government was also the port authority, enjoying taxes on trade but lacking the power or the inclination to embark on costly works for which engineering competence was still unproved. Corporations were not universally bad, but more often than not the only way forward was for harbour work to be taken over by a special public Trust. Even so, when trade had for generations been conducted cheaply in unimproved conditions it was in no one's interest to indulge in expensive works before they were absolutely necessary, and, whoever organised the work and collected the inevitable — and usually resented — tolls to pay for it, there was still the major difficulty of identifying, in the midst of trade cycles, wars and mercantile pessimism, the moment when acceptable temporary congestion plunged into permanent chaos. And finally, amid conflicting private interests protecting property values and prime trading sites, and old-established merchants objecting to expensive new works for the benefit of unnecessary new merchants, there were always plenty of obstructionists whose delaying tactics discouraged the timid and acted as a powerful drag on port improvements. In view of the physical and human obstacles to be over-come, and the pioneering nature of much of the work, the success of the major ports in coping with the trade of the industrial revolution is not only remarkable but also deserving of much greater recognition than it usually receives.

The mineral ports

For the sake of convenience the ports may be divided into three main groups: the mineral exporters, the harbours of refuge, and the general trade ports.[22] Mineral traffic was newer than the port system, and deposits of coal, copper or china clay were not always discovered near existing ports or easily improved natural harbours. In this respect the northern coalfield owed a great deal of its prosperity to its fortuitous proximity to the Tyne and Wear, particularly the latter, whose im-provement under the River Wear Commission after 1717 made Sunderland the chief coal port of the country for both foreign and coastal shipments, and at the same time enabled Sunderland to become one of the chief importing centres of the east coast. However, while every possible natural harbour was used, the mineral trades were unique in demanding — and obtaining — the construction of new ports or, more commonly, of new facilities in old-established ports. For while industrial goods and agricultural produce were exported through established routes along old or improved rivers and roads, the economics of coal transport made it not only necessary but profitable to invest in completely new works. The most spectacular in terms of trade volume was undoubtedly at Whitehaven, a place of no conse-quence before the Lowthers built piers there to facilitate the opening of their coalfield in Cumberland by exporting to Ireland. In the early eighteenth century Whitehaven harbour was handed over to a trust to maintain it, and a small harbour was built at Parton by a similar trust; by the middle of the century work was also in progress on the building of Maryport, and a small harbour was constructed at Ulverstone in the 1790s. Over on the east coast, the eighteenth cen-tury also witnessed the construction or improvement of small harbours at Blyth and Seaton Sluice serving the Northumberland coalfield, though the most spectacular, before the coming of the railways, was probably Seaham Harbour, constructed in the 1830s as a private venture by a local coal proprietor. In Wales a similar interaction between coalfield and port was already taking place in Swansea during the later eighteenth century, and would eventually transform other places. In Cornwall copper played a similar role in encouraging new harbour works at Portreath in the 1760s and Trevaunance in the 1790s, while Charlestown was built at the end of the century for the china clay trade.[23]

It was far easier to improve a port for coal than for general trade. Because ships commonly entered in ballast, and cargoes were easily assembled, turn-round times were short and the pressure of rising tonnage on harbour space was consequently less dramatic. Extensive warehousing was unnecessary. Indeed, improvements to river quays and piers were all that was needful at Sunderland and Whitehaven to accommodate a tonnage of shipping which in Liverpool or London demanded the expenditure of huge sums and the application of elaborate engineering skills. A single proprietor could build a coal port, but a dock system was beyond the means of the richest merchants.

Harbours of refuge

Harbours of refuge are usually thought of in connection with the coal trade, because they were most commonly used by colliers on the London run. In recognition of this fact Whitby, Bridlington and Scarborough each had parliamentary authority for levying dues on coal shipped from the northern ports, and built or maintained harbours that greatly exceeded the demands of local trade. In the Southeast the dangers facing ships entering and leaving the Channel was of even greater concern to London merchants, and led to the construction of a primitive but effective harbour at Ramsgate in the 1750s. In a constant battle with nature, something over £600,000 was spent between 1750 and 1816, making this place (which does not even appear in the customs list of ports) the most expensive and lavishly supported harbour in the country. If it made no direct contribution to industrialisation its indirect influence was doubtless great: no fewer than 40,000 vessels sheltered there between 1780 and 1830.[24] Improvements at Margate, after 1809, were less effective.

General trade ports: harbour improvements

The general ports were diverse in the composition, size and rate of growth of their trade. A few of them fell into disuse, but most experienced a growth in activity, and at least fifty responded by improving their facilities. There were few so fortunate as Newcastle, Lynn and Yarmouth on the east coast and Southampton on the south, where a very considerable trade could thrive without alteration to their harbour. Most ports on small and slow-flowing rivers experienced difficulties in the late seventeenth century as expanding trade rendered long-standing inadequacies intolerable. On the east coast in particular, silt or sand ruined the haven at Grimsby and threatened Sunderland, Boston and others, and while this problem was less noticeable on other coasts they were not entirely exempt, as Exeter and Chester found to their cost. In some places the answer lay in 'cleansing' the haven, as at Chester in the 1740s and Boston in the 1760s, and in others a new channel was cut, as at Grimsby (unsuccessfully) and Exeter at the beginning of the century and at Ipswich and Stockton at its end. But more commonly ports resorted to piers and breakwaters to deflect sand-carrying waves and concentrate the internal scour by narrowing the channel. Sunderland is the best example of what might be accomplished by such means, though the great harbours of refuge on the east coast and the diminutive ports of the south also relied on piers. The bigger places such as Dover and Ramsgate developed elaborate piers almost enclosing harbours fit for a fleet; the poorer places made do with a single pier at which occasional vessels might shelter or trade, and where fishing boats were commoner than merchantmen. On the whole, ports dependent on this device had no long-term future as a commercial centre. Piers constructed by man to control the elements fought either a losing or a ruinously expensive battle, and most small ports were subject to fluctuations in water depth which could detain vessels for days or even months. Indeed, one factor diverting trade to the major ports was the limited number of places where large vessels could rest in safety: the size as well as the number of vessels frequenting a port was of crucial importance in determining the nature and scale of improvements in the places that were to survive.

Whether ships frequenting the southern ports were small because they traded with France, or because larger vessels had been rejected and sent elsewhere, is a matter for debate, though the former seems most likely. There were certainly substantial differences between the ships in the different regions. The average size of ships entering the

south-east, south and Welsh ports was only half that of those entering London and the North-east, while East Anglia, the South-west
and North-west fell roughly between the highest (North-east) and
lowest (South-east) regions. The differences between the major ports
were even more marked: Hull had the highest average, at 197 tons,
in 1791, and Dover the lowest, at 55. But averages hide the very large
ships in London and Liverpool for which a permanent depth of water
was regarded by the end of the century as essential.

General trade ports: the building of wet docks

In the absence of permanent deep water in the natural estuaries of the
major ports, fleets of larger ships could be catered for only in artificial
docks similar to the Howland dock for empty ships built by George
Sorrocold and Thomas Steers. Thus when the rapid growth of her
transatlantic trade placed an intolerable strain on her Pool, Liverpool
called Steers in as adviser, abandoned her tidal frontage, and in 1715
opened the first commercial dock in the world by impounding the
Pool.[25] Here vessels could float at all stages of the tide, be protected
against damage, and load and unload in more convenient and orderly
fashion. But it was not long before ships seeking access exceeded the
dock's capacity, and there began a cycle of congestion and dock
building which lasted almost to the present (see fig. 16). Salthouse
dock was opened in 1753, George's in 1771, Duke's (at the terminus
of the Bridgewater Canal) in 1773, King's in 1788 and Queen's in 1796.
Between them they cost around £150,000, contained approximately
twenty-eight acres of water space, and allowed the tonnage of vessels
frequenting the port to rise from less than 20,000 in 1700 to 450,000
in 1800. The French wars had a more serious effect on dock-building
than on shipping in Liverpool, with the result that congestion increased around the turn of the century, and when dock construction
began again, in 1811, it was carried on with an enthusiasm, borne of
the cotton boom, which was quite unprecedented. By 1836 a further
eight docks (Canning, Union, Prince's, Clarence, Brunswick,
Waterloo, Victoria and Trafalgar) had been constructed, to add
almost seventy acres to the dock estate, which now stretched for two
and a half miles along the Mersey, and which in 1840 received almost
2½ million tons of shipping.[26]

Liverpool was undoubtedly in a class of its own as leading port of
the industrial revolution, but others played their part, and chief of
them was Hull. Her previously adequate haven became hopelessly

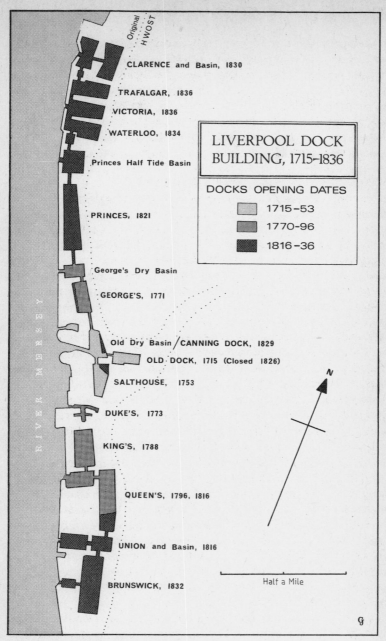

Original H W O S T

CLARENCE and Basin, 1830

TRAFALGAR, 1836

VICTORIA, 1836

WATERLOO, 1834

Princes Half Tide Basin

PRINCES, 1821

George's Dry Basin

GEORGE'S, 1771

Old Dry Basin / CANNING DOCK, 1829

OLD DOCK, 1715 (Closed 1826)

SALTHOUSE, 1753

DUKE'S, 1773

KING'S, 1788

QUEEN'S, 1796, 1816

UNION and Basin, 1816

BRUNSWICK, 1832

RIVER MERSEY

LIVERPOOL DOCK
BUILDING, 1715-1836

DOCKS OPENING DATES

1715-53

1770-96

1816-36

N

Half a Mile

G

16 Liverpool dock building, 1715–1836

congested when the importation of raw materials from the Baltic and the exportation of English manufactures expanded rapidly in the middle of the century, and after serious delays of the sort to be found in most places involved in dock-building her first dock was opened in 1778.[27] At something over nine acres it was the biggest so far constructed, and was materially different from Liverpool's docks in supplementing rather than replacing the large existing harbour, which still accommodated the coastal trade. Yet it was inadequate before it was opened, and within a decade the tonnage paying dues had doubled. A second large dock, having been long delayed by local wrangles and war, was opened in 1809, and a third in 1829.

These unfortunate delays in Hull — and subsequent troubles lasting into the present century — resulted partly from a radical innovation which turned sour. In contrast to Liverpool, where the docks were built by a public trust, Hull had chosen to hand over the work to a private company consisting initially of public-spirited merchants eager to preserve the port, and eventually of rentiers determined to preserve their income. Such companies became the norm for contemporary transport undertakings: they invested in return for monopoly rights to tolls intended to yield interest and maintain the works, and consequently proved unsatisfactory for progressively extending them. Further docks in Hull — which had not been envisaged — were resisted by the dock company because they would involve large expenditure without a proportionate rise in income; and docks which the company rejected could not be built by other bodies. The solution was substantial public subsidy of a private company, and the situation was decidedly unsatisfactory. But the difficulty was finding an alternative to private companies where public authorities could not or would not act, and nowhere was the problem greater than in London.

Congestion on the Thames had been growing as elsewhere, but it was not this alone which provoked action towards the end of the eighteenth-century.[28] The need for more Legal Quays and for secure and bonded warehouses was a telling argument put forward by various pro-dock pressure groups in the early 1790s. The trade of London, however, was so immense that no one authority — and certainly not the City fathers — was able to control the situation, yet to follow the example of Hull (and also of Grimsby and Glasson, where docks were built in the 1790s) and grant monopoly rights to a single company would have been quite inequitable: no single company could have offered accommodation to all the vessels seeking it, or pleased the supporters of diverse trades. The compromise eventually arrived at was founded on the desire for specialised warehousing, and was to attach monopoly (for twenty-one years) not to individual ships paying dues but to specific trades. In other words the way was opened for a number of separate monopolistic dock companies formed along the same lines as the Hull Dock Company. Thus in 1803 the West India Dock of over sixty acres was opened, with rights over West Indian trade; the London Dock was opened in 1805 with rights over tobacco, rice, wine and brandy (except from the West Indies); the East India Dock was opened in 1806 by the East India Company for its own trade; and to the south of the river the Commercial Dock Company, incorporated in 1810, took over and improved the old Howland dock, while the East Country Dock Company constructed a dock of similar name (fig. 17). Both these last were for the Baltic trade — chiefly timber — and both were without the sort of monopoly granted to the three earlier companies. Monopolies of all sorts were under attack as the nineteenth century wore on, and not surprisingly the rights of the original three companies were not confirmed when they came up for renewal. The immediate result was the creation in 1825 of the St Katharine's Dock Company to build a dock between London Dock and the Tower of London for general traffic, much to the annoyance of the London Dock Company, which claimed that there was no need for the dock and built a seven-acre extension of its own in case there was.

Thus by 1830 London had acquired a system of approximately 170 acres and costing well over £7 million. Swann has estimated that the total dock space in England by that time was around 397 acres,[29] so London appears to have constructed just under half the national total, while Liverpool, Bristol (with a seventy-acre floating harbour completed in 1809 by the Bristol Dock Company) and the three Humber ports — Hull, Grimsby and Goole — accounting for most of the rest. (The minor work at Glasson, Lancaster, was of no account.) Undoubtedly the major ports had undergone a revolution of considerable proportions since 1775, when the only commercial docks were at Liverpool and together contained no more than fourteen acres of water. However, while much trade growth took place before 1800, the bulk of the dock work was concentrated after that date, when money was fairly easily raised, and when the greatest of dock-builders, John Rennie, had perfected the art and inspired a generation of dock and harbour engineers whose problems, it might be suggested, were

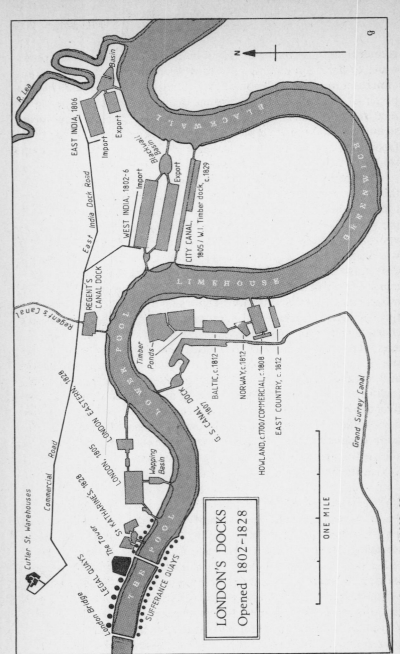

N

LONDON'S DOCKS
Opened 1802–1828

R. Lea

EAST INDIA, 1806

Basin

Import

Export

Export

WEST INDIA, 1802–6

Import

BLACKWALL Basin

BLACKWALL

East India Dock Road

REGENT'S CANAL DOCK

CITY CANAL, 1805 / W.I. Timber dock, c.1829

Regent's Canal

GREENWICH

LIMEHOUSE

London Eastern, 1828

Commercial Road

LONDON, 1805

ST. KATHARINE'S, 1828

The Tower

Cutler St. Warehouses

LEGAL QUAYS

London Bridge

THE POOL

SUFFERANCE QUAYS

Wapping Basin

LOWER POOL

Timber Ponds

G.S. CANAL DOCK, 1807

BALTIC, c.1812

NORWAY, c.1812

HOWLAND, c.1700 / COMMERCIAL, c.1808

EAST COUNTRY, c.1812

Grand Surrey Canal

ONE MILE

17 London docks opened 1802–28

greater than those facing the canal-builders.[30] However, these docks were, to a certain extent, built to offer more satisfactory accommodation to existing shipping; unfortunately for their builders and potential users they were completed at the end of a long period of relative stability in ship construction and design. Within a few years steamships had rendered most of this first generation of docks old-fashioned, and ports had to begin supplementing them with steam-ship docks.

The opening of docks did not end the old way of working, even in the major ports. Specialisation of function usually left the coasters to fend as best they could outside the docks, and in London and Hull, particularly, the rivers continued to burst with activity. Coastal trade approximately trebled in volume between 1791 and 1841, though this was partly because of the reclassification of Irish trade. Fortunately coasters still did not require expensive facilities, and coal — which many of them carried — did not require secure warehousing. The movement of foreign trade into docks usually left them with enough space in which to operate, though increasingly in the major ports the coasters also endeavoured to enter the docks. The balance was re-dressed to some extent with the arrival of the paddle steamer, which was so awkwardly shaped as to discourage docking. While port authorities argued that owners should build vessels to suit the docks (or rather the locks), steamers were increasingly accommodated at river quays and involved in rapid turn-round operation which allowed ports in the 1820s and 1830s to increase their trade rapidly without resort to dock-building. Moreover many of the unimproved ports were able to benefit in this way when coastal steamers could be persuaded to visit them.

Wet docks and trade expansion

About the expansion of foreign trade during and after the period of dock building there can be no doubt. Over the country as a whole foreign-going shipping entering and clearing each grew by a factor of 2.8 between 1789–91 and 1841, though the various regions per-formed differently.[31] As might be expected, the North-east and North-west grew from 40 to 49 per cent of entries and from 51 to 59 per cent of clearances, while East Anglia, the South-east and South-west all declined. Among the major ports, the tonnage entering and clearing at Hull grew by factors of 3.4 and 4.9, at Liverpool by 4.4 and 4.5, and at Newcastle by 8.4 and 6.0. By contrast, Bristol suffered an absolute decline of between 5 and 10 per cent, while London's shipping, despite the extensive dock-building, grew less than the national total, by factors of 2.1 and 2.3.

As has been indicated already, this growth of shipping was not entirely dependent on the construction of dock or harbour works. The two major ports with dock works in 1791 — Liverpool and Hull — handled 23.2 per cent of the tonnage entering the country from foreign parts, and the four ports with substantial docks in 1841 — Liverpool, Hull, Bristol and London — took 38.6 per cent, which still left a vast amount making use of less sophisticated facilities. Moreover half the available dock space was in London, which by 1841 had less than a third of national shipping entering or clearing, and where it was not used for traffic directly related to the industrialising regions of the country, though it may have been indirectly involved through the canal linkages and coastal trade. It would therefore seem wisest not to overemphasise the general role of docks during the period under review. The spare capacity of unimproved facilities certainly accommodated a large proportion of increasing trade, especially coastal trade, and small places could advance both coastal and foreign trade in the service of their own limited hinterlands, though even the smaller places — or at least some fifty of them — had recourse to harbour works from time to time.

However, while docks were clearly unnecessary for the considerable trade growth diffused around the country, it is important to stress their vital contribution to the performance of the major ports. Without them (given the constraints of the internal transport system and the need for mercantile enterprise and initiative) it is difficult to envisage how the industrial heartland of England could have developed as it did. So long as internal transport depended on rivers and canals there was little danger of traffic being diverted from the major ports, especially since they already occupied the prime water sites. Those traders in the eighteenth century who believed they could steal a march on their fellows by finding new and cheaper ports were disappointed. For example, the landowners who built the huge floating harbour at Grimsby after 1796 expected to fill it with ships attracted by cheaper dues from Hull, but the range of services offered by the latter was a greater attraction, and Grimsby had nothing to offer in terms of contact with the hinterland.[32] From the point of view of national trade, Grimsby Haven Company was a misdirection of resources which would have been better spent elsewhere. Unfortunately such profitable knowledge is most commonly learned by hindsight. On the other hand Goole successfully competed with Hull because her dock, opened in 1828 by the Aire & Calder Canal Company, was directly connected with an important internal waterway system.[33] The similar decision of the Stockton & Darlington Railway Company to by-pass Stockton and build a railway port at Port Darlington encouraged developments by several railway companies (including a further development at Grimsby), but this group of new ports played no significant part in the trade of the country during the industrial revolution.

There was, therefore, a threat hanging over the major ports at the end of our period. Although they had served well during the past fifty years, they had been almost choked by their own success, and it is doubtful whether the building of small-scale docks for hosts of small vessels could have continued for much longer without bringing chaos to even the best organised ports. Waiting in the wings were the railway companies, eager to avoid the confusion of enclosed docks, with their inadequate quay space, by applying the most advanced engineering skills to new sites. What in the end relieved the situation and saved the major ports from their potential rivals was the quite sudden and continuous increase in the size of ships in the second quarter of the nineteenth century, which brought economies of scale and demanded larger docks which were best provided in the major ports. It was this new phase of dock building, attracting the railways into the ports, which finally separated the major ports from the rest so far as their role in the economy was concerned, and, incidentally, secured the triumph of the dock over the harbour.

The docks and improved harbours of the industrial revolution, like other features of the transport system, were developed under a particular set of influences (such as volume of trade and size of ship) which changed over time, and works which had carried the brunt of trade at the start of the industrial revolution were already moving towards obsolescence (at least for the purposes for which they were built) at its end. Nevertheless the fact that they were soon to be overtaken by new works more appropriate for the 'workshop of the world' should not be allowed to detract from the important contribution made to economic life in this period by the 'old' docks at Bristol, Liverpool, London and Hull, and by the harbours of Tyne and Wear. It was not simply that a number of mercantile communities had applied their wealth and expertise in the service of industrialisation. The scale on which new and elaborate engineering skills were brought in to solve previously insurmountable practical problems would seem to justify the claim that the docks at least were themselves part of a momentous technical revolution.

Notes

1 See R. Jarvis, 'The appointment of ports', *Economic History Review*, XI, 1958–59, pp. 460–3.

2 E. E. Hoon, *The Organization of the English Customs System, 1696–1786*, new edn., David & Charles, Newton Abbot, 1968, pp. 168–9, lists twenty-two 'additional' ports, 1696–1786, but her earlier list is defective, omitting, for example, the Welsh ports, Gloucester (a head port) and Scarborough (a major ship-owning port). But in any case, none of her 'additional' ports played any part in the trade of the industrial revolution region, and would not affect the case that no new ports were created to accommodate it before 1800.

3 *Ibid.*, p. 125.

4 J. A. Chartres, *Internal Trade in England, 1500–1700*, Studies in Economic and Social History, Macmillan, London, 1977, chapter 3.

5 T. S. Willan, *The English Coasting Trade, 1600–1750*, Manchester University Press, 1938, pp. xiv–xvi.

6 The cumbersome procedure is described in Hoon, *English Customs*, pp. 245–64.

7 R. Davis, *The Industrial Revolution and British Overseas Trade*, Leicester University Press, 1979, pp. 77 ff.

8 This survey is based on R. Davis, 'English foreign trade, 1660–1700', *Economic History Review*, VII, 1954, and 'English foreign trade, 1700–1774', *Economic History Review*, XV, 1962.

9 Davis, 'English foreign trade, 1700–74', p. 289.

10 R. Davis, *The Industrial Revolution*, p. 15.

11 Based on tables in B. R. Mitchell and P. Deane, *Abstract of British Historical Statistics*, Cambridge University Press, 1962, p. 282.

12 E. B. Schumpeter, *English Overseas Trade Statistics, 1697–1808*, Clarendon Press, Oxford, 1960, tables xvi and xvii.

13 Mitchell and Deane, *Statistics*, pp. 289–90.

14 Calculations based on tables in Public Record Office, Customs 17/1 for 1772 and 17/9 for 1785.

15 G. Jackson, *Hull in the Eighteenth Century*, Oxford University Press, London, 1972, chapter II.

16 T. C. Barker, 'Lancashire coal, Cheshire salt and the rise of Liverpool', *Transactions of the Historic Society of Lancashire and Cheshire*, CIII, 1951, and F. E. Hyde, *Liverpool and the Mersey*, David & Charles, Newton Abbot, 1971, chapter II.

17 Calculations based on P.R.O., Customs 17/12.

18 Calculations based on P.R.O., Customs 17/11 and 17/13.

19 Schumpeter, *Overseas Trade*, p. 9.

20 Jackson, *Hull*, chapter IV.

21 It should not, of course, be forgotten that in a good harbour the cheapest mode of 'improvement' was simply to relieve pressure on its expensive handling facilities and quays by removing light (empty) ships; the Howland dock, and

the Seamills dock on the Avon about which little is known, were variations on this theme. The Brunswick dock, built at Blackwall after 1789, was similarly not a commercial dock but a fitting-out basin. See J. G. Broodbank, *History of the Port of London*, O'Connor, London, 1921, I, pp. 67–70.

22 The best general survey is probably still D. J. Owen, *The Ports of the United Kingdom*, Allman, London, 1939. The larger places are discussed at length in J. Bird, *The Major Seaports of the United Kingdom*, Hutchinson, 1963.

23 Details of harbour and dock building are in D. Swann's pioneering article 'The pace and progress of port improvement in England, 1660–1830', *Yorkshire Bulletin of Economic and Social Research*, XII, 1960. Some of the new mineral harbours, such as Seaton, Maryport and those in Cornwall, did not become legal ports during our period but were supervised from their nearest port; they did not handle dutiable goods, and did not engage in 'normal' trade. (See fig. 15.) Two interesting articles dealing with Cornish 'ports' are C. H. Ward-Jackson, 'The ships of the port of Fowey at the turn of the eighteenth century', and D. M. Trethowan, 'Porthleven harbour: its commercial growth and decline, 1811–1958', in H. E. S. Fisher, *Ports and Shipping in the South West*, University of Exeter, 1970.

24 Swann, 'Pace and progress', p. 37.

25 Hyde, *Liverpool*, pp. 13–14.

26 *Ibid.*, p. 247.

27 Jackson, *Hull*, chapter X, *passim*.

28 C. Capper, *The Port and Trade of London*, London, 1862, pp. 144–7, largely following P. Colquhoun, *A Treatise on the Commerce and Police of the River Thames*, London, 1800, *passim*, and P. Colquhoun, *A Treatise on the Police of the Metropolis*, London, 1796, chapter III.

29 Swann, 'Pace and progress', p. 38.

30 A list of engineers and their work is in D. Swann, 'The engineers of English port improvement, 1660–1830', *Transport History*, I, 1968.

31 Figures for 1841 are in *P.P.*, 1842 (409), XXXIX, 624.

32 G. Jackson, *Grimsby and the Haven Company, 1796–1846*, Borough Libraries Committee, Grimsby, 1971, *passim*, and 'Port building on the Humber, 1770–1850: a survey of local motivation', *Bulletin of Economic Research*, XXIII, 1971.

33 B. F. Duckham, *The Yorkshire Ouse*, David & Charles, Newton Abbot, 1967, chapter 5.

BIBLIOGRAPHY

The turnpike trusts

General works
The three classic treatments of the turnpike trusts are S. and B. Webb's *English Local Government: the Story of the King's Highway*, London, 1913, and chapters in the same authors' *English Local Government: Statutory Authorities for Special Purposes*, London, 1922, and W. T. Jackman's *The Development of Transportation in Modern England*, Cambridge, 1916 (repr. 1962). Although soundly based on contemporary sources and parliamentary papers, the authors did not have access to trust documents. The first account to use these documents on a national level is W. Albert, *The Turnpike Road System in England, 1663–1840*, Cambridge, 1972. More recently E. Pawson, an historical geographer, has added *Transport and Economy: the Turnpike Roads of Eighteenth Century Britain*, London, 1977.

Local studies
There are a considerable number of local studies, of varying quality. Perhaps the best is K. A. MacMahon, *Roads and Traffic in Eastern Yorkshire*, East Yorkshire Local History Series, No. 18, 1964. L. A. Williams, *Road Transport in Cumbria in the Nineteenth Century*, London, 1975, is another useful and scholarly study. A. Cossons's numerous articles are primarily descriptive, containing lists of local turnpike Acts: *The Turnpike Roads of Nottinghamshire*, Historical Association leaflet 97, London, 1934; 'The turnpike roads of Warwickshire', *Transactions of the Birmingham Archaeological Society*, LXIV, 1946; 'The turnpike roads of Northamptonshire, with the Soke of Peterborough', *Northamptonshire Past and Present*, I, 1950; 'The turnpike roads of Norfolk', *Norfolk Archaeology*, XXX, 1952. Other local works include J. Scott, 'The turnpike roads of Derbyshire', *Derbyshire Miscellany*, 1973, F. G. Emmison, *The Turnpike Roads and Tollgates of Bedfordshire*, Bedfordshire Historical Record Society, 33, 1936, and G. H. Tupling, 'The Turnpike Trusts of Lancashire', *Memoirs and Proceedings of the Manchester Literary and Philosophical Society*, XCIV, 1953; M. J. Freeman, 'Turnpikes and their traffic: the example of southern Hampshire', *Transactions of the Institute of British Geographers*, new ser., IV, 1979, pp. 415–16.

Individual trusts
There are a few useful accounts of individual trusts, including F. A. Bailey, 'Minutes of the Trustees of the Turnpike Roads from Liverpool to Prescot, St. Helens, Warrington and Ashton in Makesfield 1725–1789', *Transactions of the Historical Society of Lancashire and Cheshire*, LXXXVIII and LXXXIX; P. L. Payne, 'The Bermondsey, Rotherhithe and Deptford turnpike, 1776–1810', *Journal of Transport History*, II, 1956, and J. H. Chandler, *The Amesbury Turnpike Trust*, South Wiltshire Industrial Archaeology Society, Historical Monograph, No. 4, March 1979. W. Albert,

'The Metropolis Roads Commissions as attempts at turnpike trust reform', *Transport History*, IV, 1971, considers the formation of the large London trust in the 1820s, and the same author (ed. with P. D. A. Harvey), *Portsmouth and Sheet Turnpike Commissioners' Minute Book, 1711–1754*, Portsmouth Record Series No. 2, 1973, provides the only published complete example of this type of document.

The road builders
This topic is fairly well served, although all the works are on nineteenth-century improvers. Thomas Telford's career is considered in A. Gibb, *The Story of Telford: the Rise of Civil Engineering*, London, 1935, and his activities on the Holyhead Road are discussed by M. Hughes, 'Telford, Parnell and the Great Irish Road', *Journal of Transport History*, VI, 1964. The other Scottish road builder, J. L. McAdam, has recently been the subject of a biography by W. J. Reader, *Macadam: the McAdam Family and the Turnpike Roads, 1798–1861*, London, 1980. There is also an account of his activity in the West Country in R. H. Spiro junior's 'John Loudon McAdam in Somerset and Dorset', *Notes and Queries for Somerset and Dorset*, XXVII, Part 262, No. 64, 1956, and of his son James in H. C. F. Lansberry, 'James McAdam and the St Albans Turnpike Trust', *Journal of Transport History*, VII, 1965.

Other
There are two works which address themselves to the question of popular opposition to the turnpike trusts. D. Williams, *The Rebecca Riots: a Study in Agrarian Discontent*, Cardiff, 1955, and W. Albert, 'Popular opposition to turnpike trusts in early eighteenth century England', *Journal of Transport History*, new ser., V, 1979. For probably the most informative contemporary account of the turnpike trusts in the early eighteenth century see D. Defoe, *A Tour through the whole Island of Great Britain*, London, 1962. E. Gay, 'Arthur Young on English roads', *Quarterly Journal of Economics*, XLI, 1927, gives a useful quantitative assessment of Young's comments on the condition of turnpike roads.
W. Albert

Road transport
No separate bibliography is included for this chapter, since all the important literature available at the time of writing has been cited in the notes. However, important research is proceeding in this area, and readers should consult the bibliographies published regularly in the *Journal of Transport History* for guidance to subsequently published work.
J. A. Chartres and G. L. Turnbull

Canals and river navigations
Although the scholarly literature of the history of the canal age cannot rival in bulk that inspired even by early railway development, it is still quite appreciable in quantity. The possible list of references has therefore had to be pruned. Regretfully articles published in the *Journal* of the Railway and Canal Historical Society have been omitted, and a number too which have appeared in local history publications. Ultimately selection is arbitrary but within the limitations of space this bibliography is intended to be reasonably comprehensive.

Contemporary works

A few contemporary books on inland waterways retain some usefulness for the serious enquirer, particularly the lengthy (though not always accurate) compilation of essential facts by J. Priestley, *Historical Account of the Navigable Rivers, Canals, and Railways throughout Great Britain*, London, 1831, reprinted with an introduction by W. H. Chaloner by Cass in 1967. Of lesser moment, though still interesting for its enthusiastic reactions to canal-building, is John Phillips, *A General History of Inland Navigation, Foreign and Domestic*, London, 3rd edn., 1795. The poorer though updated fifth edition of 1805 has been reprinted by David & Charles, Newton Abbot, 1970. (See also W. H. Chaloner, 'John Phillips: surveyor and writer on canals', *Transport History*, V, 1972.) An even earlier reference still worth consulting is Anon. (Thomas Bentley?), *The History of Inland Navigations*, London, 1766, 1769 and 1779.

General histories

of British inland waterways have multiplied considerably since 1950, when the only modern reference was L. T. C. Rolt's lively *The Inland Waterways of England*, Allen & Unwin, 1950. Charles Hadfield, doyen of canal historians, has produced an excellent overall survey: *British Canals: an Illustrated History*, David & Charles, Newton Abbot, 4th edn., 1969, while several chapters of his world-ranging *The Canal Age*, David & Charles, Newton Abbot, 1968, are very relevant to the period covered in the present book. Scotland now possesses its own relatively recent general assessment in Jean Lindsay, *The Canals of Scotland*, David & Charles, Newton Abbot, 1968. Ulster is adequately covered by W. A. McCutcheon, *The Canals of the North of Ireland*, David & Charles, Dawlish, 1965. Welsh canals form the main subject of Charles Hadfield's *The Canals of South Wales and the Border*, 2nd edn., David & Charles, Newton Abbot, 1967, and are of course exclusively dealt with by Ian L. Wright, *Canals in Wales*, Bradford Barton, Truro, 1977.

Engineering and construction

The engineering and constructional aspects of river and canal projects have received special attention from A. W. Skempton, 'The engineers of the English river navigations, 1620–1760', *Transactions of the Newcomen Society*, XXIX, 1953, and 'Canals and river navigations before 1750' in Charles Singer *et al.* (eds.), *A History of Technology*, III, Cambridge, 1957. A reasonably popular yet highly informative general account is supplied by Anthony Burton's *The Canal Builders*, Eyre Methuen, London, 1972. Some of the many troubles engendered by poor contractors are described by S. R. Broadbridge, 'John Pinkerton and the Birmingham Canals', *Transport History*, IV, 1971, who also deals with a perennial difficulty of canal engineering in his 'Water supply on the Birmingham Canal Navigation, 1769–1830', *Industrial Archaeology*, X, 3, 1973. The largest civil engineering partnership of the canal age is reviewed by H. W. Dickinson, 'Joliffe and Banks, contractors', *Transactions of the Newcomen Society*, XII, 1931–32. Other useful references in this general sphere are H. Clegg, 'The third Duke of Bridgewater's canal works in Manchester', *Transactions of the Lancashire and Cheshire Antiquarian Society*, 65, 1955; Humphrey Household, 'Early engineering on the Thames and Severn Canal', *Transactions of the Newcomen Society*, XXVII, 1949–51; B. Trinder, who looks at a famous example of canal innovation in *The Hay Inclined Plane*, Ironbridge Gorge Museum Trust, 1978; and Robert Harris's admirably illustrated *Canals and their Architecture*, Hugh Evelyn, London, 1969. A useful introduction, with brief gazetteer, to the industrial archaeology of canals is represented by L. T. C. Rolt, *Navigable Waterways*, Longman, London, 1969. Much information on canal construction can also be extracted from the biographies of the great engineers. Samual Smiles's *Lives of the Engineers*, 2nd edn., 5 vols., 1878, must always remain a readable, though occasionally infuriating, classic. Modern studies include C. T. G. Boucher, *John Rennie, 1761–1821*, Manchester University Press, 1963; L. T. C. Rolt, *Thomas Telford*, Allen & Unwin, London, 1958 (which almost supersedes Sir Alexander Gibb, *The Story of Telford: the Rise of Civil Engineering*, London, 1936); B. Bracegirdle and Patricia H. Miles, *Thomas Telford*, David & Charles, Newton Abbot, 1973; and Charles Hadfield and A. W. Skempton, *William Jessop, Engineer*, David & Charles, Newton Abbot, 1978, a book which at last does justice to John Smeaton's great pupil. Charles Hadfield's 'James Green as canal engineer', *Journal of Transport History*, I, 1953, outlines the achievement of a lesser known though still important figure, while Hugh Malet's 'Brindley and canals, 1716–1772', *History Today*, XXIII, 4, 1972, deals in a popular fashion with one of the founding fathers of canal construction. C. T. G. Boucher writes at greater length, though possibly a little over-enthusiastically, in *James Brindley, Engineer*, Goose, Folkstone, 1968. Some of the earliest and most local of Brindley's canal works are covered in A. G. Banks and R. B. Schofield, *Brindley at Wet Earth Colliery': an Engineering Study*, David & Charles, Newton Abbot, 1968. David Owen's *Canals to Manchester*, Manchester University Press, 1977, surveys essentially the physical record, including Brindley's original Worsley Canal. The geography (and politics) of canal routes usually find extended treatment in the works on particular waterways (see below), but two useful references are J. H. Farrington, 'The Leeds and Liverpool Canal: a study in route selection', *Transport History*, III, 1970, and *id., Morphological Studies of English Canals*, University of Hull Occasional Papers, 20, 1972.

Promotion and finance

The promotion and finance of canals can likewise be followed in the studies on individual navigations, but a number of specialist writings exist. Hugh Malet's *Bridgewater: the Canal Duke, 1736–1803*, Manchester University Press, 1977, now supersedes his own earlier account of the creator of England's first really famous canal. T. C. Barker carefully investigates the origin of deadwater navigations in 'The beginnings of the canal age in the British Isles', in L. S. Pressnell (ed.), *Studies in the Industrial Revolution: Essays presented to T. S. Ashton*, London University Press, 1960, a reference which should be supplemented by the same author's 'Lancashire coal, Cheshire salt and the rise of Liverpool', *Transactions of the Historic Society of Lancashire and Cheshire*, CIII, 1951. Baron F. Duckham looks at the aristocratic ownership and extension of a waterway in 'The Fitzwilliams and the navigation of the Yorkshire Derwent', *Northern History*, II, 1967. Some of the problems of estimating waterway capitalisation are sketched in J. E. Ginarlis, 'Capital formation and canal transport', in J. P. P. Higgins and S. Pollard (eds.), *Aspects of Capital Formation in Great Britain, 1750–1850*, Methuen, London, 1971. There is now, however, an excellent specialist study of the actual investment in inland navigations: J. R. Ward, *The Finance of Canal Building in Eighteenth Century England*, Oxford University Press, London, 1974, which largely supersedes (at least up to 1815), the work of G. H. Evans, *British Corporation Finance, 1775–1850*, Baltimore, Ohio, 1936. At the intensely local level the late K. A. MacMahon permitted a fascinating glimpse into the waterway involvement of an unreformed corporation: 'Beverley and its beck: borough finance and a town navigation, 1700–1835',

Transport History, IV, 1971. One analysis of the geographic distribution of shareholders occurs in E. A. Wilson, 'The proprietors of the Ellesmere and Chester Canal Company in 1822', *Journal of Transport History*, III, 1957. How far the income record of inland navigations (and turnpike trusts) can provide reliable evidence of regional economic growth is considered (for the West Riding) by R. G. Wilson, 'Transport dues as indices of economic growth, 1775–1820', *Economic History Review*, XIX, 1966. The issue of voluntary legal limitations on canal dividends is raised in S. R. Broadbridge, 'Monopoly and public utility: the Birmingham Canals, 1767–72', *Transport History*, V, 1972.

Canal and river ports
The subject of canal and river ports — some of which were modest urban creations of the canal age — has recently received a fair degree of attention from historians and historical geographers. The following are the chief references: I. S. Beckwith, *The River Trade of Gainsborough, 1500–1850*, Lincolnshire Local History Society, 1968; Baron F. Duckham, 'Selby and the Aire & Calder Navigation, 1774–1826', *Journal of Transport History*, VII, 1965, and the same author's 'The founding of Goole: an early nineteenth-century canal port', *Industrial Archaeology*, IV, 1967. The subject of Goole is also dealt with in a bright popular vein by Joyce Mankowska, *Goole: a Port in Green Fields*, York, 1973, and at a more academic level by J. D. Porteous, *The Company Town of Goole: an Essay in Urban Genesis*, Hull University Occasional Papers in Geography, 12, 1970. The same author has also written on the Forth & Clyde Canal's own port in *Grangemouth's Modern History*, 1768–1968, Burgh of Grangemouth publications, 1970, and has published what was in essence his doctoral dissertation: *Canal Ports: the Urban Achievement of the Canal Age*, Academic Press, London, 1977. A slighter, but useful, reference is D. Semple, 'The growth of Grangemouth — a note', *Scottish Geographical Magazine*, 74, 1958.

Traffic
The commodity flows which inland waterways facilitated generally receive consideration in the studies of particular navigations (see below), but a few specialist investigations into the carrying trade also exist. Harry Hanson looks at more than just the social picture in his *The Canal Boatmen, 1760–1914*, Manchester University Press, 1975, a book which contains valuable information on the ownership of canal fleets. For living conditions on canal craft the reader should consult George Smith's polemical classic *Our Canal Population*, 1875; R. M. McLeod, 'Social policy and the "floating population", 1877–99', *Past and Present*, 35, 1966; S. R. Broadbridge, 'Living conditions on Midland canal boats', *Transport History*, III, 1970; and Harry Hanson, 'Living conditions on Midland canal boats: some qualifications', *Transport History*, VII, 1974, and the same author's *Canal People*, David & Charles, Newton Abbot, 1978, which also deals with canal navvies. G. L. Turnbull's 'Pickfords and the canal carrying trade, 1780–1850', *Transport History*, VI, 1973, is a pioneering study whose outlines are now filled out in chapter 5 of the same author's *Traffic and Transport: an Economic History of Pickfords*, Allen & Unwin, London, 1979. The surprising variety of vessels in use on inland navigations is reviewed visually in Hugh McKnight, *Canal and River Craft in Pictures*, David & Charles, Newton Abbot, 1970.

Regional studies
Much of the best scholarship on inland navigation is to be found in the authoritative regional studies of Charles Hadfield and in some of the longer works on individual waterways or local canal webs. In what follows many of the articles of Professor T. S. Willan are omitted as falling in chronological span rather before the period covered by chapter 3. Those interested in river navigation before 1750 can be safely referred to T. S. Willan's little classic, *River Navigation in England, 1600–1750*, Manchester University Press, 1936, and to the list of his relevant articles itemised in W. H. Chaloner's introductory guide to W. T. Jackman, *The Development of Transportation in Modern England*, 1916, 3rd edn., Cass, London, 1966, itself a monumental work of continuing value. The undermentioned works of Charles Hadfield are now fundamental to every serious student of canal history: 'The Thames navigation and the canals, 1770–1830', *Economic History Review* (old ser.), XIV, 1944–45; *id., The Canals of Southern England*, 1955, but subsequently wholly recast as *The Canals of South West England*, 1967, and *The Canals of South and South East England*, 1969 (both David and Charles, Newton Abbot); *id.*, 'The Grand Junction Canal', *Journal of Transport History*, IV, 1959–60; *id., The Canals of South Wales and the Border*, University of Wales, Cardiff, 1960; *id., The Canals of the East Midlands* and *The Canals of the West Midlands*, both David & Charles, Newton Abbot, 1966; *id., The Canals of Yorkshire and North East England*, 2 vols., David & Charles, Newton Abbot, 1972–73; *id.*, with Gordon Biddle, *The Canals of North West England*, 2 vols., David & Charles, Newton Abbot, 1970.

Individual waterways
The other chief studies of individual waterways (or of regional systems) which cover the period of the industrial revolution are: Anon., 'End of an enterprise: the Forth & Clyde Canal', *Three Banks Review*, 6, 1964; T. C. Barker, 'The Sankey Navigation', *Transactions of the Historic Society of Lancashire and Cheshire*, C, 1948, and *id.*, 'Lancashire coal, Cheshire salt and the rise of Liverpool', *ibid.*, CIII, 1951; D. E. Bick, *The Hereford and Gloucester Canal*, Pound publication, Newent, 1979; S. R. Broadbridge, *The Birmingham Canal Navigations*, I, *1768–1848*, David & Charles, Newton Abbot, 1974; K. R. Clew, *The Somersetshire Coal Canal and Railway*, David & Charles, Newton Abbot, 1970; *id., The Kennet and Avon Canal*, David & Charles, Newton Abbot, 2nd edn., 1973; I. Cohen, 'The non-tidal Wye and its navigation', *Transactions of the Woolhope Naturalist Field Club*, XXXV; E. Course, 'The Itchen Navigation', *Proceedings of the Hampshire Field Club and Archaeological Society*, XXIV, 1967; D. A. E. Cross, 'The Salisbury Avon Navigation', *Industrial Archaeology*, VII, 1970; Baron F. Duckham, *The Yorkshire Ouse: the History of a River Navigation*, David & Charles, Newton Abbot, 1967; *id., The Inland Waterways of East Yorkshire, 1700–1900*, East Yorkshire Local History Society, Hull, 1973; A. H. Faulkner, *The Grand Junction Canal*, David & Charles, Newton Abbot, 1973; A. W. Goodfellow, 'Sheffield's waterway to the sea', *Transactions of the Hunter Archaeological Society*, V, 1943; Helen Harris and Monica Ellis, *The Bude Canal*, David & Charles, Newton Abbot, 1972; H. Harris, *The Grand Western Canal*, David & Charles, Newton Abbot, 1973; J. R. Harris, 'Liverpool canal controversies, 1769–1772', *Journal of Transport History*, II, 3, 1956; G. G. Hopkinson, 'The development of inland navigation in south Yorkshire and north Derbyshire, 1697–1850', *Transactions of the Hunter Archaeological Society*, VII, 1956; *id.*, 'The Inland navigation of the Derbyshire and

Nottinghamshire coalfield, 1777–1856', *Journal of the Derbyshire Archaeological and Natural History Society*, LXXIX, 1959, H. Household, *The Thames and Severn Canal*, David & Charles, Newton Abbot, 1969; Jean Lindsay, *The Trent and Mersey Canal*, David & Charles, Newton Abbot, 1979; H. Pollins, 'The Swansea Canal', *Journal of Transport History*, I, 3, 1954; G. Ramsden, 'Two notes on the history of the Aire and Calder Navigation', *Thoresby Miscellany*, XII, 4, 1954, W. N. Slatcher, 'The Barnsley Canal: its first twenty years', *Transport History*, I, 1968; P. A. Stevens, *The Leicester Line: a History of the Old Union and Grand Union Canals*, David & Charles, Newton Abbot, 1972; H. Spencer, *London's Canal: the History of the Regent's Canal*, Putnam, London, 1961; Dorothy Summers, *The Great Ouse: the History of a River Navigation*, David & Charles, Newton Abbot, 1973; Jennifer Tann, 'The Yorkshire Foss Navigation', *Transport History*, III, 1970; A. Temple-Patterson, 'The making of the Leicestershire canals, 1766–1814', *Transactions of the Leicestershire Archaeological Society*, XXVII, 1951; D. H. Tew, *The Oakham Canal*, Brewhouse Press, Wymondham, 1968; F. S. Thacker, *The Thames Highway: General History*, 1914, and *Locks and Weirs*, 1920, repr. David & Charles, Newton Abbot, 1968; G. Thomson, 'James Watt and the Monkland Canal', *Scottish Historical Review*, XXIX, 1950; V. I. Tomlinson, 'Salford activities connected with the Bridgewater Navigation', *Transactions of the Lancashire & Cheshire Antiquarian Society*, 66, 1956–57; *id.*, 'The Manchester, Bolton and Bury Canal', *ibid.*, LXXV–LXXVI, 1965–66; R. W. Unwin, 'The Aire & Calder Navigation', I, 'The beginning of the navigation', *Bradford Antiquary*, November 1964; II, 'The navigation in the pre-canal age', *Bradford Antiquary*, September 1967. P. A. L. Vine, *London's Lost Route to Basingstoke*, David & Charles, Newton Abbot, 1968; *id.*, *London's Lost route to the Sea*, 3rd edn., Newton Abbot, 1973; *id.*, *The Royal Military Canal*, Newton Abbot, 1972; E. Welch, *The Bankrupt Canal* [Southampton to Salisbury Canal], City of Southampton Papers, 5, 1966; T. S. Willan, *River Navigation in England*, Manchester University Press, 1936; *id.*, *The Navigation of the River Weaver in the Eighteenth Century*, Chetham Society, Manchester, 1951; *id.*, *The Early History of the Don Navigation*, Manchester University Press, 1965; E. Wilson, *The Ellesmere and Llangollen Canal*, Phillimore, Chichester, 1975; R. G. Wilson, 'The Aire & Calder Navigation', III, 'The navigation in the second half of the eighteenth century', *Bradford Antiquary*, July 1969; A. C. Wood, 'The history of trade and transport on the river Trent', *Transactions of the Thoroton Society*, LIV, 1950.   B. F. Duckham

Coastal shipping

Guides to source material
E. A. Carson's *The Ancient and Rightful Customs*, Faber & Faber, London, 1972, gives, in appendix B, details of ports which have shipping registers for the period from 1786. R. Davis, in appendix A of *The Rise of the English Shipping Industry*, David & Charles, Newton Abbot, 1962, gave a critical appraisal of the Musgrave manuscript statistics. R. S. Craig's 'Shipping records of the nineteenth and twentieth centuries', *Archives*, No. 7, October 1966, though mainly concerned with ships in overseas trade, does include some references to the coastal trade. G. E. Farr's *Records of Bristol Ships, 1800–38*, Bristol Record Society Publications, No. 15, 1950, limits investigation to ships over 150 tons, thus excluding all but the larger coasters and Irish Sea packets. R. C. Jarvis's 'Ship registry, 1707–86', *Maritime History*, II, 1972, may be used to

supplement Carson, while his 'Sources for the history of ships and shipping', *Journal of Transport/History*, III, 1958, is an indispensable survey of the main printed and manuscript sources.

Primary sources

(a) *Literary* include C. Lamb, 'Old Margate Hoy', *London Magazine*, July 1823, a well known account of passenger travel on the popular London–Margate station, and R. L. Brett (ed.), *Barclay Fox's Journal*, Bell & Hyman, London, 1979, which reveals the frequent use of early steam packet services in the English and Bristol Channels by an energetic Quaker businessman of Falmouth.

(b) *Statistical.* Both J. R. McCulloch, *A Dictionary of Commerce and Commercial Navigation*, rev. edn., London, 1882, and G. R. Porter, *The Progress of the Nation*, London, 1836–38, contain statistical information, incidentally rather than systematically presented, on the volume and character of coastal shipping and coastal trade.

General surveys

There is no comprehensive account for the period of the industrial revolution, but T. S. Willan, *The English Coasting Trade, 1600–1750*, Manchester University Press, 1938, is an authorative account for the period covered and provides an essential introduction to the study of later developments. P. S. Bagwell, *The Transport Revolution from 1770*, Batsford, London, 1974, contains in chapter 3 the fullest account so far available of the coaster trade of more recent times.

Topography

The advantages and limitations of coastal shipping as compared with land or inland waterway transport can be better understood given some knowledge of coastal topography, J. Collins, *Great Britain's Coasting Pilot*, London, 1693; R. Ayton, *A Voyage Round Great Britain*, London, 1814–25, and J. A. Steers, *The Coastline of England and Wales*, Cambridge University Press, 1964, reveal the mariner's and geographer's assessment of the areas of greatest danger to coastal shipping.

The coal trade

T. S. Ashton and J. Sykes, *The Coal Industry in the Eighteenth Century*, Manchester University Press, 1929, includes an account of the organisation of the east-coast coal trade, including statistics of shipments to London. R. Smith, *Sea Coal to London*, Longman, London, 1961, though written primarily from the viewpoint of the Coal Factors' Society, has much valuable information on this all-important trade. R. Finch, *Coals from Newcastle*, Terence Dalton, Lavenham, 1973, is useful for its examination of the links between coastal and inland navigation in the distribution of coal.

Steam shipping

The rapid improvements in the technology of steam shipping and their application to the needs of coastal shipping are considered in H. P. Spratt, *The Birth of the Steam-boat*, Charles Griffin, London, 1958; E. G. Smith, *A Short History of Naval and Marine Engineering*, Cambridge University Press, 1938; and R. T. Rowland, *Steam at Sea*, David & Charles, Newton Abbot, 1970. Passenger accommodation is described and illustrated in B. Greenhill and A. Giffard, *Travelling by Sea in the Nineteenth Century*, A. & C. Black, London, 1972.

Regional studies

(a) *North-east.* S. Middlebrook, *Newcastle on Tyne: its Growth and Achievement*, 2nd edn., SR Publishers, Wakefield, 1965, gives some information on the town's coastwise trade. The best account of the coastwise trade of Hull is to be found in G. Jackson, *The Trade and Shipping of Eighteenth Century Hull*, Yorkshire Local History Society, York, 1975. W. G. East, 'The port of Kingston upon Hull during the industrial revolution', *Economica*, XI, 1931, pp. 190–212, includes information on coastal shipping and considers reasons for the rise of Hull's rival, Goole.

(b) *East coast.* F. G. C. Carr, *Sailing Barges*, rev. edn., Davies, London, 1951, is an authoritative account of the vessels that carried most of the short-distance coastal trade. E. R. Cooper, in 'East coast brigs', *Mariner's Mirror*, XXXI, 1945, writes of the ships which carried coal from the North-east to London and beyond. R. Camden, *The History of the Town of Gravesend in the County of Kent and of the Port of London*, London, 1843, is valuable for the detailed description of the huge growth of passenger traffic in the area.

(c) *South coast.* F. T. O'Brien, *Early Solent Steamers*, David & Charles, Newton Abbot, 1963, is a popular but well documented account of the role of early steamboats in opening communications between the Isle of Wight and the mainland. R. C. Jarvis, 'Eighteenth century Dorset shipping', *Proceedings of the Dorset Natural History and Archaeological Society*, 92, 1970, contains information on the ownership of coastal vessels based at Poole, Weymouth and Lyme.

(d) *The South-west, including the Bristol Channel.* H. E. S. Fisher (ed.), *Ports and Shipping in the South West*, University of Exeter, 1971, is a symposium including papers on the shipping of Fowey, Porthleven and Salcombe. The maritime history of Cornwall has been the subject of many books, of which the most useful to the student of the coastal trade are R. Pearse, *The Ports and Harbours of Cornwall*, Warne, St Austell, 1963, and R. Larne and C. Carter, *Cornish Shipwrecks: the South Coast* and *Cornish Shipwrecks: the North Coast*, both published by David & Charles, Newton Abbot, 1969, 1970. The first two chapters of R. M. Barton, *A History of the Cornish China Clay Industry*, Bradford Barton, Truro, 1966, highlight the importance of coastwise transport of china clay from south Cornwall to the Potteries and South Wales. Other studies which help to fill out the picture of maritime activity in the area include R. S. Craig, 'Shipowning in the South West in its national context, 1800–1914', *Exeter Papers in Economic History*, 7, University of Exeter, 1973, and C. H. Ward Jackson, 'The ships of the port of Fowey at the turn of the eighteenth century' *Exeter Papers in Economic History*, 4, University of Exeter, 1970. The passenger and merchandise trade of the Bristol Channel is treated in three works by G. E. Farr: *Chepstow Ships*, Chepstow Society, Chepstow, 1951; *Ships and Harbours of Exmoor*, Exmoor Press, Dulverton, 1970, and *West Country Passenger Steamers*, Stephenson, Prescot, 1967.

(e) *Wales.* A. H. John, *The Industrial Development of South Wales*, University of Wales Press, Cardiff, 1950, and P. H. Stainer, 'The copper ore trade of south-west England in the nineteenth century', *Journal of Transport History*, new ser., V, 1979, show the importance of the exchange of coal and copper for the growth of the coastal trade of the area. Two unpublished theses of the University of Wales — M. E. Hughes, 'The Historical Geography of the Sea Trading Industry of the Coast of Cardigan Bay during the Eighteenth and Nineteenth Centuries', 1962, and D. Pritchard, 'The Slate Industry of North Wales', 1935, are indispensable for an understanding of the coastal trade of the west coast, while A. H. Dodd's, *The Industrial Development of North*

Wales, University of Wales Press, Cardiff, 1951, brings into perspective the rapid growth of Beaumaris as a coastal port. A. Eames, *Ships and Seamen of Anglesey*, Anglesey Antiquarian Society, Llangefni, 1973, is a meticulously researched labour of love extending to over 670 pages.

(f) *The North-west.* The history of coastal shipping in this region still awaits the fuller treatment afforded to Wales and the South-west, but G. Chandler's *Liverpool Shipping*, Phoenix House, London, 1960, devotes a chapter to the port's coastal trade with important references to the ownership of vessels. Two articles by R. S. Craig — 'Some aspects of the trade and shipping of the river Dee in the eighteenth century', *Transactions of the Historic Society of Lancashire and Cheshire*, CXIV, 1963, and 'Shipping and shipbuilding in the port of Chester in the eighteenth and early nineteenth century', *Transactions of the Historic Society of Lancashire and Cheshire*, CXVI, 1965, help to fill in some of the gaps.

(g) *The Irish Sea.* D. B. McNeill's *Irish Passenger Steamship Services*, I, *North of Ireland*, and II, *South of Ireland*, David & Charles, Newton Abbot, 1969 and 1970, give a comprehensive description of the passenger routes and the ships which served them but do not examine the background economic developments. P. S. Bagwell, 'The Post Office steam packets, 1821–26, and the development of shipping on the Irish Sea', *Maritime History*, I, 1971, reveals the Post Office as a pace-setter in Anglo-Irish communications. H. S. Irvine's 'Some aspects of passenger traffic between Great Britain and Ireland, 1820–50', *Journal of Transport History*, IV, 1964, covers both a long span of time and a wider area. For the growth of Anglo-Irish trade the most useful sources are L. M. Cullen, *Anglo-Irish Trade, 1660–1800*, Manchester University Press, 1968, and the same author's *An Economic History of Ireland since 1660*, Batsford, London, 1972.   *J. Armstrong and P. S. Bagwell*

The ports

General trade background
There is no comprehensive work on trade during the eighteenth and early nineteenth centuries, but an excellent summary of the evolution of trade leading up to the industrial revolution is to be found in the writings of the late Ralph Davis: 'English foreign trades, 1700–74', *Economic History Review*, 2nd ser., XV, 1962; *A Commercial Revolution: English Overseas Trade in the Seventeenth and Eighteenth Centuries*, Historical Association, London, 1967; and the relevant chapters of his *The Rise of the English Shipping Industry*, Macmillan, London, 1962. The later period is covered more substantially by his *The Industrial Revolution and British Overseas Trade*, Leicester University Press, 1979. Statistics, though not for individual ports, may be found in E. B. Schumpeter, *English Overseas Trade Statistics, 1697–1808*, Clarendon Press, Oxford, 1960, and B. R. Mitchell and P. Deane, *Abstract of British Historical Statistics*, Cambridge University Press, 1969.

General surveys of ports
The most comprehensive survey, with brief accounts of all the significant ports, is still D. J. Owen, *The Ports of the United Kingdom*, Allman, London, 1939, though it is very slight on the early period. J. Bird, *The Major Seaports of the United Kingdom*, Hutchinson, London, 1963, looks in greater depth at a more limited number of ports and offers the best historical survey in print. Of older works, E. Cresy, *An Encyclopaedia of Civil Engineering*, London, 1847, pp. 306–403, is a useful introduction to

work undertaken during the industrial revolution period, and Anon., *Reports of the Late John Smeaton*, 2nd edn., 2 vols., London, 1837, and Sir J. Rennie, *The Theory, Formation and Construction of British and Foreign Harbours*, 2 vols., London, 1854, contain much useful information about those ports on which Smeaton and Rennie were consulted. Although difficult to find, R. Ayton, *A Voyage round Great Britain*, 8 vol., London, 1814–25, merits attention for its superb illustrations (by W. Daniell) as much as for its illuminating comments on the various ports.

On specific topics, R. Jarvis, 'The appointment of ports', *Economic History Review*, 2nd ser., XI, 1958, and E. E. Hoon, *The Organisation of the English Customs, 1696–1786*, Appleton-Century, London, 1938, repr. David & Charles, Newton Abbot, 1968, refer to the legal status and creation of ports; and engineering and finance are surveyed in D. Swann, 'The engineers of English port improvement, 1660–1830', *Transport History*, I, 1968, pp. 153–68 and 260–76, and D. Swann, 'The pace and progress of port investment in England, 1660–1830', *Yorkshire Bulletin of Economic and Social Research*, XII, 1960. Studies of individual engineers include H. Peet, 'Thomas Steers, the engineer of Liverpool's first dock — a memoir', *Transactions of the Historic Society of Lancashire and Cheshire*, LXXXII, 1932; S. A. Harris, 'Henry Berry (1720–1812): Liverpool's second dock engineer', *Transactions of the Historic Society of Lancashire and Cheshire*, LXXXIX, 1938; C. T. G. Boucher, *John Rennie, 1761–1821, the Life and Work of a Great Engineer*, Manchester University Press, Manchester, 1963 (though slight on his dock work); and B. Bracegirdle and P. H. Miles, *Thomas Telford*, David & Charles, Newton Abbot, 1973.

Individual ports
There is a large bibliography relating to ports, but many of the earlier books were not interested in port functions or industrialisation, and some of the modern ones are concerned chiefly with the railway and post-railway periods. Most of those listed below deal with the eighteenth century, though some may only be incidentally concerned with the period of this book.

(a) *The North-east.* Volumes dealing with the coal trade in general and with the various shipping places include W. Fordyce, *History of the County Palatine of Durham*, 2 vol., Newcastle, 1857; W. Whellan, *History, Topography and Directory of the County Palatine of Durham*, London, 1856; and, especially for development of rail-borne traffic, the early chapters of W. W. Tomlinson, *The North Eastern Railway*, London, 1914, repr. David & Charles, Newton Abbot, 1967. J. Guthrie, *The River Tyne: its History and Resources*, Newcastle, 1880, is still the best work on the major port; and Sunderland is covered by T. Potts, *Sunderland: a History of the Town, Port, Trade and Commerce*, Sunderland, 1892, and W. C. Mitchell, *History of Sunderland*, Sunderland, 1919. P. Barton, 'The port of Stockton-on-Tees and its creeks, 1825–61: a problem in port history', *Maritime History*, I, 1971, is an interesting review of port competition for the coal trade at the end of our period. G. Head, *A Home Tour through the Manufacturing Districts of England*, London, 1836, repr. Cass, 1968, contains vivid descriptions of contemporary shipment methods in the North-east (and at Whitehaven).

(b) *The Humber ports.* Modern studies of Hull are G. Jackson, *Hull in the Eighteenth Century*, Oxford University Press, London, 1972; Jackson, *The Trade and Shipping of Eighteenth Century Hull*, East Yorkshire Local History Society pamphlet, York, 1975; and *Victoria County History of Yorkshire, East Riding*, I, *Kingston-upon-Hull*, Institute of Historical Research, London, 1969. The origins of Goole are fully recounted in B. F. Duckham, *The Yorkshire Ouse*, David & Charles, Newton Abbot, 1967; J. D. Porteous, *Canal Ports*, Academic Press, London, 1977; and Porteous, *The Company Town of Goole*, University of Hull Publications, Hull, 1969. Grimsby is covered by E. Gillett, *A History of Grimsby*, Oxford University Press, London, 1970, while the building of the first dock is examined in detail in G. Jackson, *Grimsby and the Haven Company, 1796–1846*, Grimsby Borough Libraries Committee, 1970. An 'up-river' port is described in I. S. Beckwith, 'The river trade of Gainsborough, 1500–1850', *Lincolnshire History and Archaeology*, II, 1967.

(c) *East Anglia.* The standard work, and starting point for the whole region, must be W. J. Wren, *Ports of the Eastern Counties*, Terence Dalton, Lavenham, 1976, which also contains an excellent bibliography. M. J. T. Lewis and N. R. Wright, *Boston as a Port*, Lincolnshire Industrial Archaeology Group, Boston, Lincs., 1973, is a superb short study.

(d) *London.* The standard work remains vol. 1 of J. G. Brookbank, *History of the Port of London*, 2 vol., O'Connor, London, 1921, though in almost every respect it is old-fashioned. More recently W. M. Stern, 'The first London dock boom and the growth of the West India Docks', *Economica*, XIX, 1952, and 'The Isle of Dogs Canal', *Economic History Review*, 2nd ser., IV, 1952, dealt with specific areas of interest, while two recent illustrated books devote a fair amount of space to the early docks, though both rely heavily on Brookbank: J. Pudney, *London's Docks*, Thames & Hudson, London, 1975; and R. Douglas Brown, *The Port of London*, Terence Dalton, Lavenham, 1978.

(e) *The south coast.* J. B. Jones, *A History of Dover Harbour*, Dover, 1892, is a reasonable introduction, while excellent surveys of the Sussex ports are in J. H. Farrant, 'The seaborne trade of Sussex, 1720–1845', *Sussex Archaeological Collections*, CXIV, 1976, and *The Harbours of Sussex, 1700–1914*, published by the author, 12 Dudwell Road, Brighton.

(f) *The South-west.* W. G. Hoskins, *Industry, Trade and People in Exeter, 1688–1800*, University of Exeter Press, 1935, is a classic study. Several of the smaller ports are covered in H. E. S. Fisher (ed.), *Ports and Shipping in the South West*, University of Exeter, 1971.

(g) *Bristol.* There is no modern history of Bristol. C. Wells, *A Short History of the Port of Bristol*, Bristol, 1909, is passable; C. M. MacInnes (ed.), *Bristol and its Adjoining Counties*, British Association, 1951, slightly better. Specific topics are discussed in W. E. Minchinton, *The Trade of Bristol in the Eighteenth Century*, Bristol Record Society, XIX, 1957; A. F. Williams, 'Bristol port plans and improvement schemes of the eighteenth century', *Transactions of the Bristol and Gloucestershire Archaeological Society*, LXXXI, 1962; and R. A. Buchanan, 'The construction of the floating harbour at Bristol, 1804–9', *Trans. Bristol and Glos. Arch. Soc.*, LXXXVIII, 1969. W. E. Minchinton, *The Port of Bristol in the Eighteenth Century*, Bristol Historical Association, is reprinted in P. McGrath, *Bristol in the Eighteenth Century*, David & Charles, Newton Abbot, 1972.

(h) *Liverpool.* There is a large bibliography, but most of it is old or old-fashioned. C. N. Parkinson, *The Rise of the Port of Liverpool*, Liverpool University Press, 1952, stops as the industrial revolution was gathering momentum. T. C. Barker, 'Lancashire coal, Cheshire salt and the rise of Liverpool', *Transactions of the Historic Society of Lancashire and Cheshire*, CIII, 1951, puts the town in its local context, but by far the best study of the port is F. E. Hyde, *Liverpool and the Mersey*, David & Charles, Newton

Abbot, 1971. The comparative struggle of Chester is illustrated in R. S. Craig, 'Some aspects of the trade and shipping of the river Dee in the eighteenth century', *Trans. Historic Society of Lancs. and Cheshire*, CXIV, 1962.

(i) *Whitehaven*. An excellent summary is J. E. Williams, 'Whitehaven in the eighteenth century', *Economic History Review*, 2nd ser., VIII, 1956.

Postscript

E. M. Sigsworth (ed.), *Ports and Resorts in the Regions* (Hull College of Higher Education, for the Conference of Regional and Local History Tutors in Tertiary Education, Hull, 1980) usefully contains articles on a range of ports. Gordon Jackson, *The British Ports: a History and Archaeology* (Worlds Work, forthcoming), while not intended as an academic work, is an informative and wide-ranging general survey.

G. Jackson

INDEX

Italics indicate illustrations

General

Canals and inland navigations